M J —

You who read my raw draft
can now enjoy "my India" in
completed form!

Bon voyage !!

xo

Michael

Paris, 5 May 2010

INDIA *by* DESIGN

The Pursuit of Luxury & Fashion

INDIA *by* DESIGN

The Pursuit of Luxury & Fashion

MICHAEL BOROIAN
AND
ALIX DE POIX

WILEY
John Wiley & Sons (Asia) Pte. Ltd.

Other Wiley Editorial Offices

John Wiley & Sons, Inc., 111 River Street, Hoboken, NJ 07030, USA
John Wiley & Sons, Ltd., The Atrium, Southern Gate, Chichester, West Sussex P019 8SQ, UK
John Wiley & Sons (Canada), Ltd., 5353 Dundas Street West, Suite 400, Toronto, Ontario M9B 6H8, Canada
JohnWiley & Sons Australia Ltd., 42 McDougall Street, Milton, Queensland 4064, Australia
Wiley-VCH, Boschstrasse 12, D-69469 Weinheim, Germany

Library of Congress Cataloging-in-Publication Data

ISBN: 978-0470-82396-5

Typeset in 11.5/15pt Legacy Serif ITC Book by Macmillan Publishing Solutions, Chennai, India.
Printed in Singapore by Saik Wah Press Pte. Ltd.
10 9 8 7 6 5 4 3 2 1

TABLE OF CONTENTS

FOREWORD

No one has understood "India" in one lifetime. Even an immodest Indian would not make such a preposterous claim. Yet it is worth making the effort to understand, as this book does, for the rewards are plenty.

TWO INDIAS

In a land where the cities may well have succumbed to luxuries and "limited-edition" novelties, someone in a village will surprise you with the simple wisdom that possession of rare, expensive things is not the path to happiness—that all this is only *maya,* the illusion of possession. For nothing really *belongs* to us. *Gita,* the ancient Indian epic, concludes: "What belongs to you today belonged to someone else yesterday, and tomorrow it will belong to yet someone else. Change is the only steadfast rule of life." Yet some of the rarest material possessions, such as the Peacock Throne and the Koh-i-noor, Golconda, and Jubilee diamonds were once crafted for, and possessed by, Indians.

It was the courage of Indian creativity and patronage that attempted communion with the Buddha at Ajanta, carving amazing frescoed caves across a mile and a half; that venerated the Hindu deity Shiva by scooping out 200,000 tons of rocks at the Kailash temple at Ellora; that raised the 700-feet-high eleventh-century Brihadeshwara temple in Tanjore. To honor a Jain *tirthankara* with 1,444 different marble pillars enclosing 29,000 feet of double-storied space at Ranakpur, Rajasthan, or even conceive of laying the garden of paradise on earth around the Taj Mahal, requires the same royal license for religious and spiritual luxuries.

If both *yesterday* and *tomorrow* can be called by the same word "*kal*" in a cyclic, cosmic understanding of time, then it is easy to understand how for most of India's rural communities, both their identity and security lie in their "continuous editions" of fashion: except for weddings or festivals, they always dress the same. A watch, a bag, or even a cell phone can only be an item of necessity or utility, not a "limited edition" from a brand, which demands an escalation in spending. Also, much of what *this* India uses, even, say, in perfumes is usually the generic rose, jasmine, and vertiver. The henna on the hands is an unbranded henna from the grocer.

THE SECOND INDIA

Fortunately for brands seeking new markets here, a parallel India also exists: complex, but ready to change and consume all they have to offer.

So when someone wants to delve into this fascinating land of paradoxes and parallel truths, what sort of lenses does it demand? A double lens for sure, as this Franco-American collaboration demonstrates. They have certainly put together an incisive and exhaustive book on luxury and fashion in India, not just for outsiders, but for Indians as well. Michael Boroian is American, and Alix de Poix is French. Though both have European roots and many similarities in their respective career paths, they adopt different approaches: one through business expertise in people, situations, and organizations; the other using a cognitive approach. Some chapters take on an aerial view, while others focus on detailed analyses.

Writing about such a comprehensive subject is a daunting task, and many books have recently been written about India (some are even quoted in this book). The issues raised in *India by Design*—to date the only book devoted solely to this subject—may inspire others and serve as a foundation for further exploration. Having been interviewed ourselves in the process of the authors' research for this book, we have had the pleasure of sharing their challenges throughout this ambitious undertaking. The result is one of contrasts: interesting and provocative, refreshing and enriching.

The authors have addressed the most relevant issues and aspects that affect luxury and fashion in the emerging and challenging environment that is India today. The focus is on a specific sector of the economy and how that market is evolving. Where will the growth of the big brands come from given that Europe, America and Asia are already established destinations for these consumers? Where will the industry wish to invest for future expansion, sourcing, and manufacturing? And what of the clientele, ready to spend the price required to fulfill their dreams (real or not)?

The cultural diversity of India is equivalent to—if not greater than—its European counterparts. It has taken the Europeans nearly 50 years to build an economic force to compete with the other two giants, Asia and America. Europeans are proud that the roots of fashion and luxury are found among their many brands, and it is with a sense of respect for this heritage that the authors address their subject. They bring to the subject an insider's perspective on the workings of the world of luxury and fashion and illustrate, interviews in Europe, America, Asia, and India, their vision of the situations and their understanding of the environment. Both are recognized as gurus in their respective fields: they have embarked on a journey both to learn and to share their findings with others who have a comparable interest in India.

They have covered their topic in a style that is both narrative and informative, allowing the reader to gain a conceptual framework of the issues confronting the Indian market. For companies entering India today, or indeed for those already present, the challenges are formidable. The authors present an integrated vision that we believe will give the purveyors of luxury and fashion a better understanding of India and the complex and ever-evolving market they are seeking to explore.

Aman Nath & Francis Wacziarg
Co-chairmen, Neemrana Hotels

PREFACE

The genesis of this book on luxury and fashion dates back to 1999; the issues were the same, but the focus was on a different country: China. As partner and European practice leader for the fashion, retail, and luxury goods sector at TMP Worldwide Executive Search, I had been requested to complete several senior-level recruitments in China. With limited knowledge of the Chinese market at the time, I needed efficient and speedy instruction regarding the nature of, and challenges for, the luxury business there, and found very little information. I therefore proposed to my management to conduct an in-depth study, which could be used as the basis for a book on the subject matter. Whereas management approval was granted, presenting the project to publishers received a consistently negative response: "Is there even a market for luxury in China? Is it not premature to write about such a subject, and who would really be interested?" Thus discouraged by three different editors, I decided to shelve the study.

Fast forward to 2006. As founder of Sterling International, a leading niche executive-search firm specializing exclusively in the fashion and luxury goods sector, I had by now conducted many China-based search assignments, and had always harbored some regret over not having pursued the book-writing project. Yet an old familiar opportunity was presenting itself, because the clients who had previously requested recruitment services for the Chinese market were now contacting me with similar needs for India. "India is the next China" is a comment I would hear again and again, and to a lesser extent there are some parallels with regard to the luxury goods industry. With limited knowledge of the market, I set out to increase my exposure to India to learn the many facets of its fashion and luxury goods paradigm.

Given the complexity of the many contradictions that serve as a backdrop to luxury and fashion in India, the subject matter was daunting. Indeed, it prompts the question: How pertinent is the subject in a country whose 60 years of independence has its leaders addressing the more relevant past and present challenges of poverty, caste, illiteracy, and sectarian violence in an ever-growing population of one billion plus? Contradictions abound in a country where approximately half of the people are illiterate, yet it houses the world's second-largest pool of trained scientists and engineers. Against a backdrop of an evolving democracy and growing economy, per capita income is increasing and an ever-growing youth majority is looking for ways to channel its aspiration.

Enter the luxury brands, identifiable to the discerning eye, quality driven and tempting the consumer to be a part of the foray of the happy not-so-few. My primary objective for choosing this subject matter is to provide the reader with a reference on the evolution that India is undergoing in branded fashion and luxury goods and, in particular, the impact of the major European houses, whose success in India will come at a price: an opportunity cost for the local Indian businesses and design talents who have not yet learned the essentials of fashion and luxury branding, and thus risk losing sizeable market share in the increasingly competitive arena.

Michael Boroian

Why India? This dates back to 1961. To Ootacamund (Ooty), in the south of India, where my father lived while setting up an important manufacturing operation for the film industry. In addition, my husband, Jacques-Etienne de T'Serclaes, has been traveling to India doing business regularly since the late 1990s, so I have never disengaged from the country. I had been asked to speak on luxury issues at global forums, such as the Regional World Economic Forum in Delhi, and when Michael asked me if I would be interested in writing something on the subject of luxury, I saw a real opportunity to share some of the thoughts I had on this continent.

As a former senior partner with the renowned executive search firm Heidrick & Struggles, I ran the worldwide luxury practice for several years. Since then, I have been contacted regularly by friends, former candidates, and clients for information and advice on the global luxury market. Since my DNA and specialty are the family business and the luxury sector, I see an interesting parallel between the brands in India today and the emerging brands in continental Europe in the late 1950s. The arrival of a new breed of managers and the emerging role of women are also strong signs of obvious potential growth in the sector.

Will India remain in the spotlight? Is it the next destination for the old developed world, for talents, market opportunities, and brand development? The answer is "yes." Is it a new El Dorado? Potentially, yes; there is a lot of money in India. Is it for now? Probably not: too many things are missing for the moment, but it will come quicker than anyone thinks or believes. All the work and research I am now doing on leadership issues in my new role of executive search coach and consultant in Europe as well as in Asia, India, and the Emirates confirm the potential surge of this continent. All my instincts say "yes", there is room for India to be on the podium one day.

The Indians have a unique sense of time and the timeless, which in and of itself is a representation of luxury; they have the colors, the music, the fabric, the crafts, the hands, the link between temporality and spirituality, and the women... It is a continent of "bespoke" culture, with a coexistence of extreme wealth and extreme poverty, of individuality and collectivity. Will they make it? Do they want it? Can our Western eyes understand the Oriental vision? Do they need us or do we need them? These are some of the questions inspiring my co-writing of this book.

Alix de Poix

During the writing of this book, we were faced with several challenges:

- the musical chairs of the luxury brands ever-changing partnerships with India distribution groups, data for which are valid as of October 2008
- the question of how to present economic data by virtue of currency choice. Given that our readers are Indian, American, and European, we have selected one of the three currencies according to the original data provided for a specific currency. N.B. the exchange rates are as of December 31, 2007, as follows:

US$1 = €0.67942 /€1 = US$1.47285
1 € = 58.08184 Indian rupees/1 Indian rupee = €0.01722
1 Indian rupee = US$0.02536 /US$1 = 39.42750 Indian rupees.
(source: The Currency Site, www.oanda.com)

Acknowledgments

During the course of writing our book, we were privileged to meet with many individuals whose input was facilitative, and whose participation was greatly appreciated. Many thanks to the following:

- for their contribution and/or insight:
  all the designers, Pialy Aditya, Amar Agrawal, Kajal Aijaz, Harry and Claudia Ajwani, Sujata Assomull, Harmeet Bajaj, Sanjiv Batra, Rakesh Biyani, Anna Bredemeyer, Yves Carcelle, Fiona Caulfield, Radha Chadha, Kalyani Chawla, Vishal Chawla, Anil and Sabina Chopra, Anil and Mehul Chowksi, Aishwin Deo, Sobha Dé, Luca Ferro, Fergus Fleming, Irène Frain, Umesh Ganjam, Parmeshwar Godrej, Oliver Goessler, Didier Grumbach, Abhay Gupta, Pradeep Hirani, Neelesh Hunderkari, Farhat Jamal, Tarini Jindal, Tarun Johsi, Anand Kabra, Dilip Kapur, Thomas Kastgen, Rattan Keswani, Ajay Khaitan, Dietmar Knoess, Kamal Kant Koner, Ravi Krishnan, Alex Kuruvilla, Florence Lesché, Jean-Marc Loubier, Judith Leiber, André Maeder, Anuradha Mahindra, Fern Mallis, Pradeep Mansukhani, Nikhil Mehra, Vivek Mehra, Bertrand Michaud, Maneesh Mishra, Maximiliano Modesti, Françoise Montenay, Albert Morris, Gilles Moutonet, Abhijit Mukerji, Vijay Murjani, Sumeet Nair, Vinod Nair, Saloni Nangia, Kamal Nath, Amit Oberoi, Marie-Lou Philips, Marie-France Pochna, Véronique Poles, Gaurav Pokhriyal, Anil Prabhakar, Rahul Prasad, Avneesh Raghuvanshi, Deyani Raman, Sergio Ramirez, Sanjeev Rao, Chandralekha Roy, Megha Roy, Charu Sachdev, Priya Sachdev, Eric Saurage, Philippe Schaus, Anjana Sharma, Harsimran Singh, Maharaja Jai Singh, Malvinder Singh, Tikka Singh, Pranay Sinha, Rishab Soni, Srinath Sridharan, Soumistra Srivastava, Geff Staines,

Simone Tata, Bandana Tewari, Sujata Tyagi, Yanchee Vadhera, Rathi Vinay Jha, Manmeet Vohra, Ness Wadia, Max-Jean Zins

- for their particular contribution, feedback and endorsement: Xavier Bertrand, Michel Chevalier, Binita Cooper, Ritu Kumar, Uché Okonkwo, Ashok Som, Aman Nath, Francis Wacziarg
- for their guidance: the team at John Wiley & Sons
- for their help with the artistic direction: Sathya and Shiv Saran
- and a very special thank you to Ruchita Sharma and Charlotte Cookson whose endurance and invaluable contribution helped make this book become a reality

LIST OF TABLES AND FIGURES

LIST OF PHOTOGRAPHS

CHAPTER 14

The photographs in this book are sourced by Sathya Saran and are reproduced with permission.

PART I
OVERVIEW

CHAPTER 1
DEFINING LUXURY AND FASHION

CONTEXT

In defining "luxury and fashion" in India today, we perhaps need to consider the concept from two distinct perspectives.

On the one side is the almighty consumer, who, for the most part, has been a passive spectator in the world of luxury, viewing India's rich tradition and heritage of fine craftsmanship and creativity only from a distance, and consequently paying little heed to the increasing number of Indian fashion designers who have reigned within that closed circle to which such things were restricted. This consumer has, until recently, been fairly oblivious to the idolatry accorded to select designers (similarly to the star system in Bollywood). Now, however, fueled by a changing demographic, which has provided greater means of access to this refined world, the consumer has begun to awaken to the finer things in life. At the top of this consumer pyramid are both old and new money, which provide the means to travel the world and to hone the taste for the best in luxury and fashion that the many global brands have to offer. These very goods are now becoming available locally—albeit at higher prices.

On the other side are the companies—either present in India already or whose future presence is imminent—with a global reach in luxury and fashion, seeking ever-greener pastures where they may attract more consumers to the world of the marketed pleasure. These are shrewd operators who, foreseeing consumer trends in luxury and fashion moving toward the spiritual, elusive, and enigmatic, view India as having a singular allure by virtue of its history, culture, and, most importantly for the global marketers, the economic outlook and changing demography of its people. Considering the number of consumers in India with an ever-increasing means of buying from the purveyors of these goods, the stakes are high, and the stage has been set for establishing territory. And therein lies a future conflict. Why would a country with its own proven resources in the sector—both material and creative—be opening wide its doors to foreign investment, let alone encouraging the entry of brands that risk cannibalizing its very own?

"Opportunity" might be the most obvious answer, but for whom? We are witnessing a progressive evolution both for the foreign brands and the country hosting them. It is noteworthy that, with the exception of the hotel category, currently there is no globally recognized Indian luxury brand. The country is now on the world stage and is ripe for an authentic India-influenced luxury-lifestyle brand—perhaps an Indian version of China's Shanghai Tang. India's long history and diverse people make it an ideal backdrop for fashion and luxury lifestyle brands across all categories. Furthermore, India is known for its exceptional handiwork, whether in its intricate woodcarvings or the delicately embroidered couture ensembles.

Other categories in which India could compete on a global level are health and beauty. These are vast subjects worthy of studies in themselves, but they are beyond the purview of this book; so in later chapters the reader will note the exclusion of fragrances, cosmetics, and the like. However, it is worth mentioning that as the world is increasingly focused on honoring our bodies with non-Western medicines and rituals such as ayurvedic and homeopathic treatments, yoga, and meditation, India has introduced some of its own homegrown brands. Biotique, on the mass level, and Kama Ayurveda, on the luxury level, have increased national distribution, and are currently toying with regional distribution in Asia. Biotique is the brainchild of Vinita Jain, a New Delhi-based entrepreneur whose family had tea plantations in Darjeeling and Assam. There she learned about the 5,000-year old science of ayurveda[1] and saw the market to modernize those ancient herbal remedies by blending them with Western biotechnology. In less than 15 years, Biotique has achieved a wholesale distribution estimated at US$150 million, mostly within India. Furthermore, Vinita is now competing on the global luxury level with an eponymous premium skincare line, launched in March 2008 in New York City's Saks Fifth Avenue, which has been projected to reach US$100 million in five years.

During the course of our research for this book, we interviewed many individuals and companies—the key international players, as well as the local firms aspiring to build a presence—and have witnessed a growing paradox. While the growth and development of luxury and fashion companies in India are being fought out more among the global players than the local Indian ones, with few exceptions at this stage, all are forced to confront the same barriers to success. Both face many challenges ranging from the banal—the environment and climate—to the more pertinent—retail and distribution issues. While we will explore these in later chapters, they warrant immediate mention in the context of defining luxury and fashion in India, because the future success of the sector will be affected by these factors: the lack of any high street, the restrictive property regulations, the lack of infrastructure and logistics, the paucity and high cost of real estate, the pervasive fraud and potential growth for counterfeit products, and, finally, the complexities of talent hunting and employee retention. But as difficult as these barriers may seem, they are not unlike the comparable challenges faced in other emerging markets where fashion and luxury companies have become predominant. These foreign companies have one distinct advantage over their local counterparts in the form of applying the tools that have been the key to both opening the door of success in luxury and fashion, and allowing them to become masters of the house: branding.

Whereas luxury and fashion have been prevalent and a part of life in India for centuries, the notion of branding in these categories is a concept where local knowledge and practice have been limited.

The tradition and heritage of being Indian and buying Indian-made luxury and fashion items have, until very recently, not created a market filled by the formidable local Indian talent. Local businesses may have understood the technical aspects of market share and competitiveness, but taking them to the formal level of branding has eluded the great majority. This has not been emphasized either in the educational system or in the training of the people running these businesses. Hence there is a major opportunity in the making and extraordinary potential for companies that master the required branding techniques and processes to capture the ever-growing market of consumers—provided those consumers are willing to behave in a way similar to their counterparts in the rest of the world.

There are clear historical precedents to show that a divide is created when global brands come into emerging markets. Those who have had success have achieved it at the expense of a short-term opportunity cost for the local companies, whether they are branded or not. The very factors that fuel the branded companies' success in India may lead to the downfall of the local businesses. In the long term, this may work to the advantage of some Indian companies, particularly those in jewelry and high-end designer wear. These companies may upgrade their product and service offerings, and then master the rules of branding themselves. In an almost Darwinian "natural selection" process, it is the consumer who will decide who survives. In this, it is the local Indian companies who run the greatest risk over time, with the potential impact upon the very essence of what makes India different from any other emerging market: its heritage and sense of tradition with intricate craftwork, an impressive platform in breadth and depth in both jewelry and textiles, and a captive audience already in place and willing to spend.

But there is no guarantee that the wave of luxury spending in India will build the industry as quickly as the major global players would have us believe. There remain economic concerns affecting certain markets outside India, not to mention India's own challenges: the lack of luxury retail space, a nascent administrative infrastructure, a worldly and sophisticated few who do not wish to relinquish their status, and the masses who have yet to be educated in the pleasures of international luxury and fashion brands. Indeed, the masses will be the motor and determining factor behind luxury in India's evolution in the years to come. And there to help them, of course, are the global players, with their proven management and branding techniques.

BRANDING

There is a big difference between fashion and luxury goods as products, and what goes into the making of brands. In her book, *Luxury Fashion Branding*, Uché Okonkwo, the Paris-based luxury branding consultant, has outlined a succinct and pertinent perspective that may serve as a foundation for branding in the sector:

> The branding aspect of luxury goods management is integral to a luxury brand's sustainability. The brand is the reason that consumers associate themselves with a luxury company. It is what creates and sustains the attraction and desire for products. The strong attachment that luxury consumers have to brands, which often defies logic, is the result of branding. Brands are not products and should not be managed like products. Brands are a complete package that provides a source of identity for products. This identity becomes a springboard for the associations and perceptions eventually developed in the mind of consumers. This is what draws consumers to luxury brands and remains their source of satisfaction—of the journey of branding begins from crafting a clear brand concept and brand identity and projecting it to the public through an equally clear brand personality and brand image. What the public sees and interprets through the brand image leads to a positioning of the brand in their minds through perceptions and associations. This further leads to the allocation of a space for that brand in their minds according to their sentiments towards the brand. This is called the brand share and influences future purchase decisions and, subsequently, brand loyalty.[2]

The total branding concept (and not just the brand image) is the source of a luxury fashion brand's wealth. When the sum of all distinctive qualities of a brand results in continuous demand for and commitment to the brand from consumers, the brand is said to have high brand equity. The brand equity is what translates to brand value, which is the financial gain that a luxury company eventually accrues as a result of its brand strength. The brand equity ought to be painstakingly managed and nurtured to retain its ability to create value. Brands are invaluable creators of wealth for companies, and luxury brands that aim to attain a competitive edge ought to be fanatical about managing their brand strategy. This is the most important tool the luxury fashion sector has.

Developing and managing a luxury brand effectively are part of a painstakingly long process. They require a consistent integrated strategy, innovative techniques, rigorous management control, and constant auditing. This is the reason that there are few brands that claim true "luxury" status. Although several brands aim toward attaining a "luxury and prestige" rank, and every talented designer aspires to creating his or her own luxury brand, only a few brands eventually succeed. The successful brands are those that understand the challenge of finding a balance between being timeless through a firm brand concept and heritage; being current and relevant to the moment through strong brand positioning; and being innovative in crafting a future—all at the same time.

The confusion in India about what constitutes luxury may be put at an even more basic level. Only a few years ago, any foreign brand coming into India from France and Italy carried connotations of luxury: "foreign" became almost synonymous with the perception of luxury. Thus most consumers' perception of Benetton products in India was unlike that anywhere else in the world. Table wines from France were considered to be luxury when they were anything but. And with the exception of a handful of international luxury and fashion players of vision, courage, and perspicacity, most of the other "legitimate" players have tended to adopt a wait-and-see strategy. The success of several of the first pioneers, coupled with India's economic advances, has convinced the industry's global brands that the ground is now fertile for building brand equity in India.

THE NUMEROUS DEFINITIONS OF "LUXURY"

Where to start when defining what luxury is or, more importantly for some, what luxury is not? Even among the "expert" professionals from the industry, there are many variations on the theme. For many of those interviewed for this book, the initial reference is historical—from the ancients: Egyptian, Greek, and Byzantine to the Italian Renaissance through the European royal courts in the seventeenth century and on to the aristocracy, to the domination of the French in the eighteenth and nineteenth centuries, to the gradual expansion of the concept in the twentieth century, and, finally, to the current modernization and watering down of the concept in the twenty-first century. From the historical context comes a direct link to product.

From its origin (the Latin *lux*) comes the notion of light, literally reflecting the brilliance of certain objects. This aspect was at the foundation of many items deemed *lux* from the earliest signs of civilization. Copper, bronze, silver, gold, and gemstones reflected the light and, at various times, became items of currency. The ownership and accumulation of such objects conferred wealth, and came to reflect the owners' social status. So the derivation has carried down over the centuries to applications of the term *luxury* linked to these very items and concepts. The consumption and display of these rare products brought with them another notion, one of sumptuousness, splendor, and wealth (to the point of excess). But a luxury product does not make a luxury brand.

In their book, *Luxury Brand Management*, Michel Chevalier and Gérald Mazzalovo define a luxury brand as follows:

> One could say that a luxury brand is a selective and exclusive one; that is, it is almost the only brand in its product category, giving it the desirable attributes of being scarce, sophisticated and in good taste. It also has a slightly understated and aristocratic dimension ... This restrictive definition of luxury makes sense, but it doesn't represent the situation as we know it today ... we believe there is a need for an operational definition that takes into account the location of brands in stores and how they are perceived by the consumer. So, we might say that a luxury brand is the one that is selective and exclusive, and which has an additional creative

and emotional value for the consumer. This definition is much broader and includes a larger range of fashion products ...

The final factor to consider in forming a definition of "luxury" is the level of luxury epitomized by a brand. Danielle Alleres distinguishes three different levels of luxury. First is *inaccessible* luxury, which corresponds to exclusive models, sometimes hand-made in single units. Next is *intermediary* luxury, which corresponds to objects that are, in fact, expensive replicas of individual models. In the fashion field, haute couture would be the inaccessible luxury, while specially made outfits, duplicating all or part of a *couture* model, would fall into this intermediary category. Finally, *accessible* luxury represents all those products made in factories or workshops ...

This analysis is interesting, but in a way it misses the point that 98% of the luxury business today corresponds to the accessible luxury category ... Having failed to discover a definition that clearly explains what makes a product a 'luxury item,' we have evolved our own. For us, *a luxury good must satisfy three criteria*: it must have a *strong artistic content*; it must be the result of *craftsmanship*; and it must be *international*.[3]

For the masses, these three terms do not evoke the notion of luxury and are more conceptual. When applied in this way, we come to understand that the term eludes the great majority. Consulting firm KPMG's conclusions were comparable:

Luxury is a constantly evolving and subjective concept, and not easy to define. But more often than not, the word is used to define an inessential but desirable item or a state of extreme comfort or indulgence. What sets luxury brands apart is that they command a premium without clear functional advantages over their counterparts. Yet consumers are willing to pay the significant price difference because they have a unique set of characteristics including premium quality, craftsmanship, recognizability, exclusivity and reputation.[4]

Into the luxury recipe may be blended additional ingredients such as comfort, aesthetic quality, historical or traditional work from the human hand, and exoticism. In this way we form a grouping that begins with the more general use of the term and then moves into the more specific, for example:

- a universe, a lifestyle
- a concept that is highly personal or intimate in its application ("Luxury for me is …")
- a product or group of products, as qualified by the luxury industry and based upon a market and economic approach
- a business model, according to the companies in luxury goods

During a 2007 luxury conference in India, Concetta Lanciaux, an independent consultant and advisor to the LVMH luxury group, outlined four key characteristics that qualify companies for the luxury category: heritage, quality, artisan knowhow, and selective distribution. LVMH prides itself on its store concepts, visual merchandising techniques, impeccably trained sales staff and service quality. Displaying luxury goods in an environment worthy of both the brand and the consumer is part and parcel of a key factor in luxury: *image*.

If image is the short answer to "what?," then quality is the short answer to "how?" The idea of quality is inextricably linked to luxury. Take the label "Made in France" or "Made in Italy", which provides a means of differentiating (that is, placing above) one luxury product from another with the same utility. For cost-reduction purposes, an increasing number of French and Italian companies now manufacture their goods elsewhere but they shrewdly sew the last stitch themselves to maintain the prestige attached, literally, to their label of origin. Quality is linked both to the notion of perfection in the materials used and to the service that accompany the sale of the goods.

The concept of rarity has increasingly fallen by the wayside, with the producers of luxury goods emphasizing the "exotic" (mainly in reference to materials such as animal skins or gemstones). This helps to transform the "product" into an object, not unlike the concept of art. To a Japanese consumer, a Louis Vuitton item will certainly have this exotic flavor that a local leather-goods brand does not have. This cachet was developed in a knowingly shrewd manner that brings us back to the essence of branding and creating a need for something that, although not absolutely unnecessary, becomes an object of desire.

A rather recent trend in many luxury companies has been product diversification into areas way outside their traditional specialty. As Deutsche Bank analysts put it in a July 2007 report on luxury goods: "You can now buy Armani chocolates …" and an accompanying illustration (see figure 1.1) shows an increasingly adventurous product diversification. Brand diversification has met with some success, and the trend toward lifestyle luxury has seen creative variations on the theme, such as in the hotel sector.

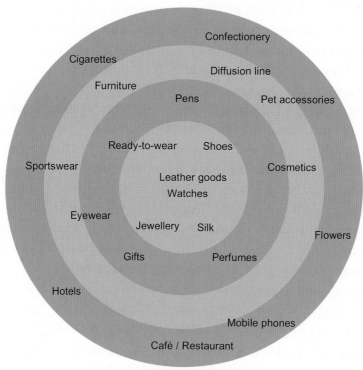

Figure 1.1: Product diversification of luxury brands
Source: Deutsche Bank 2007, *Luxury goods*

The financial crisis of 2008-2009 has had an impact on the perception of luxury. Greg Furman, founder and chairman of the Luxury Marketing Council, states that:

> The definition of luxury is changing. The words that I hear most now are Experience (unique and memorable); Story (the ability to talk about a great product or experience that is truly unique); Value (bespoke craft as in a Brioni or Chanel suit will always mast, style-wise and wear-wise); Wellness (it's no longer about "stuff"; it's about how wonderful products or experience makes us and our families and loved ones feel); Service (not the same old same old; see Jack Mitchell's Hug Your Customers for the definitive point of view on this); Time (all of us, rich or poor, desire more of it and all the most affluent require a new sensitivity and respect for their time as a favored client's time in all transactions in person and online); The simple things (dry fire wood; an hour's spa treatment; a run in the park; quiet time on the screened porch; time with family and friends; a great meal or a bottle of wine).[5]

THE LUXURY MARKET

The luxury market continues to offer enticing opportunities for companies looking for profitability drivers and returns on investment. A market study by consulting firm Bain & Company estimated that the global luxury goods market in 2006 was worth €160 billion, up 9.5% from the previous year (€146 million), with the newly rich from the BRIC countries (Brazil, Russia, India, and China) accounting for a great part in that growth.

The September 2007 launch party for the Indian edition of *Vogue* was a vibrant symbol of the attraction that emerging countries today represent for luxury and fashion houses. The stock price of luxury goods companies provides another indicator of this attraction, with recent valuations of companies nowhere near what the inner fundamentals of the brand would suggest. Take Hermès, for example. In July 2007, it was valued at 17.3 times its earnings before interest and tax (EBIT), demonstrating multiples that companies in other industries cannot compete with.

If the luxury market is to yield even higher returns, the quality of the management will be crucial. The global players have mastered their branding techniques, which start with marketing strategies that are specifically geared toward the geographies they are targeting. Owning a piece of the pie in the BRIC territories will become an increasingly competitive scenario, and here's where both the branding and marketing synergies are required to make for success. According to Uché Okonkwo:

> The luxury fashion marketing strategy comprises the branding mix as its main component which will be tagged here as "the six Ps of Luxury branding". The branding mix contains recognized marketing elements that drive the branding process forward. Like the famous Four Ps of the marketing mix, the Six Ps is a tool that propels the marketing and branding strategies of luxury brands in the direction of market success. The Six Ps are the following:
>
> 1. The Product
> 2. The Pricing
> 3. The Place of Distribution
> 4. The Promotion
> 5. The People
> 6. The Positioning.[6]

Whereas all Ps have their place in the marketing and branding strategies, the first three may serve a further use because they relate to market segmentation, a more pertinent issue for today's India. To this list we might add another P that is crucial in today's fashion and luxury world: Partnerships.

Segmentation by product category is standard when trying to identify the most dynamic market segments and to position companies on the market in accordance with their core activities. Bain & Company's 2006 study segmented the world luxury market, as shown in figure 1.2.

Segmentation by pricing becomes more difficult in a world where the rich are getting richer, where inequalities in wealth distribution are growing, and where luxury goods are more affordable to the masses as a result of both lower entry prices and an increased demand by high-end luxury consumers to maintain exclusivity and trade up to higher price points. With the term "luxury" continuing to evolve,

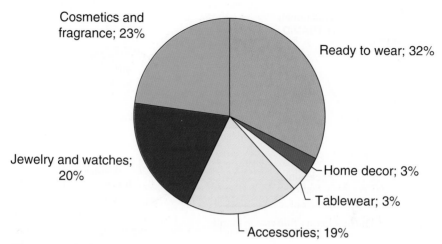

Figure 1.2: The luxury market by product category
Source: Bain & Company 2006, *Market Study*

according to Deutsche Bank's July 2007 report, the luxury goods universe has gone from a pyramid format into a pear-shaped format (see figure 1.3), and may be divided into three pricing categories:

- Super-luxury: These are goods for the very rich with money beyond imagining, and when they spend it they may do so in a personalized version of luxury to accommodate a lifestyle expressed in the form of multiple homes, yachts, private planes, and so on.
- Luxury: What the general public has come to understand as being able to buy the best or, at least, the latest. Customized up to a certain point but "the happy few" are increasing in number.
- Accessible luxury: Here is where the luxury brands have cleverly hooked the masses into their world by offering prices at lower entry levels. Coupled with the multiplicity of brand diversification (cosmetics, mobile telephones, and so on), the brands are increasingly accessible.

Segmentation by the place of distribution goes beyond the standard logic of marketers. The luxury goods companies are concentrating on the several issues that relate to geographies, among them the location of

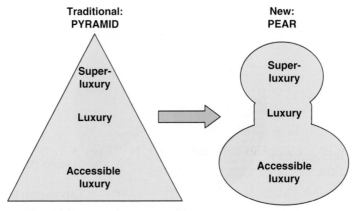

Figure 1.3: The new luxury universe pyramid
Source: Deutsche Bank 2007, *Luxury goods*

high-net-worth individuals (HNWIs). The greatest real growth of these wealthy individuals is in the BRIC countries, and they are buying the luxury goods faster, and better, in a more knowledgeable manner than they do any other category. But luxury marketers are careful to cherish the Japanese, whose longstanding, loyal consumption of luxury goods—be it in their country or while traveling abroad—accounts for 41% of the global turnover generated by luxury products, as shown in figure 1.4.

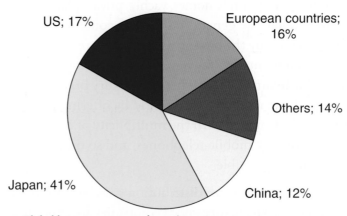

Figure 1.4: Global luxury consumers by region 2005
Source: Ernst & Young cited in Deutsche Bank 2007, *Luxury goods*

The cost differential for luxury brands in India and the limited luxury retail infrastructure open up the possibility of an additional form of product segmentation, which is product mobility. The market for luxury brands in India is growing quickly, but Indians will retain their reputation for price sensitivity and value perception. However, if the product cannot be acquired overseas and brought into India (e.g. luxury cars or music systems), then the price and environment of acquisition will matter less. If the product (e.g. watches or bags) can easily be acquired overseas and brought into India at a substantially lower cost, and if the environment of acquisition (Madison Avenue or Bond Street) provides a "feel-good" cachet, then price and environment will matter far more. The consequence of this is that for as long as the tax regime and infrastructure remain largely as they are, the value of highly mobile luxury goods sold in India may disappoint while the value of less mobile luxury goods may surprise.

We have been asked the question: Why are these luxury consumers buying more French brands than any other? In addition to the sheer number of French luxury brands compared to those from other countries, there is a simple explanation. Exportability is a great asset for these companies because the French market is so small, obliging French brands to look toward other markets. Some French luxury brands have been in existence for centuries, and most control their production, distribution, and creation, which lay the foundation for a luxury brand. Firms in countries like India have not been pressed to look outside their own immense market to proliferate. But with the advent of luxury and fashion brands, it will take more than simply desiring to become a luxury brand for this to become a reality. This may occur gradually over the years with a solid control strategy.

Many of the elements are now in place to make the argument for the growing presence of the luxury brands in India, setting the stage for local companies to learn the tricks of the trade and enter into the world of luxury branding. For both foreign and local companies, success will remain a function of how consumption continues and how the companies attract a captive market that has increasing wherewithal to afford their products.

There remains one last characteristic of luxury brands, and this is linked to their history of demonstrating sustainable growth through their high profit margins. Luxury brands have been built over time, and base their success on a strong, sustainable heritage. Almost all of them are or were a family business, passed down from generation to generation. Luxury goods have a sense of timelessness, a concept built in large part on the classical and traditional values associated with luxury, as well as the substantial investments that go into the launching of products, be they old or new. The lead time required for creation and production is also of consequence. As the hand-made aspect remains a key element in qualifying a luxury product in today's world, it is both the accelerator and the brake in the luxury brand companies, which create increased demand by forcing the consumer to wait. They would have us believe that the human hand can work only so quickly. Further, customization is a driver of business for many luxury brands, and the more individualized the process, the more the unique aspects and emotional elements that tie the consumer into a loyal relationship. Thus a luxury product should reflect a brand's dedication to tradition, heritage, and, above all, quality. After all, unlike fashion, these products are meant to last beyond the lifetime of the bearer. As Christian Blanckaert, a former senior Hermès executive put it: "A Luxury Good is something that you can retain for ever."[7]

Indeed, it is not uncommon for the original owner of a Kelly Bag to hand down this beloved object to a daughter, who in turn will hand it down to hers ...

FASHION WITHIN THE LUXURY CONTEXT

Drawing a distinction between what is luxury and what is fashion was succinctly addressed in *Luxury Brand Management*, where Chevalier and Mazzalovo put the issue squarely to the reader[8]:

There is also some debate about the distinction between luxury and fashion. According to this point of view, a brand in the textile and accessory field, for example, might start out as a fashion brand, and would only be given the status of a "luxury" brand when it has achieved some stability and a quality of being timeless. A new fashion brand has to be creative and come up with new ideas, new concepts and new products for every season, in order to attract the interest of consumers. However, as it develops "classical" models with a signature style, its status will move from fashion to luxury. While this distinction between fashion brand and luxury brand is a valid one, it is also misleading and possibly even dangerous. It is misleading because even when it has achieved "luxury" status, a fashion brand such as Chanel or Dior must still come up with new designs each season, and present them in new ways, in order to retain customers' interest. It is also dangerous because it implies that a luxury brand doesn't have to innovate to the same extent as a fashion brand, which is obviously not the case.

It is interesting to note that among the more seasoned professionals in the luxury and fashion industry, the luxury component is widely perceived as having as its core and very essence the notion of accessories. The shelf life of these items taken in their entirety is significantly longer than clothing. Fashion reflects a way to dress, hence the term "fashionably dressed," and is related to trends in any given area and at a certain point of time; namely, in the here and now. That something may become "unfashionable" or "out of fashion" is part and parcel of its very nature.

Fashion, like art, is an ever-evolving movement inspired by its time. It relates to a state of mind, a style of living, and the social atmosphere that prevails in a specific place at a particular time. At its core is the notion of clothing: the body is to fashion what the hand is to luxury. But the hand is used in most every manner, both in fashion and luxury. *Somewhere along the way the worlds of luxury and fashion overlap, to the point where it is almost impossible to distinguish between them.* If we were to draw the line between these, in which category would the following brands be placed? Chanel, Chloé, Ermenegildo Zegna, Gucci, Hermès, Louis Vuitton, Yves Saint Laurent, to name just a few. Would we call them fashion brands or luxury brands? Which belong to which universe? The trend has been to market a brand as being in the luxury category to capitalize on the cachet of prestige, the ever-important image as presented to current and prospective consumers.

Where would we position these companies when considering that luxury brand products are meant to last a lifetime and to transcend notions of transient fashionability? If we consider that luxury's bywords—quality, rarity, and service—are anchored in a sense of heritage, how would this affect our perspective? If history is at the root of a luxury brand, then what of those self-proclaimed luxury brands creating jewelry, watches, and leather goods that do not have such a rich provenance?

Fashion

Fashion brands market products that are not meant to have a long shelf life. The collections are constantly evolving and looking toward the future. It is difficult—though not impossible—for a brand whose eponymous designer is still alive to go from being a fashion brand to becoming a luxury brand.

Didier Grumbach, president of the French Federation of Couture and author of the renowned *L'Histoire de la Mode*, is one of the fashion industry's most respected authorities on the subject. During an interview with the authors, he provided his take on luxury and fashion, which is pointed and provides a broad perspective:

> Luxury is what remains when Fashion has moved on. A luxury product is one meant to last a lifetime, and by definition, luxury never goes out of fashion. Fashion brands may grow old while luxury brands mature over the years. This is generally not the case for fashion brands, which are born from the world of clothing. Luxury brands are born from the world of accessories.

As we have observed, fashion brands grow old, whereas luxury brands evolve and become timeless, like Hermès, and maintain their artisan roots. One does not think of fashion when stepping into a Hermès store; one thinks instead of buying an object of perfect quality. Conversely, one does not speak of "wearing" Louis Vuitton or Hermès, since these brands produce more accessories than fashion. There are Louis Vuitton stores where there is no fashion in the sense of "apparel." But in India a Chanel store without a Chanel suit is unthinkable; it is the incarnation of the brand's origins, which are essential. Ideally a time comes when all elements of a brand attain the same level of excellence. At Chanel, accessories, jewelry, and fashion are all at the same level for the same consumer.

The French luxury brands that have a history are those that have stood the test of time. This history is part of the brand equity and a definite asset for a brand such as Chanel, which is incontestably a luxury brand. Chanel was always avant garde, at the cutting edge of fashion. At what point did it evolve and transform itself into a luxury brand? *When Chanel started to create perfumes, it evolved and transformed itself into a luxury brand.* And it set the standard for others.

Chloé, founded in 1956, is the youngest of the Richemont group brands, and is now positioning itself as a luxury brand. We can see that the brand is bigger than the DNA from which it comes, and is a typical example of a brand in the process of change. As CEO Ralph Toledano explains, it would not sell any handbags if it was not selling fashion, just as the founder of the house, Chloé herself, launched her brand of bags through the same channels as her dresses. Fashion brands are instantaneously transversal: they have instant legitimacy in all domains, and a few of them will become luxury brands. But for decades, fashion houses have overexploited their products by issuing licenses indiscriminately, and they did not want to hear about a "creator". Today, brands are a series of Creators who, each in turn, help to make the brand "timeless," such as Gucci as an accessories brand, Yves Saint Laurent as *haute couture*, Ermenegildo Zegna as a luxury brand, or Louis Vuitton as sole provider of its goods.

Contemporary fashion brands have the potential to one day become luxury brands, but it will take time and skillful brand management.

Table 1.1   The major luxury and fashion group companies (excluding fragrance and cosmetics, wines and spirits)

LVMH France	Richemont Switzerland	Gucci Group Italy	Prada Italy
Berluti	A. Lange & Söhne	Alexander McQueen	Car Shoe
Celine	Alfred Dunhill	Balenciaga	Church's
Chaumet	Baume & Mercier	Bédat & Co.	Miu Miu
De Beers Diamond	Cartier	Bottega Veneta	Prada
Jewelers (JV)	Chloé	Boucheron	
DFS	IWC	Gucci	
Dior	Jaeger-LeCoultre	Sergio Rossi	
Donna Karan	Lancel	Stella McCartney	
Emilio Pucci	Montblanc	Yves Saint Laurent	
Fendi	Montegrappa		
Fred	Officine Panerai		
Hublot	Piaget		
Givenchy	Purdey		
Kenzo	Shanghai Tang		
La Samaritaine	Vacheron Constantin		
Le Bon Marché	Van Cleef & Arpels		
Loewe			
Louis Vuitton			
Marc Jacobs			
Sephora			
StefanoBi			
Tag Heuer			
Thomas Pink			
Zenith			

Some luxury brands, if they do not abide by the parameters within which luxury brands must optimize their management, may dilute their image and with ever-lower brand equity may be relegated to the status of fashion brands. The global luxury brands are acutely aware of this, particularly with regard to the potential cost to their image of engaging in product diversification through brand extensions or launching entry-level priced products to broaden their consumer base. The four key luxury groups have dozens of brands in their portfolios, both in luxury and fashion. LVMH's flagship luxury brand is Louis Vuitton, and among its fashion brands are Kenzo, Celine, and the like. Richemont

Table 1.2   BrandZ top ranking—Luxury category[9]

#	Brand	Brand value US$m	Brand contribution	Brand momentum	Brand value change
1	Louis Vuitton	19,395	4	7	5%
2	Hermès	7,862	4	6	13%
3	Gucci	7,468	4	5	15%
4	Chanel	6,219	4	6	−3%
5	Rolex	5,532	4	5	35%
6	Hennessy	5,403	5	7	0%
7	Cartier	4,913	4	3	−12%
8	Moët & Chandon	4,847	5	7	−2%
9	Fendi	3,469	4	4	5%
10	Prada	2,704	4	5	0%

Source: Millward Brown Optimor (including data from BrandZ, Datamonitor and Bloomberg)

group's undisputed luxury houses of Cartier and Van Cleef & Arpels are operating alongside their fashion brands such as Chloé. The Gucci Group's flagship luxury brands, Gucci and Boucheron, sit alongside fashion brands such as Sergio Rossi and Balenciaga. And Prada's eponymous flagship luxury brand is complemented by Miu Miu in fashion.

Luxury within the fashion houses

The French say that there is an exception to every rule and, in the case of some of today's fashion brands, it goes by two words: *haute couture*, the one-of-a-kind creations of the couturiers, representing the ultimate in fashion design. *Haute couture* is a protected "appellation," a designation put in place by the Ministry of Industry since 1945. *Couture* is the capacity to make to order a particular model for a particular client, and it is a skill that has been preserved. It is a service, an instrument that serves to individualize, to legitimize, and to institutionalize a brand. *Haute couture* is not an industry like any other. Since 1943, *haute couture* has become an institution in alignment with the economic situation, and there are brands that have kept with a tradition established at a time when ready-to-wear did not exist. For the following 50 years, the *haute couture* label was used as a brand license, and thus survived where it should have been toppled by ready-to-wear, as was the case in other countries. *Haute couture* was the only means to dress women at a time when women of a certain social standing dressed only in made-to-measure clothing. It was also an industry with 300,000 artisans. Now there are only 7,000. Elsewhere, *haute couture* is simply the superior part of ready-to-wear; it is only in France that it is considered as an industry in and of itself. It is a skill that the French managed to preserve, a "label" still conferred by the Ministry of Industry. *Haute couture* is an asset for Paris in spite of the difference between ready-to-wear and *haute couture* being at times difficult to discern these days.

Applying an Indian perspective to this, Didier Grumbach distinguished between the two during an interview with the authors:

> The Sari is an interesting case because it is a traditional garment and the way it is worn is governed by various codes. I cannot call it *haute couture*, it is more like the equivalent of the kimono to the Japanese. There are Indian designers who have a feeling for the spectacular such as Rohit Bal and Manish Arora, both who could also be part of our own *haute couture*.

As he specified, today's *haute couture* follows a specific calendar and requires skills and talent. And he added:

> I mean creative talent, which is why the Sari could not be part of it. *Haute couture* has to be original creation.

Indians come close to the Western ideas for products. Their luxury is more natural than our own version, which has been "polluted" by marketing. In India, the designers are idolized like soccer stars. This fascination existed in Europe decades ago, as Didier Grumbach explained to us:

> There is a real identification with the designer that does not exist in China. In India there is a certain knowledge regarding luxury products, quality is sought after, insisted upon, more than in Europe, where the

sense of quality has been lost with the onslaught of press releases. We think that in India there is a capacity for service, an understanding of quality, and a great sense of hospitality. There is already something in India, and some of their designers may try to go global. The problem is they lack expertise in cutting. The pieces are fabulous, but at present a local luxury industry does not exist in India.

Foreign brands taking a market by storm may occur in many countries. India is a latecomer to this phenomenon. Cities all over the world want to become like Paris or London. The transformation to luxury in Moscow was planned by the local authorities, and the same thing may happen in Delhi. Everyone wants to be a "player" and part of the international community. What is happening in India today happened in Japan 50 years ago. Globalization is more than just a word. It engenders organization and structure. One can no longer be 100% French any more than 100% Indian. Says Didier Grumbach:

> Today the "brand" with its content, its history, its territory, is vital. There will never be thousands of international brands. Even during the "time of the French brands," there were only three or four that really mattered. Brands that are known the world over in fashion and accessories will always be limited in number. Barriers are breaking down and soon Indians will be wearing French designer brands. They will become closer to us and we will become a little Indian ourselves. In this mixing of cultures lies the future of the luxury brands.

However, the roots of these various brands will remain identifiable. Globalization increasingly imposes an international approach. Talking of a French, Italian, or even an Indian brand will one day become a thing of the past. It is inevitable that local and national brands will be consumed by international brands. To speak of a brand exclusive to one country is to turn one's back on the future. To be a luxury brand today means to be strong the world over. A brand that is oriented toward only one market is not adapted to the neighboring markets. This is something the Indians will be bearing in mind with the continued arrival of more global players in their country. This may also set the tone for understanding India's own history of luxury and fashion.

NOTES

1. Ayurveda is the ancient system of health care native to the Indian subcontinent. It includes healthy living along with therapeutic measures that relate to physical, mental, social, and spiritual harmony.

2. Uché Okonkwo 2007, *Luxury Fashion Branding*, Palgrave Macmillan, pp. 4–5.

3. Michel Chevalier & Gérald Mazzalovo 2008, *Luxury Brand Management*, John Wiley & Sons, Introduction (pp. vii, x, xi).

4. *Business Horizons* 1998, "The Mass Marketing of Luxury", vol. 41, no. 6, cited in KPMG 2006, "Luxury Brands in China", *Consumer Markets Report*, November. introduction, p. 2.

5. Greg Furman 2009, "CEO Talk", *Business of Daily Newsletter*, June 27.

6. Okonkwo, op. cit., p. 83

7. *Hindustan Times* 2007, "Delegate Speak", April 1.

8. Chevalier & Mazzalovo, op. cit., pp. vii, viii

9. Millward Brown Optimor created the BrandZ Top 100, a ranking that identifies the world's most powerful brands measured by their dollar value. The brand ranking provides key insights and actionable information for finance, marketing and business professionals on how to manage and grow their brand assets.

CHAPTER 2
FRAMEWORK AND CONTEXT OF LUXURY IN INDIA

There are some who may call it the irony of India's modern society, but it is a curious sight. In the womb of New Delhi's Connaught Place, a glamorous store named Pashma sells the most superfine cashmere products for thousands of rupees. Just outside, in the car park, a scrappily dressed vendor sells factory-surplus shirts for 100 rupees out of his handmade rickshaw trolley. Seeing the traffic that he creates, an FMCG company has even given him a branded umbrella, in the hope that it catches the eye of passers-by and, of course, in the long hope that the consumers for that 100-rupee shirt will buy a 10-rupee bottle of soft drink to quench their thirst.

For the uninitiated, India can be a distraction as one jockeys to and fro between extremes. It is said that progress is hardly ever a simple and linear process. Even as society advances in one direction, it loses much along the way. And this is certainly true of India. Indeed, Shashi Tharoor, the former UN Undersecretary General for Communications and Public Information, and author of a dozen books including *India: from Midnight to the Millennium Beyond* recounts:

> "India," Winston Churchill once barked, "is merely a geographical expression. It is no more a single country than the Equator." Churchill was rarely right about India, but it is true that no other country in the world embraces the extraordinary mixture of ethnic groups, the profusion of mutually incomprehensible languages, the varieties of topography and climate, the diversity of religions and cultural practices, and the range of levels of economic development that India does.

> And yet India is more than the sum of its contradictions. It is a country held together, in the words of its first Prime Minister, Jawaharlal Nehru,

"by strong but invisible threads ... About her there is the elusive quality of a legend of long ago; some enchantment seems to have held her mind. She is a myth and an idea, a dream and a vision, and yet very real and present and pervasive."

How can one approach this land of snow peaks and tropical jungles, with seventeen major languages ... inhabited in the last decade of the 20th Century by nearly 940 million individuals of every ethnic extraction known to humanity? How does one come to terms with a country whose population is 51 percent illiterate, but which has educated the world's second largest pool of trained scientists and engineers, whose teeming cities overflow while four out of five Indians scratch a living from the soil? What is the clue to understanding a country rife with despair and disrepair, which nonetheless moved a Mughal emperor to declaim, "If on earth there be paradise of bliss, it is this, it is this, it is this"? How does one gauge a culture that elevated non-violence to an effective moral principle, but whose freedom was born in blood and whose independence still soaks in it? How does one explain a land where peasant organizations and suspicious officials attempt to close down Kentucky Fried Chicken as a threat to the nation, where a former Prime Minister bitterly criticizes the sale of Pepsi-Cola "in a country where villagers don't have clean drinking water," and which yet invents a greater quantity of sophisticated software for U.S. computer manufacturers than any other country in the world? How can one portray the present, let alone the future, of an ageless civilization that was the birthplace of four major religions, a dozen different traditions of classical dance, eighty-five political parties, and three hundred ways of cooking the potato?

The short answer is that it can't be done—at least not to everyone's satisfaction. Any truism about India can be immediately contradicted by another truism about India. The country's national motto, emblazoned on its governmental crest, is Satyameva Jayate: "Truth Alone Triumphs." The question remains, however: Whose truth?

There is not a thought that is being thought in the West or East that is not active in some Indian mind ... That Indian mind has been shaped by remarkably diverse forces: ancient Hindu tradition, myth, and scripture; the impact of Islam and Christianity; and two centuries of British colonial rule. The result is unique, not just because of the variety of contemporary influences available in India, but because of the diversity of its heritage.[1]

CLOTHES OF THE ROYALTY OF OLD INDIA

The maharajas of pre-independence India (before 1947) were not the first to discover luxury. Indian history, dating back 5,000 years, is replete with stories of the love for fine things among the higher class of Indians, the noblemen and royalty. Threads of gold, ornate hand-carved furniture, gossamer weaves for apparel, curtains, furnishings, and exquisitely carved and created accessories such as betel-nut crackers and betel-leaf holders (and even the humble spittoon, which was exalted simply because it was a receptacle for royal spittle) were common household items that spoke of craftsmanship par excellence on rich raw material. Richly embroidered clothes, worked on with gold thread and precious stones, caps and jackets, and waistcoats and turbans to match, formed a trend that came in with the slave dynasty (tenth century) carried forward by the *Mughals* (fourteenth–fifteenth century) and continued well into pre-independence times and today's India.

Museums in India hold priceless treasures that were part of the luxurious lifestyle favored by India's rich. Portraits of the nobility, of royal princes and maharajas reveal pearls and uncut diamonds; rich silks abound, along with transparent muslins and chiffons of the finest weave. Dainty footwear, embellished to match the designs of the clothes, complete the picture of the wearer as a person of refinement and fashionable taste. Heavy brocaded, one-of-a-kind woven coats, embroidered and embellished garments hang in the halls of the museums at Jaipur and across other palace museums in Rajasthan, Mysore, Bengal, Lucknow, Punjab, and Gujarat; and in Hyderabad, the famous wardrobe museum is a long-standing testimony of the elegant lifestyle especially of the women, who mostly lived their life in purdah.

The Nizam's Museum, Hyderabad

The Nizam's Museum in the southern state of Hyderabad, in the Purani Haveli, or Old Mansion, holds a 240-feet long structure that is perhaps the world's most interesting walk-in wardrobe and also the most exquisite in its contents. Finely woven muslins of spider-web thinness, crafted into intricate garments for the ladies and men of the *nizam*'s palace, still hang in the closets. The wardrobe of Burma teak was built by Mahboob Ali Pasha, the sixth *nizam* of Hyderabad almost a century ago.

With due concern for privacy, a changing room stands at the end of every two cupboards of the wardrobe. Cut off from the rest of the cupboard area, yet within view of someone who opens the doors to choose a garment, is the top section that houses hats, shoes (all made in France), boots, other clothing accessories (including gloves), and perfumes.

The clothes themselves are a mix of Indian and imported textiles. Silks from various parts of India, delicately embroidered cottons and muslins embellished with the shadow-work motifs of Lucknow known as *chikankari*[2], known to have been created in the harem of Queen Noor Jehan, and Chinese silks in splendorous colors still hang there for the common visitor to gaze at with admiration. For the student of apparel history or design, they are a source of wonder and inspiration. Not so long ago, the doyenne of Indian fashion, Ritu Kumar, was on record as saying that the museum is a source of inspiration for some of her lines.

In the royal courts and among the nobility in pre-independence India, clothes were a great obsession. India's foundations had a strong base in the textile trade, and it had been so from times immemorial. Every city and town had its own signature weaves and fabrics, and these in turn supported a strong community of spinners, weavers, dyers, and embroiderers. More often than not, these crafts were passed down from one generation to the next.

Royalty, more than any other class, had a strict dress code, and each rite of passage was appropriately accompanied by garments made for the occasion. Drapes, for men and women, were still quite the norm in predominantly Hindi families. Indian civilization has always placed tremendous importance on unstitched fabrics such as the sari and *dhoti*, which are given sacred overtones. The belief was that such a fabric was pure, perhaps because in the distant past needles of bone were used for stitching.

Weddings and other important ceremonies were marked by changes of wardrobe across all but the poorest classes.

In her acclaimed book *Costumes and Textiles of Royal India* (2000), Ritu Kumar notes:

> The temple trusts as well as the royal families of India were great patrons of the arts; all were connoisseurs of beauty with exacting tastes. The attention to detail, the quest for perfection and the wealth and glamor displayed by the royal costumes created a kind of splendor that was unmatched anywhere in the world.[3]

WESTERNIZATION

When the British became the de facto rulers of the entire subcontinent, the Indian royalty began to change how it dressed. Those of the royalty who were allied to the Western trading companies let their political affiliations be known by their tastes in dress and manner. It was only natural that as familiarity and social intercourse increased between the West and the Indian royalty, there would be changes in behavior and lifestyle. So it was not unusual to see an ornament-encrusted turban topping a Western suit adapted to suit the wearer's tastes. Some of the innovations in dress were almost the start of what would become, in post-independence India, a tragic loss of Indianness. The textile aesthetics changed, and the blend of Eastern and Western sensibilities sometimes became something of a mish-mash of styles. Imported fabrics were used as drapes and sometimes stitched into items of apparel, and it was not unusual for a royal personage to team a British coronation robe with very traditional clothes accessorized with jewelry and traditional footwear.

Chairs and other items of furniture came into use, consigning the rich mattresses and golden cloth seats to back rooms or the realm of history. The soft gleam of hand-worked gold-thread embroidery (*zardosi*) that set the nobility apart was replaced by the rustle of mill-produced cloth.

First-time visitors to Europe soon found that being Roman in Rome was a safe bet: their style of dress and bearing created too much attention, and not always of a complimentary kind. An unfortunate courtier traveling with Jagajit Singh of Kapurtala, for example, sitting in regal livery outside the Grevin museum in Paris, was mistaken for a waxwork from the museum. Indian women such as Rani Kanari, wife of the same Kapurtala maharaja, wore Western clothes while traveling in Europe, as did Chimnabai, wife of Sayaji Rao III of Baroda, foretelling a trend that was to become almost universal among Indians by the end of the twentieth century.

Evening suits and top hats were favored and usually acquired from the outfitters on London's Savile Row. Sayaji Rao III was so regular a client of Henry Poole & Co. that he awarded the company a royal warrant. With an impetus renewed by their first-hand exposure to the treasures of the West, the princes would ensure that they ordered the very best in Dresden china, crystalware, silver, and jewelry during their visits.

The tragic story of a *rana* of Udaipur who ordered an entire houseful of crystal objects, from beds to hand fans and goblets and doorknobs, but died before his consignment could reach him, is oft repeated to the many visitors who file past the crystal gallery above the Durbar Hall at the Fateh Prakash palace in Udaipur, and shows that there was no holding back in the level of orders placed for goods that tickled the royal fancy.

THE EVOLUTION OF LUXURY AND FASHION IN INDIA

The British elite in India generally adopted an extravagant lifestyle that could be cultured as well as being indulgent in the ways lovingly recalled in the memoirs of William Hickey, who resided in Kolkata as an attorney for most of the period 1777–1808.

Take the house that Raja Rajendra Mallick built in 1835, and which continues to be a residence for his descendants. It still houses a huge cache of Western sculpture and Victorian furniture, paintings by European and Indian artists, and other *objets d'art*, including Bohemian chandeliers, Belgian glass, clocks, and literally truckloads of marble statues and busts. It still has two paintings by Rubens—*The Marriage of St. Catherine* and *The Martyrdom of St. Sebastian*—and works by Titian, Murrillo, Sir Joshua Reynolds, John Opie, and a whole room for a statue of Queen Victoria.

Indeed, the Mallick Palace is typical of the palaces and mansions built during Kolkata's golden age in the late eighteenth century, when it became the administrative center of the famed East India Company, and was subsequently named the capital of Bengal. During Queen Victoria's reign as empress of India, it became the imperial capital and evolved into a beautiful city of palaces, wealth, and culture. Once the opium trade (the center of Kolkata's economy) ended, the city went into an irreversible slow decline, especially when the capital was moved to Delhi.

Fast-forward 100 years and imagine … a poker table surrounded by gentlemen in tuxedos and elegant women in flapper dresses. A beautiful dark-haired young woman, obviously Indian, in a luscious silk sari, a long cigarette holder between her fingers, is scraping up almost every chip on the table. But that is not what seduces the people around her. It is her regal bearing, and her rather unusual mascot, a small turtle whose back is studded with precious stones. As the creature strays across the table, her beautifully manicured hand brings it back to her side, her emeralds and rubies glinting with every movement.

The lady in question is Maharani Indira Devi of Coochbehar, a jetsetter who counted Noel Coward, Douglas Fairbanks, Jimmy Stewart, and the Prince of Wales as her friends. They, in turn, often referred to her as the *maharani* of "Couche Partout" because of her penchant for scandalous love affairs. Her saris were made of pure French chiffon. Her shoes were often made by Salvatore Ferragamo, cobbler to the rich and famous, who recalled in his memoirs some extraordinary commissions, in particular a pair of pearl-encrusted green velvet shoes, and another black velvet pair set with diamonds.

In his book *Made for Maharajas: A Design Diary of Princely India*, Amin Jaffer has countless examples of the style and elegant tastes of the princely class that ruled the Indian states. These men and women straddled the two worlds very successfully, ordering their

Gandhi in Western clothing

clothes, furniture, luggage, shoes, and jewelry from the most renowned luxury houses in the West, without a second thought to price or the inconvenience it might cause the creators to adapt to their special requests and specifications.

Luxury, and the love of it, penetrated to the noble class too. Salar Jung, a nobleman of high lineage and a connoisseur of things rare and beautiful, collected perhaps the largest one-man collection of art and artifacts in recent Indian history. The collection has outlived the man and his passion, and can be viewed in a museum bearing the collector's name in Hyderabad.

Dr. S. Rangachari, perhaps the most famous surgeon in Madras in the previous century, was, despite his otherwise Brahmanical

Gandhi in traditional clothing

ways, one of the first owners of a private two-seater plane and a Rolls-Royce, and his vast collection of imported and Indian artifacts lie scattered across younger generations of relatives and at the Madras Museum. Instances such as this are many.

Not surprisingly though, clothes were a matter of personal taste; and when only the best in fittings would do, the best in the West were called upon to provide them. Motilal Nehru, barrister-at-law and father of India's first prime minister, was a connoisseur of the good things in life, steeped in Western culture, and kept an elegant home. When his clothes needed laundering, he sent them to Paris! His son, Jawaharlal, and Mahatma Gandhi were, thanks to their student days in England, also very British in their dress and speech. But where Gandhi adapted the villager's mode of dressing very early in his fight to rid his country of British rule and attended the Round Table Conference in England in a loincloth, *dhoti*, and slippers, Nehru held on much longer.

Nehru arrived in England fitted out in tweeds, hat, and smoking a cigar, as was the fashion then. And his wardrobe stayed with him until he eventually bowed to increasing criticism that his manner of dress was at odds with the anti-British movement, and abandoned them.

Nehru's love of fine clothes metamorphosed into the creation of his personal style: the Nehru jacket, with its Mandarin collar and straight, clean lines, is a style borrowed from the Sherwani, an Indian coat that many have adapted across the world, and epitomizes sheer elegance. It came into international focus after it appeared in *Vogue* and was adopted by the likes of Johnny Carson, the Beatles and Sammy Davis, Jr., who claimed to have owned more than 200 of the jackets.

Western brands come to India

The patronage of Western luxury brands by the royalty in India ensured that brands set up direct points for access to their clients. As brands began to trickle into the country, little pockets here and there served the very niche and elite with exotic jewelry and exquisite apparel. These included Gazdar in Mumbai, which has been around since 1930 and earned a reputation for itself as the Tiffany's of India, and Indian Textiles, a store that drew clients from across the world, and sold saris for the price of one lakh[4] (100,000 rupees) at a time when only a few annas[5] (16 annas to one rupee before the currency was converted to the decimal system) could support a family of three for a week. It was not long before the ability to acquire the best—previously the preserve of royalty—was extended, as other connoisseurs of beautiful *objets d'art*, jewelry and clothes began to exercise their buying power.

India starts its first Western couture establishments

A growing clientele demanded more options. Stir the memories of those who were present at the beginning of India's early links with the fashion world beyond its shores, and the stories tumble out. The shifting of the capital to Kolkata by the British brought the city into focus. The people of Kolkata, much influenced by the style and manners of the British, laid great emphasis on dress and bearing, often juxtaposing Western wear and Indian, with great elegance. A team of homegrown designers grew in this fertile climate, cutting and stitching rich fabrics to create clothes to suit all needs. Deftness with scissors and needle, using *kantha*[6] stitch and sequin, brocade, and chain stitch, formed the inspiration for a new breed of talented designers that the city seems to throw up with each season. In fact, Sabyasachi Mukherjee, perhaps the first of Kolkata's designers to make it in international events and stores, has often acknowledged the seamstresses of Kolkata in the days after independence as one of the main sources of his inspiration.

If Kolkata was a studio of busy dressmakers, Mumbai was not far behind. Three still-remembered names from that period are Madame Pompadour, who ran a very exclusive shop at the Taj Mahal Hotel and took special orders for wedding gowns for Christian ceremonies, Madame Pope, and Madame Ghalleb, whose talents saw her selected to create a dress for Queen Elizabeth. Mistresses of their craft, they designed and created ball gowns and evening dresses for the gentry who dined and danced at the Taj Mahal Hotel and at lavish private dinner parties. The exquisite embroideries and cuts executed by the battery of seamstresses they employed were priceless in the fineness of detail and finish. Some of their work survives today, and is an indication of their genius.

Madame Ghalleb—the early years

The Nationalist movement and its fallout

Fashion, as it is understood today, languished in the decades immediately preceding and after independence in 1947. The *Swadeshi*, or Nationalist, movement emphasized the importance of using goods made in India and rejecting Western modes of dress and imported textiles. *Khadi* had become a nationalist symbol, and there were still many who spun their own yarn, inspired by Mahatma Gandhi, and wore the result of their labors with pride and elegance.

Effects of industrialization in independent India

However, India's tryst with industrialization quickened the pace of an intrinsically agriculture-based nation. From the late 1950s, with Prime Minster Nehru creating a clear mandate for moving the economy toward industry and agriculture as twin routes to progress, the nation was on the move upward. The surging middle class, seeking its place in the emerging nation, had little time now to make its own clothes, and the office worker preferred to have his or her clothes made by someone who specialized in the craft. Men, particularly, preferred to patronize the local tailor, rather than trust the cutting of pants and shirts to their womenfolk (which may explain why menswear today sells more than women's wear).

The women, however, still took pride in the fact that their *cholis*[7] and their children's garments were still hand stitched at home. The trend lasted for a while at least, and if the levels of talent showed up in the elegance, or lack of it, of those for whom the clothes were made, no one knew enough to complain or remark about it. That was then ...

The French have a saying, *"Plus ça change, plus c'est la même chose,"* meaning that the more things change, the more they stay the same. After a period of austerity, the face of fashion and luxury has made a comeback and much has been said and written about A-list parties on a grand scale. The *couture* shows are talked about, the unusual settings and runway ramp. Not too long ago, by far the most exciting thing on show at the Chanel launch in New Delhi was the jaw-dropping fine jewelry—from unblemished multifaceted diamonds to blue sapphires being showcased in a limited edition exhibition. The irony, most of their guests, which included industrialists, politicians, society mavens, fashion designers, and so on, were wearing far superior eye-popping creations from all over the world.

India today, together with China and Russia, has become part of the so-called Golden Triangle, attracting Europe's biggest designer labels. "With aspiration power soaring in this segment with no socialistic bondage of India's colonial past—the modern Indians are living the maharaja's lifestyles of yore," says Anuradha Mahindra, the editor of *Verve*, India's answer to *Vanity Fair*.

Clearly, the Indian luxury retail market has a wide scope as it caters for a large spectrum of aspirations, choices, and tastes. The presence of luxury watches, apparel, accessories, fragrances, footwear, jewelry, food, and liquor is also informing those choices and aspirations. Global powerhouses such as Louis Vuitton, Bvlgari, Cartier, Hugo Boss, Burberry, Ermenegildo Zegna, Gucci, Salvatore Ferragamo, Chanel, and even the watchmaker Girard-Perregaux have been quick to get a foot in the door, and a slew of other brands are waiting to do so. India is now a compelling market because of the increasing tendency among the rich—old and new—to spend.

In the past few years, the number of multimillionaire families has been growing apace and the figure is set to double by 2010. There are approximately 1.6 million households in India that earn about US$100,000 per year, and that spend US$9,000 per year on luxury goods and services. The number of such households is growing at 14% per year. According to global management consulting firm McKinsey, the consumer-goods market in India is expected to reach US$400 billion by 2010, making it one of the five largest markets in the world.

India's luxury retail market has gained significantly from the country's changing economic environment. Luxury brand companies have been encouraged to invest in India by several factors: the growth in the younger "aspiring" population; increasing salaries; a strong economic climate; and a growing brand awareness attributed to increasing international travel. The Indian government's decision to permit 51% foreign direct investment in single-brand retailing will undoubtedly fuel more entries and growth.

The country's high import tax, which adds 45–55% to the price of foreign apparel and watches, has been a hurdle, though. Brands are absorbing some of those costs but, the higher prices mean that many affluent Indians, who travel frequently for business and pleasure, are buying such goods abroad. As for infrastructure, India's congested urban centers and rent control have produced few shopping malls, obliging brands to open their first stores in five-star hotels.

The late 1980s witnessed the emergence of the DINKs (Double Income No Kids), the new-age Indian corporate woman, who didn't necessarily wear the sari to work, and the trust-fund kids who went globe-trotting with "daddy's money." These bright sparks rejected the literal and figurative constraints of tying themselves around with six yards of material as they went about a normal day's activities from boardroom to bedroom. They could just as well wear a Chanel suit to work one day or an Indian couturier's bling-studded skirt to a family wedding the next. Curiously, from our research it seems that Indian men are the mainstay of luxury shopping, spending big on toys such as cars, planes, and yachts.

Some women, too, have experienced the Indian version of bespoke luxury, with India's top designers unveiling ready-to-wear collections rich in hand embroidery with an eye toward Western markets as well. Better known for garment factories that make clothes for big Western retailers such as Gap and Banana Republic, India is slowly gaining a reputation as a land where high fashion can be found alongside silk saris. Industry insiders know that both long-established and more contemporary international designers such as Valentino and Matthew Williamson have been coming to India for years to take advantage of the tradition and high-quality work that is available in beading, silk chiffon, and lace.

Ritu Kumar

Movie stars such as Nicole Kidman and Judi Dench have worn Indian creations. Indian designers sell their labels at high-end boutiques in London, New York, and Paris, and a handful of Indian labels are available at Browns in London and Saks Fifth Avenue in New York. Keeping the market in mind, Indian designers such as J.J. Valaya, Ashish Soni, and Rohit Bal have diverse lines that range from couture to ready-to-wear to home accessories.

Ritu Kumar's Label line is a case in point; it appeals to the younger set and yet has the classic Ritu Kumar touch and standard. Ritu, like many of the others, has also ventured into home furnishings, which promises to grow into a big market. In early 2008, the French government bestowed upon Ritu Kumar the prestigious award of *Chevalier des Arts et des Lettres* (Knight of the Order of Arts and Letters) a deserved recognition of her contribution to Indian textile crafts and traditional techniques and her interaction with the French fashion world.

As Ritu Kumar pointed out in an interview with us about accepting the award:

As the world loses its crafts, India is ensuring that its rich traditional textile crafts do not become a profession that is practiced only in a studio. This tradition lives in the hands of an estimated 16 million craftspeople and master craftsmen. Today, India is no longer associated with cheap labor, but is recognized internationally for the sophistication, richness, and diversity of its highly skilled techniques.

The new millennium took India's star designers to foreign shores. Manish Arora, for example, has been showing in Paris for several seasons, and has had outings at London Fashion Week. He has also started line extensions of his brand, with a portfolio of shoes made by Reebok, sunglasses by Ispecs, and a cosmetic range for MAC. Since starting his own brand in 1997, he has seen sales evolve from exclusively domestic to almost global.

The real impetus to fashion retailing came in 1987 when Tarun Tahiliani opened Ensemble in Mumbai, followed by Kavita Bhartia with Ogaan in Delhi, and Sanjay and Yashodhara Shroff with Ffolio in Bangalore. Today, there are literally hundreds of dedicated fashion stores and multibrand fashion stores such as Kimaya, Aza, and so on. Even the bigger department store brands—Pantaloon, Shopper's Stop, Lifestyle, Westside, Wills Lifestyle—have started fashion-focused retailing.

The trigger for all this upscale fashion fervor, say retailers, was the new money that middle-class entrepreneurs began to make following domestic capital market reforms. When Rajesh Jain sold IndiaWorld to Sify for more than US$100 million, it was catalyst of sorts. Up till then, mega-money deals only happened to the global Indian (Sabeer Bhatia and Hotmail, for example). Jain's deal effectively told Indians that it was possible be a success in their backyard. Once the preserve of the non-resident Indians, Indian entrepreneurship at home could just be as robust at home as it is abroad.

Some of the finest examples of entrepreneurship are embedded within India's share of small-scale industries. These are companies with very small, virtually insignificant, capital investment and a handful of employees, operating in skill-based industries such as handicrafts and diamond polishing. The Indian diamond industry was founded in the

1960s and covers more than 700 firms. India is the biggest diamond-exporting nation and nine out of 10 diamond pieces in the world are processed in India. The Gujarati[8] community dominates the sector, with the Palanpuri Jains and the Kathiawari Patels pre-eminent.

LUXURY HOTEL DEVELOPMENT

As India came into international focus as a tourist destination and luxury market, the hotel industry found itself on an upswing. Five-star hotel chains have set themselves on a clear course of adding properties and increasing the offerings to the well-heeled traveler who comes to the country for leisure or business, or both.

Spas and restaurants offering specialty cuisines that match the best in the world are the lures that tempt clients.

The history of luxury destinations in India dates back to when the Taj and the Oberoi groups started building on their properties to create a regal and unique ambience for the overseas visitor, and a watering hole for the local elite. When the maharajas, led by Arvind Singhji of Udaipur and others from Rajashthan started converting some of their palaces into hotels, The Lake Palace and Shiv Nivas Palace in Udaipur, The Umaid Bhavan in Jodhpur are some prime examples, others quickly followed suit.

The Taj Group soon boasted of a chain of royal homes that under its management became luxury retreats for visitors, The Oberoi followed suit with its chain of Vilas hotels, situated in tourist hotspots, the Vanya Vilas at Ranthambore and the Udaivilas at Udaipur being two prime examples.

Following the path of this success story, enterprising people such as Aman Nath and a Frenchman, Francis Wacziarg, bought and restored old forts in places that were off the beaten track, creating wonderfully luxurious getaways like the Neemrana properties and the Devi Garh Fort in Rajasthan, in the process.

Shiv Nivas

Neemrana Fort Palace

The Neemrana chain of hotels beginnings read like a fairy tale. To quote from *The Hindu*, the oldest newspaper in south India:

> During a research tour of the Shekhawati region in Rajasthan for a book, Aman Nath and Francis Wacziarg stumbled upon a ruined fort, which sat atop a hill, overlooking the Aravalli range. Looked like the once imposing 15th Century fort was waiting for someone to give it a facelift. And what a facelift it got, even if it took nearly 15 years! Today, the flagship of the Neemrana Hotels, the Neemrana Fort-Palace, about 120 kilometers from Delhi, is a heritage hotel that draws the likes of Hollywood actress Kate Winslet and Lady Nadira Naipaul.[9]

The Neemrana chain now boasts 14 hotels built on lease agreements, across the country, and these boutique hotels range from one rooted in the fourteenth century to others that are thoroughly modern.

However, it is to Ananda in the Himalayas that the credit goes for bringing the spa experience into the luxury format. Started as a Raphael Hotel, that was later transformed into a Mandarin, the property now run independently by Gautam and Ashok Khanna, from the PRS Biki Oberoi family, has set the standard for Indian spas, by winning international awards for its blend of Indian spirit with Western professionalism. Its location high up in the misty foothills of the Himalayas, overlooking the city of Rishikesh and the Ganges spread below, and its emphasis on yoga, ayurveda and a holistic plan for peace and well-being has been a trendsetter and motivator for many other properties to add high-profile spas and programs into their bouquet of offerings.

The Taj hotels in the south, specifically in Kerala, have capitalized on the idea, and have built their spas around ayurveda, which has its origins in that state, and offer intensive, purely ayurvedic treatments and programs that are extremely popular with the European visitor, and has done much to drive high-end tourist traffic to that region. The latest change in the hotel sector is the fact that most of the five-star hotels are offering their shopping areas to luxury brands.

Louis Vuitton, Salvatore Ferragamo, Omega, Zegna, and Dior are some of the brands that are, in the absence of a High Street in Mumbai at least, nestled in five-star hotels.

Of course, not everyone has had equal success in their business endeavors, and many entrepreneurs have rejoined companies again. But this has been a huge learning period in all sorts of things and all sorts of ways—how to take risks; how to look for opportunities; how to break out of the "safe job" mindset; and how to make money—setting the stage for an economy receiving considerable global attention and with a demographic unlike any other in the world.

NOTES

1. Excerpt from Shashi Tharoor, *India: From Midnight to the Millennium*, Harper Perennial, 1998; Nehru quote is excerpted from Jawaharlal Nehru 1946, *The Discovery of India*, Oxford University Press, 1998.
2. *Chikan* or *chikankari* is a traditional embroidery style using one or more bloclets to block-print a pattern on the ground fabric.
3. Ritu Kumar 2000, *Costumes and Textiles of Royal India*, Antique Collectors' Club.
4. A lakh (also written lac) is a unit in the *Indian numbering system*, widely used both in official and other contexts. When used to denominate money, one lakh is equal to 100,000 rupees.
5. Annas are former coins worth one-sixteenth of a rupee before the decimal system was introduced.
6. This is a type of embroidery that forms or outlines decorative motifs with a running stitch.
7. Midriff-baring blouses with short sleeves and a low neck; cut to fit the body tightly.
8. The Gujarat region is in India's northwest, bordering Pakistan.
9. Savita Gautam 2004, "Ruins Revisited", *The Hindu*, <www.hindu.com/mp/2004/07/29/stories/2004072900680300.htm>.

CHAPTER 3
DEMOGRAPHICS, ECONOMY, SPENDING HABITS, AND PURCHASING POWER

It is a land where they make the Mercedes Benz and BMW, yet on the roads these luxury cars jostle for space with hand-pulled carts, cycle-rickshaws and solar-powered mini-coupes. It might be tempting here to lapse into the old cliché that India is about striking contrasts: the rich and the poor, the haves and have-nots ... That is why it's important to open a short parenthesis on the demographic and economic issues specific to India, for a full grasp of the country's diversity. Actually, there are plenty of data on the subject, and we have tried to gather the most significant to give a comprehensive view of what India is today, and what it is set to become.

The latest economic survey released by the government in February 2008[1] clearly indicates that the economy has moved decisively into a higher growth phase. Until a few years ago, there was a debate among informed observers about whether the economy had moved above the 5–6% average growth seen since the 1980s. Now, however, there is no doubt, with GDP growth exceeding 8% in every year since 2003/04. The projected economic growth of 8.7% for 2007/08 is fully in line with this trend. There was acceleration in domestic investment and saving rates to drive growth and provide the resources for meeting the 9% (average) growth target of the Eleventh Five-Year Plan (2007).

Macroeconomic fundamentals continue to inspire confidence, and the investment climate is full of optimism. Buoyant growth of government revenues made it possible to maintain fiscal consolidation as mandated under the Fiscal Responsibility and Budget Management Act (FRBMA) (July 2004). The decisive change in growth trend also meant that the economy was, perhaps, not fully prepared for the different set of challenges that accompanied it. Inflation flared up in the latter half of 2006/07 but was contained, despite a global hardening of commodity prices and an upsurge in capital inflows. An appreciation of the rupee, a slowdown in the consumer goods segment, and infrastructure constraints (both physical and social) remained of concern. Raising growth to a double-digit figure will therefore require additional reforms.

This stated, the news since March 2008 has not looked rosy. As corporate earnings reports started trickling in, tight liquidity conditions coupled with soaring costs seemed to have taken the wind out of corporate India, one the biggest engines of growth. According to the Dun & Bradstreet Optimism Index, sales optimism is proving to be another issue. In April 2008 it was at a five-year low, according to a news report in India's leading magazine *India Today*[2]:

> Consumers are vacating plush malls and automobile showrooms; durables manufacturers are desperately wooing traffic to their dealers with combination offers and realtors are offering to share, and even delay, EMIs till apartments are ready to be delivered. Thanks to the drop in private consumption which fuelled the +9% GDP growth, 11 of the 17 manufacturing industry groups in the index of industrial production showed slower or negative growth in the first half of financial year 2007–2008.

On the face of it, the slowdown is the direct result of inflation. Private consumption is not only 60% of the GDP growth; it makes or mars the economy. And the boom, to all intents, was triggered by the interest-rate cut of 2003, which led to a spurt in demand and growth. Consumption created demand-triggered output, delivered profits, and fueled expansion that generated employment. But this virtuous cycle didn't last long, and was interrupted by a phantom called inflation. By the summer of 2006, Reserve Bank of India had issued the warning signals that too much money was chasing goods. Or that demand was outstripping supply, both in inputs and food articles, which hurt the poor. It wouldn't be an understatement to say that the situation is simmering, and has turned fiercely political since the slowdown has begun to show across sectors.

There are two very strong pulls in the economy: the rising cost of money and the rising cost of living. Even those padded by the wealth effect of the immediate past (largely from rising asset prices) are feeling the pinch. Then there are those who save to pay monthly installments on loans for houses or cars. The gap between their income and savings is being squeezed ever tighter. According to reports, consumers are shunning the glossy showrooms that have sprung up in malls in India's urban centers. Even in the fastest-growing sector—handheld phones—consumers are now changing handsets every nine months, in sharp contrast to the earlier six-month change.

The slowdown is bound to hit India's consuming class hard. This highly diverse continent is mainly rural, with only 30% of its 1.1 billion population living in an urban area. With a young demography, Indians speak 18 official languages and have 1,652 dialects.[3] Hindi, however, is the official language, and English is commonly used in business. Most Indians practice Hinduism (80.5%), but there are many other religions, such as Islam (13.4%), Christianity (2.3%), Sikhism (1.9%), and others (1.8%) (see figure 3.1).

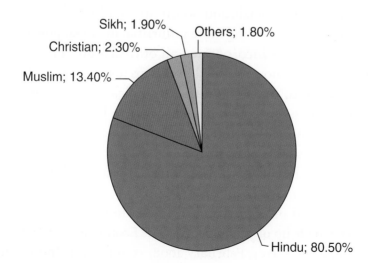

Figure 3.1: Religious beliefs

India is the world's fourth-largest economy, the third-largest in Asia, and the second-largest among emerging nations. The Indian market reflects considerable diversity in income levels and lifestyles. Although India's per-capita GDP is one of the lowest among the developing countries, a significant segment of the population (an estimated 200 million people) has significantly higher income. Along with the shift of the lower-income households to the high-income categories, consumer credit is growing by 35–40% annually; new cardholders are increasing by 25–30% annually. Buying has become a year-round phenomenon.

India today accounts for one in six of the world's population, but nearly 72% of it lives in rural areas. While both are growing significantly, the rural market is estimated to be growing approximately twice as fast as the urban market. The rural share of total consumer purchases rose from 62.6% in 1998 to 64.7% in 2004. Some economists have argued that India is shaping its own version of "reflexive modernity," the phrase coined by German sociologist Ulrich Beck to mean the second phase of modernity, a renaissance of modernity through a realization that *we can't control every risk.* In that respect India isn't very different from other aspiring economies such as China, Brazil, and South Africa, which, as their economies develop, are becoming more influential in global politics. Even the G8 Summit has incorporated an outreach program for these countries. India is now included in this exclusive club. No business can afford not to understand the dynamics of the relationships between business, government, and society in India's national context. As Beck pointed out in 1994, the intensification of globalizing influences has significant disruptive effects on these relationships. Sometimes it scratches both the political and societal feel-good and well-being factor.

The pyramid of population in India shows the base—almost 70%—to be made up of young people. The Economic Survey of 2007–2008[4] (*Economic Survey*, February 2008) states that if India can get its skill development right, the country will be harnessing a "demographic dividend." In India, the "demographic dividend"—a reference to the proportion of the population in the working age group (15–64 years)—will increase steadily from 62.9% in 2006 to 68.4% in 2026. But to take full advantage of this will require proper healthcare provision and a major emphasis on developing skills and encouraging labor-intensive industries.

Conventional wisdom says that the country's youthful population will soon be in the purchasing group. Already with their earned outsourcing money or call-center "get-rich-quick" pay scales, the young are ready to move into the higher segments of consumption.

According to McKinsey & Co.[5], India's households are classified into five economic groups based on real annual disposable income, as follows:

- *Deprived* usually earn their livelihoods though unskilled or low-skilled activities, and are often engaged in seasonal or part-time employment.
- *Aspirers* are generally small-time shopkeepers, small-holding farmers, or low-skilled industrial or service workers. They tend to spend almost half their income on basic necessities.
- *Seekers* (also considered lower middle class) are the most varied in employment, attitudes, age, and other factors. Could include young college graduates who have just started working, traditional white-collar employees, mid-level government officials, or medium-scale traders or businesspeople.
- *Strivers* (also considered upper middle class) are regarded as very successful; working, for example, as business traders in urban areas, senior government officials, medium-scale industrialists in towns, or rich farmers in villages. Generally, they have done well financially over a period, have stable sources of income, and have a reasonable wealth base.

- *Globals* (the cream of society) are senior corporate executives, large business owners, politicians, big agricultural-land owners, and top-tier professionals. More recently, the rapid emergence of a new breed of the upwardly mobile has been seen: mid-level executives or graduates from India's top colleges who are able to command premium salaries from international companies. McKinsey predicts that by 2025, this group will comprise 2% of the population, numbering more than 23 million. This segment of Indians is truly international in its tastes and preferences, and enjoys a very high standard of living.

Indeed, according to *Forbes* magazine[6] India was home to the most billionaires in Asia in 2007. Lakshmi N. Mittal, the London-based steel magnate who spearheaded the takeover of European steelmaker Arcelor SA, is the richest Asian—and the world's fifth-wealthiest individual—with a net worth estimated at US$51 billion.[7,8] India added 14 new billionaires to the list in 2007, to bring its total to 36, whose wealth contrasts sharply with the 400 million Indians who still live on less than a dollar a day. In second place, Japan had 24 billionaires (with an estimated combined net worth of US$64 billion), followed by Hong Kong (21 billionaires) and China (20). In addition, India has 83,000 millionaires.[9]

These rankings underscore how the rapid economic growth in China and India is altering the balance among the world's wealthiest men and women. As in China, the rich in India have cashed in on nearly every opportunity presented by their increasingly globalized economies, from a boom in stock markets to soaring commodity and real estate prices. The combined wealth of the Indian billionaires (US$191 billion) far exceeds that of their Chinese counterparts (US$28.9 billion). The total wealth of the top two Indian billionaires is almost double that of the Chinese billionaires combined. Yet, the world's greatest inequalities are found in India where the wealth of 36 billionaire families exceeds that of 800 million poor peasants, landless rural workers and urban slum dwellers.

Contrary to what the world at large seems to believe, most of the India's billionaires aren't exactly young, high-tech, or very innovative. Most are more than 55 years old, one-third do not have a university degree and less than one-fifth have a master's degree. Almost half inherited a substantial part of their fortune. The great majority of Indian billionaires started as millionaires—that is, as part of the privileged upper class—and parlayed their long-standing family and political connections toward maximizing their profits. More than half (54%) accumulated their initial wealth through their monopoly positions in manufacturing, mining and construction and then took advantage of the liberalization, deregulation and privatization policies of the Congress and BJP ruling parties to construct their billion-dollar empires. The much-publicized high-tech software Indian billionaires are a distinct minority (approximately 20%) of the super-rich, outnumbered even within the service sectors by media moguls and financial and real estate developers.

Yet despite the continuing disparities in income and wealth, there can be no denying the advances being made. Positive improvements over the years include the alleviation of poverty, from 93% in 1985 to 54% in 2005. McKinsey & Co. has forecast that this figure will be reduced to 22% by 2025. The literacy rate was at 62% in 2005 and will continue to increase. The unemployment rate has also seen improvements and was at 8.9% in 2006. Female workers comprised 31.6% of the workforce, according to the latest Indian National Census in 2001.

Furthermore, according to McKinsey & Co.,[10] aggregate consumption in India is forecast to grow in real terms from 17 trillion rupees today to 70 trillion by 2025. Average real household disposable income will triple from 113,744 rupees in 2005 to 318,896 by 2025 (a compound annual growth rate (CAGR) of 5.3%)! There is a current trend towards the privatization of infrastructure assets, opening trade barriers, encouraging greater foreign direct investment (FDI) for mono retail brands (with 51% FDI ownership today), and the entry of multinationals in all sectors. The globalization of the Indian economy is the result of the availability of skilled manpower and English-speaking professionals, and increased FDI, which contributed US$5 billion out of US$12 billion (2004–2005). In addition, there is a strong position for foreign exchange reserves (US$309.16 billion for the week ended 28 March 2008) and a strengthening of the Indian rupee.

The robust economic growth of the past couple of years has led to many people being able to move above the poverty line and into a lifestyle unheard of by previous generations. It is projected that more than 291 million people will move from desperate poverty to a more sustainable life, and India's middle class will undergo a 10-fold increase from 50 million today to 583 million people by 2025 (41% of total population, or 128 million households) (McKinsey & Co.)[11] The employed population in India increased from 397 million to 431 million (2001–2006), with the bulk having an average age of 30 years old. This corresponds to the increase in the average annual disposable income from 15,000 rupees to 20,000 rupees.

The new India abounds with stories of entrepreneurship: the opening of a carpet store in Gurgaon; a former luxury hotel chef who has launched a Mexican eatery in Kolkata; the MIT student who has returned home to farm vanilla in the Tamil Nadu state that lies on the eastern coast of the southern Indian peninsula; the marketing executive who has started a design hotshop in Delhi; the cricketer who has put money into a "restobar." Yes, they are taking a risk. All they are doing is what has been done many times before. In the new world, entrepreneurship has become part and parcel of the ordinary, the norm, if not routine.

The new economy opportunities have increased the upside, and diminished the element of risk. The Internet boom spawned so many wildly successful new companies that "entrepreneur" is no longer a euphemism for "trying something small and insignificant" in India. The trickle effect is that the downside of entrepreneurship has improved along with the upside, and this change is probably permanent. Indeed, if anything, the boom has educated a lot of people to the real meaning of the word. India's entrepreneurs are change experts, and they understand better than others how technological change can be applied to redefine how the world views India. The energy and innovation of the new generation of entrepreneurs are not just redefining how India works together to become a global player, but also help resolve social issues.

The immense potential of the Indian luxury retail market is now increasingly evident. More international brands associated with fine living and haute couture are planning to venture into the Indian market. The current luxury market in India is estimated to be worth between 15 billion and 20 billion rupees and, over the next five years, it has the potential for registering annual growth of 15–20%.

International brands seeking to enter the Indian market should do so now, assuming that their development strategy is clear, and a key component to success is choosing the right partners. The reliability of Indian partners is very variable. There is a general tendency to promise too much and, in many instances, foreign partners have been let down by local partners who are unable to deliver. Two categories of partners can be found: bigger, well-established corporations and smaller startups. Therefore, it is important to define the type and terms of joint venture very carefully.

OVERVIEW OF INDIA'S ECONOMY

Here is a selection of economic indicators as reported by Morgan Stanley in June 2006[12]:

- National income (GDP) to grow from US$912 billion in 2007 to US$1,063 billion in 2008.
- Exports to amount to US$131 billion in 2008.

- Imports to amount to US$203 billion in 2008.
- Foreign investment is valued at US$17 billion in 2008.

Political situation

India's political situation can be regarded as relatively stable. The Indian government adopted the English common law system from its former colonial masters, which could ease a foreign company's dealings with regard to the law. Furthermore, in 2006, the government increased FDI limits for particular industries (e.g. retail and hotels). This has increased interest in India, and new companies are lining up to invest.

From a socialist-inspired economy to the early 1990s, India made slow progress away from the previously British-led economy, which left India's local economy in a poor state. It was only after extensive economic reforms in the early 1990s (initiated by current prime minister, Dr. Manmohan Singh) that India's economy began to grow at a high rate. Today, India is considered an emerging economic superpower and is currently the tenth-largest economy in gross GDP terms, and stands as the world's largest democracy, with a population exceeding 1 billion. It is self-sufficient in food, and is a fast-growing, economically strong country, the fourth-largest when accounting for purchasing power parity (PPP).[13]

One of the great strengths of India's democracy is that it is truly representative at a local level. Historically, the Indian political landscape has been dominated by two strong national parties: the Congress party of Gandhi and Nehru, and, more recently, the BJP nationalist party. However, during the tenure of the past few governments, the emergence of increasingly strong local state-based parties has brought a significant change in the political landscape. One of the important consequences of this political fragmentation of central control has been the inevitable dilution of tough policy measures, because India's coalition governments are now dependent on cross-party support. Because this tends to be state-based and ideological, it is increasingly difficult to push through new economic and socially sensitive legislation. Fuel and food subsidies, protection of domestic industry, and restrictive labor practices are some of the areas in which urgent national reform is required but is being blocked because of lack of coalition consensus. This position is not likely to change. This will have considerable ramifications for luxury and fashion brands in the areas of restrictions on foreign ownership, inflexible labor markets, business conflict resolution, and the tax regime.

Spending patterns and lifestyle and shopping habits

Several surveys predict that India will emerge as one of the largest consumer goods markets in the world. The very affluent class is predicted to become a much larger group than similar classes elsewhere in the world.

India's economy has grown by an average of 8.1% over each of the past three years. The boom has given tens of millions of people a disposable income for the first time, and is estimated to have more than doubled to 50,000 the number of households with incomes above US$225,000. The new money has helped foster a Western-style urban consumer culture (28% of Indians live in urban areas), which in turn has loosened many conservative traditions.

Indeed, according to Indian Council for Market Research (ICMR), which studied the market between 2002 and 2007:

> [C]onsumer spending can be categorized into regular spends and lifestyle spends. Regular spending includes the basic necessities of life, while lifestyle spending includes spending on a computer, Internet, car, cell phone, etc. Analysis of consumer spending in the past 10 years reveals that the average consumer has been spending on an increasing number of different goods. There are a number of factors affecting the consumer spending pattern in India; these include growing income levels resulting in more disposable income with individuals, changing attitudes towards consumption, changes in prices, introduction of new

products, availability of credit such as loans, mortgages and credit cards,
rising aspiration levels, increased literacy, growing brand consciousness
and rapid urbanization.[14]

Spending habits are different for people belonging to different
sections of society. For instance, people belonging to the middle
class consider basic necessities and education and spending toward
the future of their children as their top priorities including weddings, religious spendings, etc., followed by lifestyle goods. The rich
spend more on luxury goods and international brands. The super-
rich spend on ultra luxury goods. As disposable income increases,
people prefer more of branded goods, they shift to processed foods,
and their expenditure on food, beverages, tobacco, and transport
and communication also increases. A comparison of consumer
spending habits in 2002 with those in 2007 revealed that expenditure on food, clothing, and personal care has remained more or less
constant, but expenditure on entertainment has increased.

The shopping habits of Indians are changing as a result of their
growing disposable income, a relative increase in the younger population, and a change in attitudes toward shopping, where the previous emphasis on price is giving way to considerations of design,
quality, and trendiness. The desire to look and feel good is also a
guiding factor in making purchase decisions. The growing levels of
disposable income are propelling demand for consumer durables
and eating out in restaurants. Spending decisions are also influenced by age, with people in the 20–24 age group spending more on
electronic and home appliances and movies, while those in the 45–48
age group spend more on vacations and assets.

Some of the challenges companies will face with these new consumers will be educating them, creating brand awareness, and tailoring service and support toward their needs. However, some of
the benefits to these are that they have few brand loyalties, and their
patterns and tastes are not yet established. Indeed, one of the questions most often asked in India is why luxury marketers haven't

been able to convert professional, upwardly mobile consumers into big luxury buyers of fashion or accessories in the same way as Brazil, Russia, and China have. It seems that, though fairly flush with money, this segment first wants to invest in assets such as homes, cars, art, high-end jewelry, and all things experiential, such as travel and dining out.

Total private consumption expenditure in India amounted to US$475 billion in 2005, compared to US$370 billion in 2003. It has been growing at almost 10% annually over the past few years, with changes in spending preferences towards more nonessential, lifestyle-oriented purchases. Indian consumers' lifestyles and shopping habits are rapidly evolving. Discretionary spending continues to witness increases for the urban upper and middle classes. Lifestyle habits are shifting from austerity to complete self-indulgence, and Indians are now unapologetic about spending lavishly on luxury watches, cars, and nonessential goods. There is an easier acceptance of luxury and an increased willingness to experiment with mainstream fashion. Expenditure on personal-care items and clothing has increased since there is greater emphasis on looking and feeling good. With new shopping malls in large and smaller cities and towns offering multiplexes, restaurants and bars, and video-game centers, shopping has evolved from a need-based activity to a leisure pastime. Therefore, expenses on activities such as watching movies and eating out have increased considerably.

With the growth in middle-class families, home textiles and electronics and consumer durables have become a means of demonstrating prosperity as well as creating a comfortable home environment. Credit friendliness, falling interest rates, and the easy availability of finance have changed people's mindsets, and capital expenditure on jewelry, houses, and cars is being redefined as consumer revenue expenditure. The number of credit cards issued grew at a CAGR of 26% in the five years to March 2005, to reach 15.5 million.

A lot has been said about women shoppers in India, yet a 2008 study by the Knowledge Company indicates that the Indian male shopper too is coming of age:

> Men in a modern shopping environment are increasingly becoming explorers, losing themselves to the allure of colors, interesting packs and displays. Modern formats thus have to accommodate on their radar this vital category of shoppers who are no longer just shopping for macho products like shaving accessories or gadgets, but are just as interested in products that till now have targeted women. The male consumer seems to have developed an appetite for gourmet foods, kitchen gadgets, spa treatments, and personal products.[15]

For instance, personal-care products such as hair care and toiletries are being sought out by men as well. The study says that men spend considerable time shopping for toiletries, and are inquisitive about the latest products, researching various brands before making their purchase. Modern-format outlets, where traditional stereotypes or gender profiles do not apply, offer new-age men a non-intimidating environment in which to evaluate shopping options. As a result, both their shopping needs and rituals are becoming more complex—a fact that more manufacturers and retailers should note and respond to accordingly.

"Splintering"—the concept where families enter as one unit but go their separate ways to pursue their individual interests during the shopping process—is another phenomenon talked about in the report. The splits result in greater involvement in shopping, negating the guilt associated with having an uninterested shopper tagging along. The supermarket has been added to the family's list of social events in which there is something for everyone to do. And children are increasingly becoming part of the shopping group. Going to the mall is becoming a source of entertainment in its own right, if not to shop then simply to walk around, look, enjoy the air conditioning and visit the food court. One of the challenges being faced by mall operators and shop owners is converting this high "footfall" into actual purchasing transactions.

With so many Indian women still opting for the traditional sari, it's not surprising that menswear is the fashion category leading the subcontinent into the world of luxury. In India, shirts are considered outerwear, and the climate may also help explain the popularity of menswear brands such as Louis Philippe and Crocodile. High-scoring local brands such as Park Avenue, Allen Solly, and Reid & Taylor focus mainly on business and formal attire (although they do manufacture women's lines and traditional Indian clothing), which means that they cater to special occasions such as weddings. Wills Lifestyle may be more familiar to local fashionistas because it is a major sponsor of India Fashion Week. As foreign brands go, Swiss watchmakers have made the greatest inroads into this market, and only one foreign fashion label—Gucci—made the top 10.

The question is: Who buys luxury? The *Luxury Market Report*[16] delineates a psychographic profile of the four key types of luxury consumer:

- *X-Fluents* (extremely affluent) spend the most on luxury and are most highly invested in luxury living.
- *Butterflies* are the most highly evolved luxury consumers, who have emerged from their luxury cocoons with a passion to reconnect with the outside world. Powered by a search for meaning and new experiences, the butterflies have the least materialistic orientation among the segments, yet they spend nearly as much as the X-Fluents on luxury.
- *Luxury cocooners* are focused on hearth and home, and spend most of their luxury budgets on home-related purchases.
- *Aspirers* are consumers who have not yet achieved the level of luxury to which they aspire. They are highly attuned to brands and believe luxury is best expressed in what they buy and what they own.

Status symbols provide convenient shorthand for telling us who is who, by showing us who has got what. They merit serious thought because they sometimes work in a counterintuitive fashion. For instance, showing off a cheap or old-model mobile phone even though you can afford the latest model, still amounts to displaying a token of prestige. This stems from the logic that only those people who are anxious about their social status try to impress others with expensive objects. Thus people who choose objects that are disproportionately cheap for their wallets are demonstrating great confidence in their own social standing.

But not all status symbols are cash commodities. According to Aditya Nath Jha, global head (branding) at Infosys, for example, "things that are available are not status symbols." When the elite of the Indian corporate world is so saturated with money, possessions, and cosmopolitan experience that designer clothes and trips to Europe merit scarcely a yawn, it becomes apparent that the "new" status symbols are linked to a different category of scarce resources.

In a booming economy, time is the scarcest resource for most working people. Therefore, status symbols that represent free time such as travel and leisure accessories, luggage, golf clubs, and yachts rate highest among those who do not enjoy much of it.

The Indian consumer's purchasing habits and preferences are evolving toward a strong predilection for brands. Consumers equate brands with intangible value for which they are willing to pay premium prices to obtain. The pricing structures for branded and unbranded goods in India are very different.

The range of luxury brands in India is very diverse. It can start anywhere: with accessories like watches, luggage, handbags, and shoes, even with cars. The grab-and-run attitude that prevails in India is the biggest enemy of luxury. People do not walk. The driver stops, the client enters the shop, and goes back to the car. There is no parking, there are too many peddlers, and the calm environment that shoppers in Europe are accustomed to is lacking here.

There are also differences between urban and rural consumers. Rural consumers are economically, socially, and psychologically different from their urban counterparts, and are more sensitive to price. For example, to address this issue, most consumer-goods companies introduced products (such as tea, shampoo, and biscuits) in smaller packs and sachets both to make the product more affordable for rural consumers and to obtain a share of wallet.

According to market reports, Indians are especially affected by the trends seen in popular media—television and movies, primarily. Indians love celebrity gossip and many a fad starts from a hit movie, a high-TRP (Television Rating Point) serial, or a catchy music video. In Indian mindsets, fashion is linked with celebrity, media, and high society.

Companies have to keep track of innovations, which can be anything from the earrings worn in a new video, a hit movie, or a retro revival on the catwalk; a new invention; an unusual color range; or a garment detail or mood expressed in a distinctive style. Innovative ideas are discovered by fashion scouts (journalists, fashion directors, forecasters, and merchants) and moved from source to marketplace by tastemakers (celebrities, models, fashion stylists, and fashion leaders), who increase the visibility of the innovation and make it acceptable to more consumers.

While luxury companies will face the challenge of educating and creating brand awareness among these new consumers, tailoring service and support toward their needs, they will also benefit from the fact that these consumers have few brand loyalties, and their patterns and tastes have yet to be established.

Indeed, Santosh Desai, CEO of Future Brands in India and considered to be a branding maverick, has suggestions for multinationals entering India:

> There is no perfect solution except that you need to be ready to make solutions for India solutions. You should be willing to understand and invest in understanding Indian consumer mindset before coming. In the past ten years or so many multinationals failed initially and gradually learnt the hard way that you need to speak to India in an uniquely Indian way. If you understand that and if you are able to convert that

theoretical understanding into practice then there is a good chance for you to succeed, but if you don't do that and stick to some standard frame of yours it is very true that you will be dismantled very quickly.

In seeking answers to our questions about what Indians are spending their money on, we asked a journalist friend to give us a few pointers:

> The answer will be food, home, mobile phones, TVs, cars, and computers. Why? Because they are mostly tools of communication, getting around, and connecting people. And Indians are seeking out these in large numbers—not just the standard vanilla variety, but in the form of individually customized sundaes! Mobile phones that do a lot of things in a lot of languages; not just televisions but interactive televisions; and all kinds of cars for different occasions. The point is, the changing face of India is culturally diverse and constantly diversifying; attention spans are fleeting and flying all over the media space and, of course, media isn't only "the media" any more.

ASPIRING YOUTH

In a recently opened nightclub in New Delhi, a band of devotees made up of 20-somethings, mainly from media and advertising, were debating the merits of what may be the most explosive of cocktails, the Manhattan: three parts rye to one part vermouth. With cocktails, however, things are not that simple. There are as many ways to make a Manhattan as whiskeys to make it with and people to drink it. And Delhi's cool new customers are slowly getting the taste of all that. With bars and restaurants opening every month in Mumbai, Delhi, and Bangalore, the youth of India is eager to party.

Estimates vary on the number of Indians aged under 25, but this segment is certainly more than half of the country's population, and one that is as brand conscious as its Western contemporaries. Even more significant is the fact that the young don't want a spartan lifestyle: the young want the best, and they want it now. They have been educated abroad. They wear Western clothing. They are ready to spend on brands, yet want value for money and hence they compare prices when traveling in Paris, London, or Dubai.

According to Hong Kong-based Manoj Singh, CEO of Deloitte Asia-Pacific Region:

> One of the biggest advantages the youth of India have is mobility. It is very easy for them to move about the country and follow the opportunities—an edge Chinese youth do not currently have. The youth of India are quickly adapting to new technologies, and English is now being more widely accepted and spoken than before. India's youth have a unique advantage: a combination of mobility, language, education, a thirst for knowledge, and technology-savvy nature. Add to that a country that has an entrepreneurial spirit and a very clear intent to adapt to Western culture, and you have a very solid case.
>
> But it's not all hunky-dory for Indian youth. Parents from the burgeoning middle class are driving their children ever harder at academic and other activities. They believe this is the only way to stand out and survive in a system where competition is cutthroat because of an exploding population and as education becomes increasingly accessible to the masses.
>
> The 18–25-year-olds have now started to look at different professions besides becoming a doctor, engineer, lawyer, government official, jobs that the earlier generations were expected to pursue, and did. Alternative professions are also beginning to gain credibility amongst parents.
>
> The youth today are definitely more aware of the choices available to them. The middle-class youth seem to be grounded within the value system and culture, since it is so unique. They are also more creative. The environment that currently exists warrants that, and competition ensures that creativity is likely to be the best way to get ahead.[17]

Often called the BPO (Business Process Outsourcing) generation, the youth of the country have become a major target for luxury brands. Armed with a spending mindset and growing affluence, lacking earlier hang-ups, for this 20–30 generation money *is* the new religion. At the lowest level, they have jobs in call centers, still live at home, and spend their entire average yearly salary of US$4,000 on themselves. Further up the ladder, there is a demand for doctors, lawyers, software engineers, and accountants (jobs that offer salaries of US$8,000–16,000 per year). Salaries for MBAs, meanwhile, have skyrocketed to a minimum of US$75,000 per year, with multinationals paying twice that. They are hungry to catch up with their Western counterparts and work hard to get it. New hotels, airlines and malls offer new ways for the new generation to make money. There are 200 million Indians in the 20–30 age group and 110 million 15–19-year-olds who are ready to spend on Tommy Hilfiger or whatever else is available. It is clear, moreover, that this class of "Highly Aspirational Youth" (a new segment of affluent young Indians) will contribute to the global brands of tomorrow.

This youthful trend is manifest in the number of young men and women who have started joining gyms and wearing better clothes. Even women who had never worn makeup have invested in the newly revamped home-grown range of Lakme lipsticks. Started by Simone Tata in the early 1960s and acquired in the early 1990s by Hindustan Levers, the brand repositioned itself to meet the challenge from the international segment, adding a number of new products to its arsenal, and enlarging its market considerably.

The educative approach that many of the new cosmetics brands adopted vis-à-vis the Indian consumer, coupled with television and print advertising on, persuaded the Indian woman to value herself. India's dream run in winning four Miss World and two Miss Universe titles added its own endorsement. With the new millennium the consumer boom was well under way. The outsourcing industry gave young Indians enough spending power to make their own decisions, and to have the wherewithal to change the lifestyle of their families in the process. Eating out and buying feel-good items— clothes, perfume, makeup, and hair-care products—became the norm. In turn, more international brands began to come in, with luxury brands like Louis Vuitton and Chanel making a serious bid for the Indian buyer's wallet.

According to Anuradha Mahindra, editor of *Verve* magazine:

> There is a high level of aspiration in this segment as they have not seen the post independence India. To them the pre-color TV era is unheard of. The population has grown up in a partially global India, they have developed aspirations of being in a level playing field. The music channels have done a lot (MTV). Kids recognize the music anywhere. This advances the feelings of confidence and self-respect. In my time, one never admitted to listening to Hindi music, it was done behind closed doors. Or even seeing Hindi movies was taboo. The idea was to appear Western, to be aware of the latest Western films and music. Now Hindi music has become hip and cool.[18]

As part of this trend, it is therefore natural that the growing importance of the young in society is reflected in the offerings put out by luxury brands, both home-grown and foreign. Indeed, it is not putting it too strongly to suggest that it is crucial for any brand wishing to stay competitive in India for the long term to take segment's tastes and requirements into consideration.

Indeed, in a world where Bollywood, MTV, *Vogue*, and LV are the new gods, and materialism and self-promotion are the order of the day, it is only fitting that the young in India have more money than ever before, both due to the economic changes discussed above, as well as the fact that pocket money and pester power are a rising force.

According to a 2005 survey conducted by Images[19] (covering 11 major cities and focusing on the 16–24 age bracket) Indian youth spend most of their earnings on fashion apparel and accessories—a far cry from their parents' generation for whom education, survival, and rebuilding India were their *raison d'être*.

Young Indian consumers are unapologetic about spending lavishly on themselves, and with the advent of easier access to credit, a "buy now and pay later" culture is slowly emerging. These consumers are increasingly spending on a wide variety of products and services, including eating out, movies and theatre, clothing, consumer durables and electronics, and personal-care items.

These trends are further reinforced by the roughly 20 million Indians overseas who, until recently, were not allowed to hold dual nationality. With the November 2007 issue of *Vogue India* profiling such notables as Roopal Patel (fashion director of Bergdorf Goodman in New York), and ex-model and girl-about-town Padma Lakshmi, not to mention Hillary Clinton's election campaign chief of staff, Huma Abedin, and the publicity surrounding the wealth of the likes of Lakshmi Mittal and Arun Sarin, Indian youth have their role models both within and without.

It is the youth of India who are in the vanguard of the moves to loosen social and caste strictures, expressing themselves through their labels rather than their social castes. The brands, meanwhile, have clearly caught on to this. Indeed according to the survey conducted by ACNielsen, brands target 57% of their products at the youth of India. This means that out of a market based on 88,340 crore at the last count, nearly 50,000 crore of apparel production is based on this segment. Even more surprising, these statistics do not take into account electronic gadgets, cell phones, jewelry, footwear, and the like. It should not be assumed that methods and practices developed elsewhere will work in the Indian markets. Unlike other markets, India is finding its voice and attitude outside of the urban metros; it's the second-tier cities from which the trends driving India's prosperity are emanating. In this complex environment, what marketers need are beacons, indicators of trends in the Indian market so that they can correctly predict the behavior of potential customers and thus sell better.

To delve deeper into the attitudes of today's Indian youngsters is to appreciate the increasing importance of the dream factor, and to realize that consumption power lies in their hands. Certainly, today's youth are sensible, and set priorities at an early age. As with their Western counterparts, fashion is not confined to apparel alone. It has been extended to every aspect of life—mobile phones, CDs, consumer durables, and other electronic gadgets all make a certain fashion statement. Even more significant, the growing presence of luxury brands in the country means that young people, who intrinsically love to explore and hunt, can now take full advantage of what brands have to offer in fashion, music, food, travel, and so on.

In perhaps the biggest challenge to conventional family hierarchy, Indian youth, besides taking decisions on their personal spending, also command a fair degree of influence in matters of family purchases. Indeed Indians, whose tendency has always been to save, rather than spend, are finding more and more that their young are calling the shots, leading the way into a culture of brands. Luxury—and perceived luxury—brands are stepping in to satisfy the hunger created by satellite TV, *Vogue*, and MTV. Brand image, affordability, and quality are the attributes that attract today's youth, but it is living up to the brand promise that keeps them loyal. While consumers in the 17–24 age group crave established global brands, even if they are expensive, they are prepared to wait till the products become affordable.

In the current economic boom, the young consumer is intelligent and experienced in getting information and making informed buying decisions. With its increasing disposable income and purchasing power and its willingness to spend, this consumer segment holds out great promise to brands and marketers that offer innovative products and services.

The assertions above are all supported by the KSA *Made in India Made for a Young India!* survey, created by Technopak, the Knowledge Company. This too makes it clear that in the move away from the collectivization of their fathers, young Indians are drawing out their own consumer symbols, applying them to their own reality and identifying which so-called tribe they belong to or, more likely, aspire to belong to.

As *Newsweek International* notes, however:

> While Luxury goods makers may be able to sell to India's global consumers, with little modification to their products, those selling to India's "new middle class" will need to be innovative to square the difference between the rising aspirations of consumers and their still modest pocket books.[20]

Drivers of apparel-purchasing behavior hint at a potential retail explosion that should be felt in the next two or three years. For instance, the growing middle class will now have even more disposable income. A breed of new young consumers wanting to look and feel good is growing rapidly. There are changing standards of Western-style dress at work and are shifting from tailor-made clothing toward ready-made garments, thus becoming more exposed to international brands and more brand aware. These developments call for modern retail concepts that are currently emerging. For example, there was not a single mall in 2002 and fewer than six in 2007. Today, there are almost 50 malls, with predictions pointing to somewhere between 300 and 500 in the next few years!

DISPOSABLE INCOME

Meet Pushpita Singh. A typical day for this 47-year-old mother of two begins at 6a.m. with a short exercise routine. She then wakes her 17-year-old daughter to get ready for college. (Her 21-year-old son has been away at law school for the past two years.) She helps the maid start breakfast, and prepares the lunchboxes. She takes her dachshund for a 45-minute walk in the park near her apartment before having breakfast with her journalist husband. Through it all, Singh is mentally ticking off the things she has to do that day: pick up milk, schedule an appointment with her daughter's dance teacher, drop her visiting aunt at her mother's, pick up the laundry, send flowers for her friend's birthday, plan that night's dinner. After all this, she will start her day job. As have many urban housewives today, she has become an entrepreneur, running a fairly successful bespoke jewelry operation from her home. Over the past three years, her business has grown to the point where she employs others. As her reputation has spread by word-of-mouth, she has been featured in magazines. What's more, she says, chuckling loudly at the thought: "There was always bread, butter, and jam at the table, maybe now it's time for the caviar."

The curious thing about disposable income in India is that there really isn't any conclusive evidence of how much of it there is, or how it moves in the marketplace. If the Economist Intelligence Unit's figures are to be believed, the 2007 disposable income per head in India, in PPP terms, was US$2,303, but was expected to grow to US$3,033 by the end of 2008. According to the website of Rama Bijapurkar, the doyen of market research in India:

> Income data in India has always been a contentious issue. There is a lot of intuitive discomfort that we have with the numbers, especially when you have to explain them to someone from overseas who is evaluating the potential of the Indian market with a view to investing in it. "How can anyone who earns so little, afford to buy so many things, and still manage the living expenses of a family of five?" they ask, puzzled![21]

We can definitely vouch for the fact that the income data is generated by reputable, world-class organizations, using rigorously designed, huge sample-size surveys that would satisfy the excellence standard of any survey data, anywhere in the world. So there is no "survey science" flaw on which to hang our discomfort with the data.

CHALLENGES AHEAD

A research report by Morgan Stanley provides an interesting insight into the economy of the country. Amongst other things, it has this to say:

> By 2015, we forecast India's GDP will cross the US$2 trillion mark ... We see the greatest challenge as the need to balance the economic contribution of investment and consumption. India requires an aggressive investment and export thrust while cooling consumption ... India has to strengthen its infrastructure, improve public finances, reform its

labor laws and augment its resources through higher FDI inflows and privatization.... Both countries [India and China] require political reform to lift them to the next level of economic development.[22]

Infrastructure deficiencies

Morgan Stanley outlines its view that while infrastructure is the key to a strong growth cycle, India isn't yet at the required level. With India's infrastructure spending just one-seventh of China's, the report calls for a "national plan" to increase infrastructure spending to 7–8% of GDP—a considerable increase on the estimated 3.6% in 2005—"to push the economy onto a sustained growth path of 8–9% a year."[23]

The report notes the key role of infrastructure in job creation. Along with its natural resources and entrepreneurial expertise, India's strength is undoubtedly its large skilled and semiskilled workforce. But the country is missing a great opportunity for development simply because all of this is not being harnessed adequately. However, it does note that the Indian government is clearly making an effort and that infrastructure investment is expected to increase to US$50 billion by 2009 from US$28 billion in 2006.

Also, a general lack of basic utilities and transportation facilities (electricity, water, roads, and ports) is a hindrance to many businesses operating in India today.

Weak public finances

A second major issue identified by Morgan Stanley is a "fiscal deficit" estimated at 7.8% of GDP for the fiscal year 2006. This is attributable to the poor management of states' finances, which comprise up to 50% of the total deficit in 2005, from 40% in 1996. On top of that, debt has also risen sharply, with a ratio to GDP that rose from 59% in 1997 to 82% in 2006.

Essentially, the state finances have run out of control as a result of inefficiency, subsidies, and poor levels of tax collection, while a substantial percentage of available government funds is being used to service interest on the national debt.

Outmoded labor laws

With the youngest workforce among all the world's large economies—the median age of the population in 2005 was 24.3 years, as opposed to 32.6 in China or 40.7 in western Europe—India does not have the laws that could trigger a virtuous cycle, taking advantage of such an age pattern. The Morgan Stanley report suggests that all 40-plus of the current labor laws are outdated and no longer relevant in an ever-changing and increasingly competitive globalized world. To illustrate this, it cites the example of the laws covering the laying off of employees in the event of company reorganization:

> Currently, any employer of more than 100 people needs to go through a rigorous approval-seeking process not only for closing down the business but also for laying off employees. In this respect, the labor laws are more restrictive than they were before 1976 ... Not surprisingly, the World Economic Forum's global competitiveness report (2005) ranks India one hundred and eleven out of 117 countries on hiring and firing policies compared with a twenty-sixth ranking for China.[24]

Lack of cohesion with regards to duties and taxes

According to McKinsey & Co., there is still no uniformity in excise duties and sales tax rates across the states. This causes price differentials across product categories, which creates confusion for luxury customers and encourages them to shop abroad.

Need to encourage privatization

Last but not least is the issue of privatization, which is proceeding at a very slow pace in India. The funds raised through this process could help trigger job creation, offsetting job losses.

Despite the steps the government has taken to increase FDI, it is still slow to open up entry for multinationals. Wal-Mart, for example, had to enter with an Indian partner. Moreover, infrastructure-related industries—some of the weakest in the country—are still heavily controlled by the government. While slow decision-making and implementation may be the result of there being a coalition government (National Democratic Alliance) in power, it also seems to be a reaction against the reform agenda, especially in relation to opening up the manufacturing sector to competition, modernizing industries such as retail, and continued attempts to draw in international trade and investment. In addition, excessive bureaucracy and corruption are still very much a part of the system.

While India is acknowledged as an excellent provider of expertise in the IT field, it still suffers from a "technology brain drain" to developed countries such as the U.S. And for all its technological knowhow, the country still lacks suitable applications of automated technology in crucial areas such as highway toll booths. India is still vulnerable to breakdowns in basic utilities such as water supply and power, which can have a detrimental effect on business productivity. The Indian economy, as it opens up, is far from immune from global tractions. And this could mean bad news for luxury vendors. Despite an Indian rupee that has been gaining strength over the recent past, in 2008 it was Asia's second-worst performing currency, which impacted inflation. The rupee declined 3% in 2008, as equity purchases by overseas funds slowed amid a global credit crisis and rising oil prices pushed import costs higher. According to government figures, India's trade deficit had widened to US$10.79 billion, up 83% from $5.87 billion in the year-ago month. The shortfall in the current account, a broad measure of trade and investment flows, widened 46% to US$5.4 billion in the December quarter, from US$3.7 billion a year earlier. The rupee's 12.3% rally in 2008, the most in more than three decades, helped cool inflation to a five-year low in October before flaring up to a three-and-a-half-year high in April. In April, the Reserve

Bank of India announced that the country should be prepared to face "potentially large" outflows of capital as the global credit crisis made global investors more risk averse. Global funds, which bought a record US$17.2 billion in Indian shares, more than they sold in 2007, had at the time of writing dumped a net US$2.6 billion in 2008 as the central bank expected economic expansion to fall below 8% for the fiscal year.

If these inflationary trends continue, and growth does slow down, it might set back analysts' predictions by several years.

NOTES

1. Government of India's Planning Commission 2008, *Economic Survey*, February.
2. Malini Bhupta 2008, "Pause & Effect", *India Today*, April 17.
3. The Boston Consulting Group 2008, *Eurupee: Building a Strategic Partnership between EU & India (2008–2013)*, February.
4. Government of India's Planning Commission, op. cit.
5. McKinsey Global Institute 2007, *The Bird of Gold: The Rise of the Indian Consumer*, May, p. 42.
6. *Forbes World's Billionaires* 2007, March 8.
7. National Council of Applied Economic Research (NCAER) Projects Study.
8. McKinsey Global Institute, loc. cit.; *Forbes World's Billionaires*, op. cit.
9. *The Hindu* 2007, "A Tide of Billionaires: Lakshmi Mittal India's Richest, Again", November 16.
10. McKinsey Global Institute, op. cit., p. 14.
11. ibid., p. 46.
12. Morgan Stanley 2006, India and China: New Tigers of Asia—Part II, preface, June.
13. *Asia Pacific Post* 2006, "Luxury Goods Hit Last Frontier", June 27.
14. ICMR 2007, executive summary of *A Note on Consumer Spending Patterns in India*.
15. The Knowledge Company (Technopak Advisors' Market Intelligence Division) 2008, *India Shopping Trends 2008*.
16. Research and Markets 2004, *Luxury Market Report 2004. Who buys Luxury, What they buy, Why they buy.*
17. *Businessweek* 2005, "China and India the Challenge: Expert Roundtable 6 Chinese and Indian Youth", August 22, <www.businessweek.com/magazine/content/05_34/b3948426.htm>.
18. Interview with the editor of *Verve* magazine.

19. Images in collaboration with ACNielsen 2005, *The Indian Brand and Wallet Share, Consumption Patterns of Indians Premium Consumers.*

20. Diana Farrell & Eric Beinhocker 2007, "Next Big Spenders: India's Middle Class", *Newsweek International,* May 19.

21. Rama Bijapurkar, *Demand Drivers, Solving the Income Data Puzzle,* <www.ramabijapurkar.com>.

22. Morgan Stanley, op. cit.

23. ibid., chapter on "Outmoded Labor Laws", p. 48.

24. ibid., chapter on "Infrastructure Deficiencies", p. 40.

CHAPTER 4
CULTURAL ISSUES AND SPECIFICITIES OF THE INDIAN MARKET

Culture (klchr) n.—The totality of socially transmitted behavior patterns, arts, beliefs, institutions, and all other products of human work and thought.

In describing the country's cultural heritage, the official Indian government site (www.India.gov.in) has this to say:

The long span of Indian history covering more than 3,000 years and enumerating several civilizations has been a constant reminder of the country's rich multicultural extravaganza and world-renowned heritage. The people and their lifestyles, their dance forms and musical styles, art & handicrafts, and such other elements go on to reflect the varied hues of Indian culture and heritage, which truly epitomizes the nationality of the country.[1]

It is certainly true that India is characterized by a demographic heterogeneity, made up as it is of numerous castes, communities, religions, languages, and lifestyles. And yes, there are two parallel Indias: the aspiring, consumerist India, and the other India that aspires only to potable water and, perhaps, electricity. There are many stretches in India where a liter of milk or a pizza is luxury. Yet in the other, day-old milk gets discarded and takeaway pizza is a routine affair.

After months of research and interviews, we have attempted to summarize some of the key cultural issues dominating the Indian psyche, and which we think still plays an important role in Indian society. Indeed, we have found that Indian values intertwine between the following:

- Family and clan
  The Indian is naturally a collective being. The "other" does not exist. For the "other" to exist, it is necessary to exist oneself as

an individual. The Indian civilization does not facilitate the blossoming of the individual. The family takes priority over the individual, at all times and in every social context. The collective family ego arbitrates in all matters, to the detriment of the personal ego. It is the family that appeases the gods and is custodian of the deep soul of the country. It is the family that is the true depositary of the Law. The sense of the "personal" must lose itself within the perception of the "impersonal," and this cult of the "impersonal," which is at the heart of the Indian psyche, explains the humility that we Westerners find at all levels of society.

- Caste and community
  India is a severely hierarchical society, in which the caste system orders human beings from inferior to superior rank and allots them specific social roles. It is based on the so-called purity level and thus set the type of work one can do. When India was gradually annexed by the British East India Company from the early eighteenth century, the British attempted to equate the Indian caste system to their own class system. They saw caste as an indicator of occupation, social standing, and intellectual ability. Though the Indian Constitution has outlawed caste-based discrimination, the caste system continues to play a major role in India. It is, for example, still a major criterion for matrimonial choices. However, in the future, the increasing role of money, the higher penetration of education, and the development of an urban population less knowledgeable about this class system will create a breach in that system.
- Hierarchy and harmony
  The Indian family takes its patriarchal form through the importance it accords to the male; a sociological rather than a genetic fact (the Hindu law recognizes 12 types of filial relationships). Marriage is an agreement made between parents, whose duty is to marry their children, thereby ensuring the continuation of the family. In principle, spouses are required

to give their consent. Falling in love is not a natural behavior for Indians; not because they are incapable of love, but love is accompanied by a sort of solemn indifference in which the heart has no role to play. Deeply rooted in his or her culture, the Indian is obsessed with purity and if love of gods is everywhere preached and seen in the architecture, love between men and women is not the objective. It is the soul (and thereby God) of the other person that he or she is attracted to. Procreation is the sole purpose of marriage. Revered once a mother (especially if of a son!), a woman before marriage is an outcast. With the exception of campus life (often abroad) there is no question of flirting, nor having relationships; a woman is expected to come to her marriage a virgin.

- Respect and obedience
  India is a theocracy and for an Indian, true liberty is to be free in his or her mind. He or she only asks that his or her religious customs be respected. We need to understand that Indians do not have our sense of individuality and therefore do not share our need for independence. This has some consequences, as we will see in more detail in chapter 9.
- Religious undertone in action
  The ultimate goal of every Indian is to fuse with the Divine. Whatever we do, whatever may happen to us, we are part of this game, earthly and cosmic at the same time. This notion of game, of play, is inherent to the Indian psyche. Everything is a game, and the Gods are playing with the humans. This *lila* or "divine play" refers to many things. Religion in India has found its expression in human art, literature, and its various activities, more in the past than today, but India is still one of the most religiously diverse nations in the world, with some of the most deeply religious societies and cultures. Religion plays a central and definitive role in the life of the country and most of its people. You are born religious—there is no atheism in India.

- Karma: its duality and consequences
  Dharma, or "duty," is at the centre of the Hindu way of think-ing, with its stress on personal responsibility. As the notion of karma developed into a larger-scale device for explaining the world and its changes, it never lost this focus on the individual; ultimately, karma and its consequences remain solely the responsibility of the individual. Every human being gets what he or she deserves, no more, no less. No god or divinity controls your actions or the consequences of your actions: you at some point in the past have caused what you are today and you can still choose the manner you are going to behave and live in this present life.

  The idea of karma was combined with the idea of life after death (reincarnation) to form the concept of *samsara* or the cycle of birth, rebirth.

  In the social order, karma produces the "four colors" or "castes," which form the hierarchy of the society. This social order reflects the rewards and punishments that accrue to one life after life. This may explain why poverty in India is "accepted" by those living in such a difficult environment: a well-lived life, even as the poorest Dalit, guarantees rebirth in a higher social order and vice versa.

- Value for money
  Because Dubai and other key destinations are not too far away and Indians like a deal irrespective of their net worth, compar-ative pricing is key. "Behind every Indian customer there is a merchant, this was true even when imports were not allowed." The group with the greatest propensity to spend is the young (late 20s to 30s) and upwardly mobile group, and brands would do well to concentrate their efforts on this group. In India the current mantra is "big house, big car, big luxury, then branded clothes or ready-to-wear." The "gifting market" is a key potential market because it marks *"status."*

There is in India a principle of absolute submission to the divine order, whatever it is. We would like to believe that it is the popular concept of India, perhaps fed by years of foreign fantasy of spiritual aspects of India. India, there is no denying, is a fiercely spiritual country, but few outside understand just how democratic it can be about its true identity.

A lucid and compelling read in this matter is *The Argumentative Indian* by Nobel economist Amartya Sen, now advisor to French President Nicolas Sarkozy. In an interview with an American Ivy League college magazine, Sen explains lucidly the trigger for the book:

> In some ways people had got used to the idea that India was spiritual and religion-oriented. That gave a leg up to the religious interpretation of India, despite the fact that Sanskrit had a larger atheistic literature than exists in any other classical language. Even within the Hindu tradition, there are many people who were atheist. Madhava Acharya, the remarkable 14th Century philosopher, wrote this rather great book called *Sarvadarshansamgraha*, which discussed all the religious schools of thought within the Hindu structure. The first chapter is "Atheism"—a very strong presentation of the argument in favor of atheism and materialism. The second chapter is on Buddhism, which is treated as an offshoot of Hinduism. And then it goes through the other schools of Hinduism … One of the things I tried to argue in *The Argumentative Indian* is that there's a long tradition of philosophical argument. People ask, "Which really reflects Indian culture? Is it this or is it that?" What reflects Indian culture most are the arguments themselves, rather than any resolution in one direction or the other.
>
> I am not claiming that Akbar or Ashoka represent anything like the "essential India." My point is that they represent a very strong perspective that has come up again and again, which includes a lot of tolerance. But of course there is also a long history of extreme intolerance and nastiness. Indian culture has this variety that needs acknowledgement. Since the focus has been so much on the other side, I am using my focus as a correction. I have quite an elaborate discussion of science and mathematics in India. This is not a claim that everyone was a scientist in India. It's a claim that that tradition exists.
>
> When we try to draw on the past, we draw always in a selective basis. When the French and the British and the Americans were drawing on

the European past in saying there is a democratic tradition, and they referred to Athens and ancient Greece—over a small number of centuries from third to sixth century B.C.—they were not looking at the Goths and Visigoths and Ostrogoths. Due to the context of the debate on democracy in America in the late 18th or early 19th century, the relevant reference is Athenian democracy. Ostrogoths, Vikings, and in a different way, intolerant masters of the Inquisition are no less—"European" than ancient Greeks. Nevertheless, one could say if you're looking for representative Europe, it ain't like that.

Looking back on our history, it is not surprising that Gandhi or Nehru would emphasize those parts of the Indian tradition of public reasoning that were particularly relevant for modern India—the first poor country which chose to be an uncompromisingly democratic, multi-party state. I don't think any of them claimed that their focus was the only tradition that existed in India.[2]

Basically, what Sen argues is that recognizing the widespread legacy of heterodoxy in Indian traditions is critical for understanding the country's past: "Indian traditions in mathematics, logic, science, medicine, linguistics or epistemology may be well known to the Western specialist, but they play little part in the general Western understanding of India. Mysticism and exoticism, in contrast, have a more hallowed position in that understanding." This persistent tendency to emphasize only the "exotic" negates the rational, scientific, and nonreligious (often openly agnostic or atheistic) schools of thought that pervade ancient Indian scholarship and philosophy.

India is one of the most religiously diverse nations in the world, with some of the most deeply religious societies and cultures; religion plays a central and definitive role in the life of the country.

In researching this book, we were struck by the extent to which the Western view of India is still trapped in the image of the maharaja, despite royalty occupying a very different position in modern India. As William Dalrymple so succinctly put it in a 2007 article in the *Guardian Weekend*[3], wealth in India now lies with the businessman and entrepreneurs. Although the maharaja is still vested with mythical importance, as far as economics and the bottom line is concerned, royalty is no longer so influential. Some royal families that have been successful in liquidating their assets have turned their homes into luxury hotels affiliated to luxury hotel chains, rendering them "royal" entrepreneurs.

It is not just the royals, however, who are seeing a change. Indeed, industrial families and clans are also redefining their roles, moving away from managing and operating their businesses and toward governing the whole wealth-generating potential of their collective family enterprise. And if we take into account the movement of Indians and their presence in every sphere of business around the world—the nonresident Indians (NRIs) and persons of Indian origin such as Indra Nooyi, CEO of Pepsico, and Nirmalya Kumar at the London Business School—it is evident that the global Indian has arrived in the true sense. Recognizing this, the government has decided to grant dual passports to the Indian diaspora, bringing such luxury luminaries as Roopal Patel, fashion director of Bergdorf Goodman, the model and cookery writer Padma Lakshmi, and catwalk model Ujwala Raut back into the fold.

In modern urbanized India there are many "old school" traditions that are changing, even as they remain the same. Financial security is still a major motivator for many middle-class Indians. In some ways, saving is an imperative. Therefore, gold has both a financial and a sentimental value in India. It is a hedge against inflation and devaluation of the rupee, and, in the form of women's jewelry, it is also a traditional symbol of economic security, wealth, and social prestige. Indeed, the purchase and valuation of gold are intrinsically linked to saving and financial security, and are not seen as an investment into a brand.

As an extension of the concept of a woman displaying her husband's wealth through ornamentation, moreover, arranged marriages are still important. Marriage is an agreement made between parents, whose duty it is to marry off their children and thereby ensure the continuation of the family. In principle, the intended spouses are required to give their consent. After the age of 25, women are considered old spinsters; even if today girls can refuse a husband, family pressures are still very high.

Yet something clearly is changing on the arranged marriage front, too. According to a recent cover story in one leading magazine,[4] online matrimonial sites are changing the rules of the mating game, and are a significant pointer to the changes in urban Indian society. Today most 12 million Indians use online matrimonial searches and matrimonial sites are now the thirteenth-most popular mainstream online activity. As the news weekly points out:

> Millions of unmarried couples, especially young women, are now depending on the Net to exchange photos, videos, views and opinions before bringing in the parents to convince them they have found the person they want to marry. It's a major development in a society where mobility and opportunity is separating parents from their children much earlier than before.

Interestingly, 68% of the women want to work after marriage, 68% want NRIs as husbands and a surprising 41% are completely in favor of inter-caste marriages.

WEDDINGS

For years, weddings have been grand occasions in India, depending on the scale of the person's income, and not just for the rich. While ten years ago, they might be a few weeks long or even more, today celebrations last just three or four days. With the economy growing at more than 9% and the ranks of the middle class swelling to nearly 300 million, weddings are becoming the most clear-cut examples of conspicuous consumption. Besides ceremonies and feasts, even dowries—though legally outlawed—are becoming larger and more costly. The trendsetters, to a large extent, have been the Indian film industry which has made a Bollywood mode of the Indian wedding aped by the diaspora, middle class, and upper class Indians.

Wedding splendor

Wedding ceremony

As the Mumbai-based *DNA* newspaper reported in 2007:

> It might be a "seasonal" industry, thriving only during the auspicious months of the year but with an estimated worth of Rs125,000 crore,[5] the Indian wedding industry is getting bigger and fatter. With the industry growing at an average rate of 25% per annum, the lavishness doled out by Indians on weddings is just getting larger this season as exhibitors and even designers from Pakistan entering the market to target the customers who have begun shopping for the post October marriage season.[6]

Indian weddings are mostly paid for by the couple's parents, so the wedding is like a gift to the bride and groom. But India's middle class is turning weddings into a showcase for their growing disposable incomes and newfound appetites for the goodies of the global marketplace. According to a straw poll among wedding planners, the minimum budget for a wedding ceremony would be about US$40,000, while the upper-middle and rich classes are known to spend upward of US$2 million. This doesn't, of course, include cash and valuables given as part of a dowry.

An Indian wedding is never only about self-gratification. The guest is as central to it as the bridal couple. And food is the only level at which guests can fully participate, the truly interactive quotient. Yes, guests can stand in an interminably long queue waiting to wish the family, while balancing unwieldy packages in unwieldy clothes. Yes, they can swing at the *sangeet*.[7] But food plays the star role in the extended ritual of a wedding just as the *jaymala* does for the intimate one.

A typical traditional Indian wedding offers an insight into the region, class, caste, religion and the ethnic diversity of the predominantly Hindu India. Even Indian Christian weddings incorporate most of the traditions of their Hindu communities. Northern and southern customs vary considerably, and sometimes are in direct contrast. While the north has most ceremonies at night, day ceremonies are the norm from Maharashtra southward. Again, the custom of *ghunghat* (veiling the face) is common in the north, but considered unsuitable and even inauspicious in the south. The Indian wedding is rich with symbolism.

The dowry or *streedhan* still remains a pernicious tradition in many communities, ending in untold misery for the bride's family.

One of the foremost traditions is the *sagai* or engagement ceremony, which can be found almost everywhere although it be called by different names in different parts of the country. Traditional Indian weddings include a host of other pre-wedding ceremonies such as the *sangeet*; the *mehendi*, in which the henna is applied as decorative art on both the bride and groom; and the *haldi*, which is the ritual cleansing of both bride and groom with turmeric.

At the time of marriage, the couple walks around the sacred fire taking vows of togetherness in a traditional custom known as *saat phere*. There are many other traditions but they tend to vary depending on where the marriage is taking place.

Unlike the traditional white usually worn by Western brides, Indian wedding dresses are often red, which is considered to symbolize fertility. Because India is so diverse in culture and religion depending on what region one is in, the Indian wedding dresses will vary too. Some common styles used, however, are the sari, *gaghra choli*, and *salwar kameez*.[8] The sari is what many people have already seen Indian women wearing. The cloth is wrapped around the body, either secured by pins or tucked into the waistband. The *gaghra* is a long skirt and short blouse with a scarf, called a *dupatta*,[9] draped across the bride's chest. The *salwar kameez* is a long tunic over pants. It too has the *dupatta* draped across the chest, but the bride can specify that the *dupatta* be worn around the neck or over the head.

Indian wedding dresses are often a combination of intricate patterns, threading, sequences, and beadwork. Some Indian brides with money have their Indian wedding dresses woven with jewelry, pure fold or silver as part of the dowry. The Indian wedding dresses are usually made of a fabric that reflects light well, such as satin, silk, or chiffon. Other accessories are available with Indian wedding dresses. There can never be too many necklaces, bracelets, rings, earrings, or hair decorations on an Indian bride. It is all part of the ornamentation of the bride on her wedding day, and her Istree Dhan (women's wealth).

Clearly, there are opportunities for luxury marketers who can offer "giftable" items in their wedding-market portfolios. Customization is increasing in the form of Louis Vuitton trunks, Montblanc pens, and suits made by Canali, Hugo Boss, and Ermenegildo Zegna. "The amount of gifts given and purchases made [for Indian weddings] is astronomical," said Mohan Murjani in a *WWD* article "Homecoming,"[10] pointing to a recent wedding where each of the couple's 500 guests received a Tag Heuer watch.

According to McKinsey Global Institute,[11] as income levels grow, spending priority will move from essentials to so-called discretionary items. The market for upscale and premium clothing, watches and accessories grew at 25–30% in recent years. Yet, even here there are challenges. Though there is rising brand recognition, 50% of women still get their jewelry made by trusted family jewelers according to a study by KSA-Technopak.[12]

The urban apparel market also has a large luxury segment, which is expected to grow significantly in the future. The global consumers mentioned earlier in this report spend approximately 15 to 20 times more per capita than their lower middle class counterparts, and are a good target market for most luxury brands. The spending by this income segment already accounts for one-fifth of the total urban apparel market, and McKinsey expects that this consumption will grow steadily more than 10% in the next 20 years.

And, of course, there is a growing middle class with money and a desire to spend it! The growing trend to spend on luxury and premium products and services is being helped by the refurbishing of shopping districts and the creation of new malls. For example, jewelry already commands a large share of the luxury consumer's wallet. As women begin to earn and spend more, there is an increase in fashion and lifestyle awareness and aspirations, with a newfound comfort with branded jewelry. The new middle class is also being exposed to brands through work conferences in hotels, where many brands are located. Growing individualism among women consumers is also reflected in the jewelry they wear.

The most fundamental change in urban spending on apparel will be a shift away from tailored clothing toward ready-made garments. Another significant trend in the urban apparel market is the growing significance of Western-style clothing. The growth of formal economy over the past 20 years has consequently fed (and in years to come will feed) the greater demand for "officewear." With more and more working women, this new segment of women's wear has also recently become important for the major players in the industry. Other contributing factors include the emergence of younger consumers, especially women; the rise of the Double Income No Kids (DINKs); and changes in perception toward self-indulgence.

Less commonly spoken about, but still very significant, is the so-called cash economy (also known as black money or the parallel economy). This manifests itself in a gifting culture even among politicians and government officials. This leads to a lot of disposable income, which is not necessarily officially accounted for.

These young women are the key consumer group of tomorrow, and these shifts have big implications for marketing companies. More such transformational trends were revealed by two studies by the Grey Global Group (GGG).[13] One study examined 3,400 unmarried women aged 19–22 of different income and social levels. This involved 40 focus groups in five large metro areas and five smaller cities. The researchers sometimes lived with the women for a while to study them more closely. They supplemented their data with interviews with journalists, teachers, and psychologists. The following were among the major findings of the studies:

- *Guilt-free materialism:* 51% of young single women in major metro areas say it's necessary to have a big house and big car to be happy. In smaller cities, 86% agreed with this statement.

"This shows that the less women have, the greater are their aspirations," said Nisha Singhania of GGG. "One woman interviewed was making just US$200 a year but said she wants to own a jet plane. A typical comment in recent interviews was, 'I want money, fame, and success.'" (see figure 4.1).

- *Parental ties:* Traditionally, parents regarded girls as somebody else's future property. They arranged marriages for their daughters, and then the daughters would go away and take care of their in-laws, so parents needed and doted on sons. According to Singhania, "As a girl, you never spoke to your parents. They spoke to you."

But today's young women are rebelling against that: 67% say they plan to take care of their parents into their old age. For that, they need money.

Unilever played on that sentiment with a recent controversial— but successful—ad for its "Fair and Lovely" line of beauty products. A daughter came home and found that her parents had no sugar for coffee because they couldn't afford it. She became an airline hostess after using the company's products to make

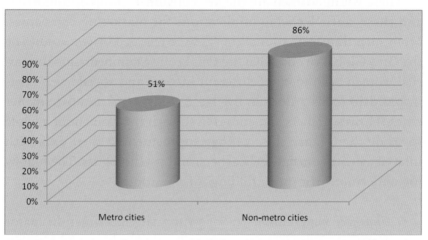

Figure 4.1: Percentage of single women who say it is necessary to have a big house and a big car to be happy

her beautiful. She then visited her parents and treated them to a gourmet meal.

- *Marital freedom:* Now many women say they'll marry when ready, not when their parents decide to marry them off. Sixty-five percent say dating is essential, and they also want to become financially independent before they marry. More than three-quarters (76%) say they want to maintain that independence afterward. Sixty percent say they'll decide how to spend their own salaries.

  What's more, 76% say they'll decide when to have children. "They now regard this as the woman's decision completely," Singhania observed. In big metro areas, 24% say they never want children, and that number reaches 40% in smaller cities.

- *Individualism:* "Female role models in Indian culture used to personify perfection," said Singhania. "Now, 62% of girls say it's okay if they have faults and that people see them. They don't want to be seen as Mrs. Perfect. Popular [television] characters are Phoebe of *Friends* and Ally McBeal. They like women who commit blunders."

- *Careerism:* A decade ago, most young women saw themselves as housewives. After that, most said they wanted to be teachers or doctors. "If they had a profession at all, it had to be a noble cause," according to Singhania. "Now, it is about glamor, money, and fame." A surprising 45% of young single females say they would like to be journalists, largely because prominent female journalists, especially TV reporters, are seen as very glamorous. Another 39% say they would like to be managers, 38% are interested in design, and 20% think they want to be teachers. Interestingly, 13% say they would like to be in the military. The percentage of those saying they want to be a full-time housewife was minuscule (see figure 4.2).

- *Modern husbands:* "The relationship with the husband used to be one of awe," Singhania said. "Now women want a partner and

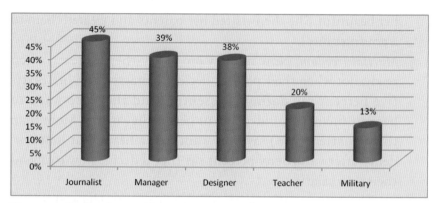

Figure 4.2: Preferred careers for young women today

a relationship of equals. They want to marry a man like Greg of *Dharma and Greg* or Chandler of *Friends.*" A recent Whirlpool ad shows a man washing the family clothes before his wife comes home from work, while a Samsung home-appliance ad shows a husband and wife cooking together.

Whereas India still remains a highly savings-oriented country, some interesting changes are undoubtedly happening. We are not sure that it is the young who are saving. It seems to be the 33–45-year-olds who have seen the greatest leap in real income as well as expectation. They are old enough to remember harder times and not too young to think things were always this good. On the flipside, the higher income levels of Indian youth, along with their exposure to Western culture, fuel their aspiration to achieve a higher standard of living, like that of their counterparts in the Western world. The influx of foreign and domestic brands into Indian markets has made consumers more conscious of what they use.

The almost instant availability of money has had an effect too. Banks haven't just introduced tools such as the debit card, but have also made the availability of credit very easy, which is tempting to consumers. Many retailers are offering EMI (Equated Monthly Installments) facilities, enabling goods to be purchased today for the promise of payment from future earnings. Consumers have responded well to this facility, which allows them to spread payments over months.

The past decade has witnessed the emergence of a sophisticated bank lending system, which has opened up the opportunity for younger people to buy property and acquire home durables (luxury and nonluxury). In addition, international travel and the emergence of satellite and cable TV have been instrumental in changing consumer aspirations. Bank credit has been the biggest enabler for a younger generation of professionals to borrow and spend with confidence about their economic future. This is one of the most transformational changes in Indian society today, as the integrated family breaks down, apartment buildings go up, and a boom in consumer durables fueled by employment growth and credit underpins consumption expenditure across all categories.

These gradual changes in an Indian's lifestyle have a much bigger impact than meets the eye.

THE BOLLYWOOD FACTOR

New money has helped foster a Western-style urban consumer culture, which, in turn, has loosened many conservative traditions. For example, one hit Bollywood movie in 2007 was about an unmarried couple living together—a phenomenon almost unheard of before.

The growing power of Bollywood (which produces more than 1,000 films per year, with 14 million Indians going to the movies each day) and the beauty-queen factor accompanying it have been reinforced by the advent of satellite television, projecting images of high fashion and beauty in features and advertising into the homes of millions. The impact on the latest fashions in India of films such as *Bunty Aur Babli* and *Bluffmaster* is therefore less than surprising.

This trend was only helped by the success of Sushmita Sen and Aishwarya Rai in the 1994 Miss Universe and Miss World contests respectively. The fame, money, and international acclaim that accompanied their success made them instant role models to a whole generation. That the winners were always beautifully presented and made up, that they wore designer clothing and sported fancy eyeshades and watches, and that international brands were vying to sign them on as brand ambassadors fueled the boom further.

Fashion and films have always been intricately linked. Hairstyles, clothes and quirky creations that were meant to set off a character trait have often caught the public imagination and become national fashion statements.

More recently, with the sweeping changes that India is witnessing in fashion (especially since the introduction of India Fashion Week in 2000 and the increasing foreign press coverage it has received) and the influence these have had on the way film stars dress, on and off screen, Bollywood has played a more serious role in the way people dress. By deftly combining their own creations with well-known international brands, designers such as Rocky S, Neeta Lulla, and Manish Malhotra have been successful in helping to create personalities on screen, and a fan following off it. Film magazines and society tabloids carry the baton to the next level, printing pictures of the stars and their designers together, with each endorsing the other's role in their success. Readers who wish to emulate the stars then take the images to their local tailors for a quick copy.

NOTES

1. Indian government website, <www.India.gov.in>.
2. Pranab Bardhan 2006, "The Arguing India", *California*, vol. 117, no. 4, July/August; Amartya Sen 2005, *The Argumentative Indian*, Farrar, Straus & Giroux.
3. William Dalrymple 2007, "The Lost World: The Rulers of Hyderabad", *Guardian Weekend*, December 8.
4. Damayanti Dutta 2008, "Netrimony: The New Mating Game", *India Today*, June 27.

5. A crore is equal to 100 lakh, or 10 million (10,000,000).
6. Snehesh Alex Philip 2007, "The Great Fat Indian Wedding is Getting Fatter This Season", *Press Trust of India*, August 21.
7. A women-only event that takes place in a banquet hall or at home two or three days prior to a Hindu or Sikh wedding.
8. This is a form-fitting overshirt worn with trousers that are cut wide at the top and narrow at the ankle.
9. This is a long scarf that is most commonly worn with the *salwar kameez*, the trouser suit, and the *kurta*.
10. *WWD* 2007, Special Report *WWD/DNR* Summit 2007, "Homecoming: Mohan Murjani Brings His Expertise to India's Booming Retail Scene", November 14.
11. McKinsey Global Institute 2007, *The Bird of Gold: The Rise of the Indian Consumer*, May, p. 16.
12. The Knowledge Company (Technopak Advisors' Market Intelligence Division) 2006, *Jewelry: Indian Affluent Consumer Trends*.
13. *Businessweek* 2005, "India's New Worldly Women", August 22.

PART II
THE INDIAN CONSUMER

CHAPTER 5
Consumer Differences Between Cities

Cities the world over attract the young, the hungry, and the ambitious, all looking for a better future. With seven cities with populations of more than four million, and 35 others with more than one million, India is no exception. Here, gated enclaves exist side by side with vibrant slums. This is the dual-faced reality of the whole Indian story, which someone once referred to as a bipolar development model. There is no overlooking the strange compost of wealth and squalor in India's cities: billboards of multinational banks offering wealth management services; sprawling slums. Almost unbelievably, at almost every major intersection in Delhi or Mumbai, young vendors sell copies of *Vogue*, the *Harvard Business Review*, or Eckhart Tolle's *A New Earth*.

"Indian's urban population will increase by 290 million people, or the equivalent of the population of the entire United States, by 2036," writes Mira Kamdar in her book *Planet India*.[1] "Despite a housing construction boom, 60 percent of Bombay's 18 million people live in slums or in the streets. That is 10.8 million people. Learning not to see dire poverty all around is a basic life skill of the affluent in India."

That may be, but the impact of India's impressive economic growth over the past few years has extended to its smaller cities as well, where a young population with rising disposable income is finding that many Western and upmarket domestic brands are increasingly accessible. According to Fiona Caulfield, CEO of Hardys Bay Consulting Group and author of several books on India, during our interview:

> The danger is that you scan cities and get into the New York–L.A. game. I think there are more interesting things going on in India. If Kolkata is

Boston, and Bangalore is San Francisco, what does that make Bombay? Who is making the decisions? Who are the people who set trends here? If I was a luxury goods player, I would not just play the Bombay game. In terms of cities, I would look beyond Bombay and Delhi.

According to *EuroMonitor*, consumer goods companies are stepping up efforts to expand to these second-tier cities:

> Nearly 35 Indian cities have a population exceeding 1.0 million and a rapidly growing consumer market with rising incomes. They are referred to as second-tier cities, and the Indian government is keen to encourage economic expansion there. As foreign and domestic investors are making the most of government incentive policies and tapping into the expanding consumer market in second-tier cities, consumers are presented with a wider range of international and upmarket domestic brands and services.[2]

In 2007, the government pledged to spend US$29.0 billion over the seven years to 2014 to modernize second-tier cities and turn them into economic hubs besides existing metropolises. Thanks to government investment and incentive policies, second-tier cities across India will gain greater importance both as engines of economic growth and as expanding consumer markets. Analysts predict that the development of these cities will be the key to boosting and sustaining India's economic growth.[3]

Apart from the small and medium enterprises (SMEs) that have been fueling growth at the next level, service providers have begun to outsource into cities such as Pune, Chandigarh, Kolkata, Indore, Ahmedabad, Cochin, Chennai, Hyderabad, Secunderabad, Jaipur, Rajkot, and Nagpur, among others. In an economy that expanded 9.4% in 2006/07, corporate tax collections from many of these cities grew faster than the national average, although better compliance and a stronger tax regulatory regime may have also contributed to this. In that year, the rate of growth in Jaipur, Hyderabad, and Ahmedabad was higher than that in New Delhi and Mumbai. Ranked by tax collected, New Delhi and Mumbai—which together account for more than 50% of total corporate taxes—are followed by Bangalore, Chennai, Meerut, and Hyderabad.

The growing importance of second-tier cities is further attested to by data collected by the National Sample Survey Organisation (NSSO) over 1999/2000 and 2004/05, which lists Varanasi, Agra, Bhopal, Indore, and Patna as the cities with the greatest number of self-employed individuals in the country. However, since the SME sector is the biggest creator of employment in the nonfarming domain, any economic slowdown will have a corresponding great detrimental effect.

In the following, we present a brief outline of the major cities, with particular emphasis on the luxury and fashion market.

Delhi

New Delhi, for all its somber capital-city status, has been identified as one of the most status-conscious cities in India. With their lavish lifestyle, competitive nature and social consciousness, Delhi's big spenders are given to outdoing each other through sheer displays of wealth.

The current luxury shopping scene in the city is widely distributed—from Hauz Khas to the Crescent Mall, and five-star hotels in between. There is a true sense of excitement in the new malls and neighborhoods, such as Emporio and Dome. The Garden of Five Senses in Sandulajab is one of the complexes that bring a special mix to Delhi retail. Set across seven buildings that house more than 20 designers, including Manish Arora, Ana Mika, and Alpana Bawa, the Magique restaurant, and a store devoted to the best of British brands, the complex offers a well-balanced international melange. There is also the Lodhi Colony Market, positioning itself to be a Soldermam (Stockholm's chic shopping area), where top design talent Rajesh Pratap Singh has already occupied one floor of his austere, clean-design store selling his lime-color eyelet skirts and simple linen pieces. He is deciding whether to place men's or women's on the second floor. There is also the indigenous Fab India, Anokhi, and

Dilli Heat which get an equal number of shoppers of all of the above put together from the "urban arrived elite".

Connaught Place is an ideal location and setting to become a true High Street. As someone said "You just need to throw everyone out," but the reality is that there is no political will, and one feels that luxury is only for the elite, a reverse pyramid. Kamal Nath, Minister of Trade and Commerce of India, understands when he says, "They don't look at the future; a sophisticated city is part of our heritage."

However, there seem to be no concerted effort to save the architectural heritage of the town, apart from the most famous monuments. According to Nehru, "New Delhi is the visible symbol of English power, with all its ostentation and extravagance."

"Delhi has two advantages compared to other big Indian cities: one is the relatively cheap cost of labor, and secondly the fact that it is the capital of the country," says Bernard Dufresne, economic attaché to the French Embassy in Delhi. It is also the home of the IIT (Indian Institute of Technology) and IIM (Indian Institute of Management) among other prestigious economic institutions. The city's Gurgaon district is home to such multinationals as Alcatel, AmEx, IBM, Citibank, Coke, General Motors, Microsoft, Nestle, Nokia, and Xerox.

Mumbai (Bombay)

According to McKinsey & Co. and the "Bombay First" business group report in 2003, titled *Vision 2020*[4], by that year, Mumbai will be the most populous city in the world, with 28.5 million people (see figure 5.1).[5] "Mumbaikars"—residents of Mumbai—have the same sense of pride in their city as New Yorkers. Its business leaders envision a Shanghai-style transformation for the city, into a world financial capital rivaling Singapore. This dream can only come true if new roads are constructed, services are privatized, and slums such as Dharavi[6] are rehabilitated or cleaned up. (As Mira Kamdar writes[7]: "[A]long the Mithi River, squeezed between the neighborhoods of

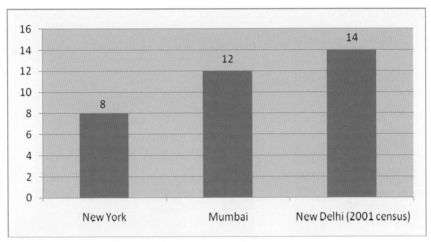

Figure 5.1: Populations of major cities

Mahim and Sion, Dharavi, an originally fishing village, is a thriving community (one million people crammed into 535 acres) where small-scale industries occupy the same tiny space where families live. Leather tanneries, scrap-metal dealers, potters, and women who toil food (*papads*[8]) at home, a popular snack food." Resources were pledged from the national government to support this goal[9] of rehabilitating Dharavi. Figures 5.2 and 5.3 show revenue per inhabitant and crime rate for various cities in comparison to Mumbai, respectively.

As shown in figure 5.4, Mumbai has a population of 12 million with an average density of 27,350 inhabitants per square kilometer, on a superficies of 440 square kilometers. As a comparison, New York has eight million with an average density of 9,550 inhabitants.

Indian giants such as DFL, Emar, and Hirandani are among those prepared to go into action. The creation of special economic zones (SEZs) within the city is favorable to large multinational corporations, but it remains to be seen how this will benefit existing microenterprise owners and craftsmen, or how the housing needs of all those people expelled in the process will be met.

Figure 5.2: Revenue per inhabitant

The economic successes of the 1990s had a direct bearing on the emergence of the new wealthy classes in this city (who now frequent the new Olive Bar and other such elite establishments as the

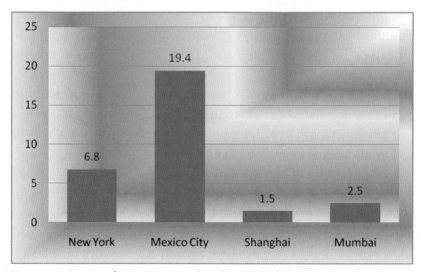

Figure 5.3: Crime rate for various cities (per thousand inhabitants)

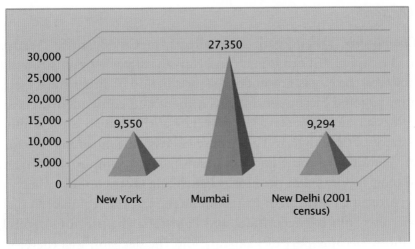

Figure 5.4: Population density of various cities (per square kilometer)

Bombay Gymkhana or the Breach Candy). The glamor of this city is further reinforced by the presence of the Bollywood film stars who frequent the Indigo restaurant and the Insomnia club at the Taj Mahal Palace.

Wealth conscious, cosmopolitan, trendy, competitive, and ambitious, Mumbai is also the last bastion of the old money coming from industrial dynasties, which are currently benefiting from the abolition of the old ideals that it was bad to make money. The new generation, schooled at Harvard, Wharton, Cambridge, London Business School, or INSEAD, are self-proclaimed "citizens of the world."

Is Mumbai's growth sustainable? Any extreme divide leads to potential turbulence, and something the business community doesn't want or need is uncertainty. Here the affluent invest in their children's Ivy League education abroad rather than the latest collections every season even if they have the means. Further south, Bangalore, Hyderabad, and Chennai consider North Indian sense of style a far cry from their austere sensibilities of fashion and luxury.

The North

Chandigarh   Chandigarh, also called "The City Beautiful," serves as the capital of both Punjab and Haryana states. Administratively, however, the city is not under the jurisdiction of either state, being administered by the central government and consequently classified as a union territory. The governor of the Punjab is the administrator of Chandigarh. The city derives its name (meaning "the fort of Chandi") from the goddess Chandi, whose temple (the Chandi Mandir) is located in the nearby Panchkula District of Haryana.

After the partition of British India in 1947, the region of Punjab was also split between India and Pakistan. The previous capital, Lahore, became part of Pakistan, and the decision was therefore made to construct a new capital for the Indian state of Punjab: Chandigarh. Because of its strategic location and with India's first post-independence prime minister, Jawaharlal Nehru, taking a personal interest in the project, the city's development quickly assumed prime significance.

Ludhiana   Ludhiana is the Punjab's largest most prominent industrial city, with a population of between 1.5 million and 2 million. Often referred to as the "Manchester of India," it is known largely for its hosiery, textiles, and bicycle industry. Most of the people are of the Sikh faith (more than 60%), with the remainder mostly Hindus, while Christians number a little more than 1%. Much of the population consists of migrant laborers from poorer states, who live in temporary settlements that lack both clean water and sanitation facilities.

The South

Bangalore   Bangalore has moved from being a city of retirees to a tech city, which is now grappling to put its infrastructure together to support the boom. In luxury spaces, there are the lifestyle mall at

Leela Palace near the airport, and the UB City Mall, with five high-rise towers set on 10 acres, that opened in late 2008, providing key position for luxury fashion brands in the city. Another project in progress is the MBD Group luxury mall and 450-room luxury hotel, called Zephyr, which plans to open end 2010.[10]

There is a lot of money in Bangalore today, which is reflected in Bang & Olufsen's (B&O) plans to open offices and production facilities there in the near future.

Bangalore has an upwardly mobile, gadget-obsessed population balanced between young, working professionals, and the retired. The IT sector experienced growth from US$50 million in 1991 to US$40 billion in 2005, and during the past three or four years has had a compounded growth rate of 30%, although this seems to be slowing down in the current worldwide economic situation.[11] Much like the original Silicon Valley in California, Silicon Valley in India has its stars, such as Narayana Murthy of Infosys and Azim Premji of Wipro.

Hyderabad   Hyderabad is the capital of Andhra Pradesh state. The region has a population of 6.1 million, and the city itself has an estimated 3.6 million people, making it the sixth-most populous city in India. Hyderabad is known for its rich history, culture, and architecture and represents a unique blend of north and south India. It is a place where Hindus and Muslims have coexisted peacefully for centuries. It is also one of the most developed cities in the country and has become such a hub of IT and biotechnology that it is now said to be "fast rivaling Bangalore as India's top IT city."[12]

Hyderabad is also the financial and economic capital of the state, with the financial sector employing some 29% of the workforce. From the 1990s onward, the economic pattern of the city has changed from being primarily service oriented to incorporating a much broader spectrum of economic activities, including trade, transport, commerce, storage, and communications. The service industry is the major contributor, with the urban workforce constituting 90% of the total.

Hyderabad is known for products such as silverware, saris, Nirmal and Kalamkari[13] paintings and artifacts, unique Bidri handcrafted items, lacquer bangles studded with stones, silkware, cottonware, and handloom-based clothing materials, which have been made and traded through the city for centuries. Hyderabad was one of the first Indian cities to renovate its urban center, widening roads, clearing sidewalks of vendors and beggars, and replacing dilapidated old buildings with modern high-rises.[14]

Chennai (formerly Madras)   Located on the Coromandel Coast of the Bay of Bengal, Chennai is the capital of the state of Tamil Nadu and India's fourth-largest metropolitan center. With an estimated population in 2007 of 8.63 million,[15] the 368-year-old city is one of the largest metropolitan areas in the world.

Chennai is the third-largest commercial and industrial center in India, and is known for its cultural heritage and its temple architecture, and as a hub for south Indian classical music and dance. The city is considered to be the automobile capital of India and is the base for many of the country's major automobile manufacturers. This has led to Chennai being referred to as the Detroit of South Asia.[16] It has also become a major center for outsourced jobs from the West.

Chennai has a diversified economic base. In addition to automobile industry, it offers software services, hardware manufacturing, and financial services, as well as petrochemicals, textiles, and apparel. Based on the "Location Ranking Survey" conducted by ECA International,[17] it was recently rated as having the highest quality of life of all Indian cities. The city is home to the Tamil entertainment (motion pictures, television, and recorded music) industry, which is the second-largest in India after Bollywood. (Because it is largely centered around the Kodambakkam area, the Tamil film industry is popularly referred to as "Kollywood.")

The East

Kolkata (Calcutta)   Located in eastern India on the east bank of the River Hooghly, Kolkata is the capital of the state of West Bengal. The city has a population of almost 4.5 million, with an extended metropolitan population of more than 14 million, making it the third-largest urban agglomeration and the fourth-largest city in India. Also known as the "City of Joy," Kolkata, considered by many to be the cultural capital of India, is renowned for its literary, artistic, and revolutionary heritage. (It was at the forefront of the struggle for independence and a center of leftist and trade union movements.) As the former national capital, it is the birthplace of modern Indian literary and artistic thought and the home of the Bengali film industry.

Serving as the capital of India during the British Raj until 1911, it was once the center of modern education, science, culture, and politics in India, but witnessed economic stagnation in the years following independence in 1947. However, since 2000, an economic rejuvenation has arrested the morbid decline. This vibrant city is the main business, commercial, and financial hub of eastern India and the northeastern states, numbering Bata India among the notable companies headquartered there. However, as do other large cities, Kolkata continues to struggle with poverty, pollution, and traffic congestion.

The West

Ahmedabad   Ahmedabad is the largest city in the state of Gujarat and the seventh-largest city in India. It has a rich historical heritage, and forms the hub of the most prominent regional corridor extending from Vapi near Mumbai to Ahmedabad. Its growth in the 1940s from a major trading center for gold, silk, and cotton in medieval times reflects the continuity of its distinct enterprise and business leadership. The establishment of the first cotton-textile mill in 1861, without any special climatic advantage and before the advent of railways, and the way in which this industry expanded over the years speaks for the high level of business acumen. As one writer has put it:

> Unlike Bombay, Calcutta, Madras and Kanpur, Ahmedabad was not the creation of the British but a city which while remaining true to itself successfully adapted to the new industrial age carrying over commercial and industrial skills and patterns of traditional social organization. In no great city of India can the continuity of past and present be seen as clearly as in Ahmedabad.[18]

Textiles still constitute the largest industrial group in the city's registered industrial sector, which accounted for 33% of the country's total exports in 1997.

There are three Ahmedabads, the first of which is the five-century-old walled city founded by Sultan Ahmed Shah. The area features several medieval mosques of Indo-Islamic architectural style and innumerable, tightly packed houses along narrow winding lanes, most of which are occupied by a homogeneous community, each with a separate subculture.

The second Ahmedabad developed around old villages on the periphery of the city during the latter half of the nineteenth century, after the emergence of the textile industry. Here, slums and multi-storied concrete buildings (*chawls*) mushroomed around the textile mills and factories. While this area retains much of the traditional caste-based lifestyle of the old villages, the slums and *chawls* also carry the imprint of the social composition and segregated diversity of the textile mill workers. Those who migrated into the second city during the nineteenth and twentieth centuries settled in *chawls*, while those who came after independence were forced to live in slums. Before 1980, almost one-third of the textile workers were classified as Dalit (literally "downtrodden"—including scheduled castes, scheduled tribes, and backward classes); another third were Muslim.

The third Ahmedabad is new, and is separated from the other two by the river Sabarmati. An elite area, it is populated by the upper and middle classes, with a very small and scattered Muslim population and a few Dalit housing colonies and slums. This part of the city hosts most of the modern institutions of higher learning, including the university. In the past decade, the character of this area has changed under the influence of communal riots principally in the old city, which has a large concentration of Muslims living alongside the Hindu community. After each riot, the middle and upper classes in the walled city felt less secure, and they, along with traders and professionals from around the city moved to the relative stability of the new Ahmedabad. The process quickened after 1985, with the rise of multistoried offices, residential buildings, and Singapore-style shopping arcades, which made the elite areas of the new Ahmedabad even more exclusive.

Pune   Located in the western Indian state of Maharashtra and its second-largest city, Pune is the eighth-largest urban agglomeration in India, with a population of 4.5 million.

Pune is widely considered the cultural capital of Marathi-speaking Maharashtrians, and its several esteemed colleges and educational institutions have earned it the nickname "the Oxford of the East." It is also home to software and IT companies.

Its strong presence in the automobile sector has seen it consolidate its position (in the minds of the locals, at least) as the "Detroit of India." It is home to one of the world's largest two-wheeler manufacturers, Bajaj Auto, and to other major players in Tata Motors, India's largest passenger car and commercial vehicle manufacturer, and DaimlerChrysler, which has an assembly line for its Mercedes-Benz brand. Electronic goods giants Whirlpool and LG have appliance manufacturing plants in the city, as do major food processors Frito-Lay and Coca-Cola. Plans are in hand to make Pune India's first wireless city.

Goa   Although Goa is India's smallest state in area and the fourth-smallest in population, it is India's richest, mostly as a result of tourism. Located on the west coast of India in the region known as the Konkan, it is bounded by the state of Maharashtra to the north and by Karnataka to the east and south. Panaji (Panjim) is the state capital, Vasco-da-Gama (Vasco) the largest city, while the historic city of Margao still exhibits the influence of its Portuguese colonial past. The Portuguese controlled Goa for about 450 years, until it became an Indian possession in 1961.

CONSUMER DIFFERENCES

From the newly rich who are still encumbered by the shackles of post-independence austerity, and who prefer to invest in a foreign education than in the faux trappings of luxury brands to the so-called butterflies of Technopak Knowledge Company's The Technopak Advisors' Market Intelligence Division, *India Shopping Trends*,[19] who are ready to shed their cocoon, the demands of the new consumer are far from uniform. Even the elite range from Bollywood glamor to subtle old money and anything in between.

Thus Louis Vuitton and other international designer brands are far more successful in New Delhi, with its more exhibitionist nature, than in Mumbai. Indeed, Zainab Nedou, formerly of World Luxury Council, says "in Delhi it's the 'bling factor' that counts, and Louis Vuitton has become like Surf (a popular detergent); everyone has it".[20]

Certainly, Delhi and Mumbai display different consumer reactions and buying patterns for luxury brands. Delhi is a media-led city where socialites make Page 3 (equivalent to a Page 6 in New York), displaying their recent acquisitions from trips to Gucci, Fendi, Prada, and LV in Europe, or in India as the case may be. Mumbai, on the other hand, is a culturally confident city in which Bollywood and the advertising industry play a prominent role. Here, high-street brands do well, as do watches and jewelry, the mainstay of luxury in India today.

Differences: North vs. south

Rattan Keswani of the Oberoi group, a premier luxury hotel chain, explains the differences between Mumbai and Delhi consumers this way:

In Delhi, money flows freely because the north has a different kind of income through trading in real estate and agricultural revenue, which is totally tax free and as a consequence black or unaccounted money. (Resources such as agriculture do not attract tax.) In Delhi, there is a different kind of customer, because the city like a cocoon and hub at the same time draws people from other cities such as Ludhiana, Chandigarh, and the cities of the North Belt of Punjab to spend this unaccounted-for money. Delhi is then possibly a hub that draws all the new money like a bee.

Delhi condenses backward and inward as a hub, attracting workforce and people into the city. Delhi feeds off other cities, which explains why the consumer behavior here is different than in Mumbai.

Mumbai doesn't have this advantage of a large consumer base from other satellite cities. It is finger-shaped and fragmented into three sections: North (near the airport); Central; and South (Nariman Point, Malabar Hill, and Colaba).

Recent consumer buying trends have demonstrated that the North and Central parts are witnessing new and emerging consumers, whereas the South has a different, old-money mindset. Even the buying behavior of Indians from these parts is very different and they might not be as besotted with logo brands, preferring the more "bespoke".

In sum, it is the status conscious in both Delhi and Mumbai who are most ready and willing to buy into the luxury dream.

NOTES

1. Mira Kamdar 2007, *Planet India: How the Fastest-growing Democracy is Transforming America and the World*, Scribner, New York.
2. *Euromonitor*, <www.euromonitor.com>.
3. ibid.

4. McKinsey & Co. and "Bombay First" business group 2003, *Vision 2020*.

5. *BBC News* 2000, "Bombay Aces Population Boom", December 30, <www.news. bbc.co.uk/2/hi/south_asia/1093424.stm>.

6. This is a mega slum and administrative ward spread across parts of the suburbs of Sion, Bandra, Kurla, and Kalina.

7. Kamdar, op. cit., p.201.

8. Also known as poppadom, this food is a dried lentil chip studded with Indian spices that comes alive when grilled or deep fried.

9. Nikhil Anand 2006, "Disconnecting Experience: Making World-Class Roads in Mumbai", *Economic & Political Weekly*, published by EPW Research Foundation Mumbai, vol. 41, no. 31, August 5–11, p. 3422.

10. *The Daily Retail* 2008, "Parsvnath, Ansal API are Firming Plans for Luxury Malls", March 7, <www.thedailyretail.com/Retail_news/Indian_rn/article/index.php?article_name=8Marchrni03>.

11. *The Indian Express* 2009, "IT Industry Facing Unprecedented Crisis: Nilekani", February 16, <www.indianexpress.com/news/it-industry-facing-unprecedented-crisis-nilekani/424232/>.

12. Kamdar, op. cit., p. 211.

13. This is a block-printing technique.

14. Kamdar, op. cit., p.194.

15. World Gazetteer, "Cities, Chennai", <www.world-gazetteer.com>.

16. *The Hindu* 2005, "Chennai Has the 'Potential' to Become Detroit of South Asia: IT Secretary", July 18.

17. ECA International 2007, *Annual Location Ranking Survey*.

18. Kenneth L. Gillion 1968, *Ahmedabad: A Study in Indian Urban History*, University of California Press.

19. The Knowledge Company (Technopak Advisors' Market Intelligence Division) 2008, *India Shopping Trends 2008*.

20. Radha Chadda & Paul Husband 2006, *The Cult of the Luxury Brand: India's Love Affair with Luxury*, Nicholas Brealey International, p. 229.

CHAPTER 6
Indian Views on Luxury

THE SARI

This most versatile Indian garment is an unstitched drape of six yards that has traditionally been woven on a handloom. Worn in many styles across the country, it was easy, until maybe the 1950s, to tell which part of India a woman hailed from by the drape and weave of her sari. Even today, purist handloom weavers hold to their patterns, colors, and designs zealously, refusing to let outside influences mingle or pollute their purity. Silk, cotton, art silk, raw silk, and silk and cotton blends, muslin as well as *khadi* are some of the traditional fabrics of which saris are made. Gold and silver thread woven embellishment is common, as are silk thread woven patterns.

Weaving saris in mills made them affordable to all classes; and created a flux in women's wardrobes, filling it with color and patterns that were new and enticing. Synthetic and mill-woven fabrics were easier to maintain and cheaper, and created a revolution of sorts even in the middle class, which started buying saris in large numbers at all times of the year, and not only for weddings and festivals, as was the norm in the past.

Today millions of saris are produced in the town of Surat for instance on rotary printing machines and churned out in synthetics across the country. Any small printing mill has a capacity of producing 10,000 saris per day and they are all pre-sold.

The sari remains an intrinsic part of India's dress sensibility, and although the Indian man has long abandoned the draped *dhoti* as daily wear, the woman takes to the sari without a second thought whenever the need or the mood arises. Formal gatherings, family functions, and important meetings in the country or abroad are usually occasions for the sari to be flaunted, even by those corporate women who are normally comfortable in an Armani suit.

INDIAN VIEWS OF LUXURY

To most Indians, luxury goods are those that cost a great deal and come from foreign markets. Needless to say, Indian views on luxury are necessarily as polarized as Indian society itself. While the maharajas indulged in Cartier and Louis Vuitton, as exemplified by Lucy Moore's *maharanis*, at the bottom end of society a decent meal and a safe place to sleep would probably do. According to McKinsey's classification (see chapter 3), Indians are just getting used to the idea of luxury brands (and potentially their usefulness as an aid in social mobility), a good education taking precedence over the fripperies and decadence of the upper classes. It is estimated that there are as many as nine million Indians who can afford to buy luxury goods but do not, because to do so would contravene the Gandhist socialist/communist idealism of post-Partition India.

The quantities of cash in India have also bred a "gold digger" attitude among certain businessmen, a kind of "grab and run" mindset. The amount of money earned is increasingly important, and Indians like to flaunt what they have. However, this concept does not meet the criteria for our definition of branded fashion and luxury goods, and the truth of the matter is that, with the exception of the international brands now implanted in the major cities, India is practically devoid of any Indian branded fashion and luxury goods today.

There is a potential dilemma here and eventual danger for Indian companies producing fashion and luxury products, because they will be competing with the savvy, global marketers seeking a way into the market. Unless they come up to speed very quickly in branding, they risk being devoured little by little as the consumers become educated by and addicted to luxury brands from the West.

At present, consumers are not as sensitive to this as they should be; as they become more affluent, they are seeking ways to spend their money, and some of the very wealthy are ready to pay any price for luxury. While these may represent a small percentage, they are a small part of a massive population and will have a considerable impact on the luxury goods industry, now and in the future.

But for most others who can afford the brands, luxury is defined as something that is an indulgence rather than a necessity, something perceived as being at the highest end of the market in quality and price, which brings a sense of being part of something select, superior, and exclusive.

Perspectives on luxury

Following are some personal perspectives demonstrating Indian views on luxury:

- *Rajesh Pratap Singh (designer):* "I wanted luxury, but I could not afford it. To me, making the perfect shirt is making luxury. It can take 40 days to make a shirt that is not a mass-produced creation, but one of its kind, a labor of effort and love. It is sold from special places, because abroad, they see it as an item of luxury, and sell it at very high prices. But it is not the price point that makes it luxury; it is the quality of the work, the fact that the product is handmade, and thus special."
- *Ashish N. Soni (designer):* "India has always been a country that has been steeped in the culture of luxury. Luxury has been the country's cultural heritage. The difference today is that luxury has become more accessible to people across the world. A growing number of affluent Indians are aspiring for luxury today that was earlier a privilege of a few."
- *Sabyasachi Mukherjee (designer):* "For me it lies in simplicity. A simple cotton sari woven on the handloom can outshine everything around. Luxury is when every component is in harmony,

and there is a sense of peace and time. It is a handmade suit. I translate luxury as intimate handmade details, when a garment is completely handcrafted, it is rarified, has an old world charm that mass-produced luxury labels cannot boast of. It lies in the perfect cut, achieved with love and care."

- *Tarun Tahiliani (designer):* "I don't think you can become a global player unless you open up your local market. Let Indian designers compete with everybody and let people buy what they want. Only then will there be vibrancy. Let me stress once again, the look, in the next century, has to be Indian. That's one thing that always works—whether in films, architecture or fashion. Whenever there has been a departure [from this], it has been disastrous."

- *Rana Gill (designer):* "A handwoven, well-draped sari is luxury to me. *Haute couture* in India is bridal. Our *haute couture* is bridal because it is hand embroidered, with every panel either woven, beaded, custom made, fitted ... so that to us is *couture*. You know, Western *couture* is all pleated and fitted, and you come for fittings. A plain satin duchess fitted dress is *haute couture* in Paris, but I don't see that in India."

- *Fiona Caulfield (CEO, Hardys Bay Consulting Company):* "It's about bespoke; India has the longest history in the world of doing bespoke. And luxury in India is all about customization. How you customize this experience. In India, it is not traditional to go shopping in the Louis Vuitton store. The Louis Vuitton store comes to your home as a personal shopping consultant. Even the shopping experience gets customized around the individual. It is not the behavior we have in the other markets."

- *Minu and Namit's (Ampersand):* "Luxury is to be free of material trappings. Luxury is time, to be able to do what I want, when I want, the way I want to. Of course, with the economy booming, there is more money in the market today. All the brands are coming in, but for it to reach a level where people are actually buying luxury it will take at least 10 years. There is no doubt that the market is there. Luxury has been in India forever, every village and city has its little royalty, a luxurious way of living—you are your own master, the way people have lived here that's luxury. The material brand luxury part is creeping in now."

- *Maharaja Jai Singh ("Joey"):* "Bit of an overall concept, how you use it, how you wear it. When we lived in the palace, it was the best of everything, food, clothing, jewels, formal attire, turbans, and necklaces for the men, cars, luxurious carpets, furnishings—which came with the Europeans, a modern concept ... Now it is Western fashion names, foreign brands, and luxury is the showing off of foreign brands."

- *Rathi Vinay Jha (former director general of the Fashion Design Council of India):* "I would still say that luxury is what I am very comfortable in: fabrics that I love, textiles that I enjoy, a lifestyle that I know I can lead—but I would like to push the envelope and try to buy a Tanjoy sari, rather than buying a cotton sari."

- *Nikhil Mehra (designer in the "Shantanu & Nikhil" fashion house):* "For me, it is selling a part of your philosophy, your culture, your art and your heritage. Not only selling, but also sharing the experience of where you come from, where you belong. For Shantanu and me, being Indians who've studied abroad and have come back here, it's about sharing what India has to offer, with a modern, tasteful philosophy. So for us it is about fabrics, which is an historical aspect of our culture. It is about embroidery that goes back hundreds of years."

JEWELRY

For many Indians, the notion of Indian luxury still revolves around gold and jewelry, and comes from a tradition of royalty and fabulous displays of wealth. India is renowned for its gems, its natural resources enabling an entire industry to thrive across many centuries. The Indian consumer sees jewelry as an investment; saving for a rainy day or bad times. Gold is perceived as being as good as cash, and constantly escalates in value; weight takes precedence over design. And yet India-made jewelry remains very design bound, with different regions preferring and repeating designs that have special meaning in that region and culture.

Traditionally, Indians have always had recourse to their family jeweler. Traditionally, jewelry firms have been family-owned businesses, which have nurtured clients through the generations and refined designs that have been handed down through the generations. Goldsmiths and other artisans also hand down their craft from father to son. Their methods of working are technically hidebound, and their skill is perfected through the generations by constant repetition and re-creation of a few basic permutations and combinations of designs and applications. Getting them to understand a new medium or technique can be a monumental task: being experts in their field and adept at their art, they are not open to suggestions from "unskilled" persons. That many of them are only semiliterate compounds the problem.

There are several jewelry houses in India with luxury products but not luxury branding, among them the renowned Gem Palace in Jaipur. But beyond its impressive array of jewelry that make it an indisputable tourist attraction, Gem Palace is not branding per se. There are, however, several companies making a foray into the ways of branding, among them:

- *Tribhovandas Bhimji Zaveri (TBZ)* has made an attempt to be groundbreaking as India's first big branded traditional jeweler. As such, it focuses on *trust*, and was one of the first to "mark" every piece. Originally, it had one flagship store and specialized in gold, but has diversified into gemstones. It now has several stores, and advertises in high-end fashion and luxury magazines.
- *Popley* is similar to TBZ, but its products are flashier and not as exclusive.

- *Orra* specializes in platinum and diamonds, although its products are lower down the luxury scale than those of some contemporaries.
- *Rose* is the new kid on the block, and openly presents itself as being "exclusive." Starting with an exclusive boutique at Breach Candy and operating by appointment only, it has since expanded—perhaps too far and too fast.
- *Anmol* was started in April 1986 by the Datwani brothers, Ishu and Sunil, neither of whom has a jewelry background. From one small store in Bandra, they now operate a big one there, with branches in Gurgaon (Gold Souk) and Delhi's Emporio Mall and plans to double the number of points of sale by 2010. With a dedicated marketing effort, they are coming close to luxury branding, and have demonstrated strong advertising campaigns using very contemporary images away from the standard bridal shots.
- *Ravissant*, set up two decades ago by Ravi Chawla as a store concept with luxury products, the Ravissant network now comprises boutiques in Delhi, Agra, and Mumbai. Whereas the stores meet some of the luxury brand criteria, including the offer of some luxury branded goods (Wedgwood, Rosenthal, and Royal Doulton, Versace, and Bvlgari), the mix of fashion apparel with sterling silverware and furniture sends a mixed message, and risks being perceived as something of a hodge-podge, an impression not alleviated by the recent addition of the high-end Jacques Dessange hair salons. While some consider Ravissant to be the closest thing India has to a Westernized luxury brand, it is the consumer who makes comparisons with the real thing and categorizes accordingly. While beauty may well be in the eyes of the beholder, in the luxury industry, things are not so subjective or clear cut. How it is created, marketed, and distributed is only one part of the equation. There remains the other and more crucial component for brand success: the purchase.

Above and beyond these, if there is one brand among the Indian jewellers that already has the makings of branding techniques as a platform for expansion to the next level, and can be considered as a branded luxury goods firm, it is Ganjam. It has been visible on the market in recent years and was the first company to undertake a marketing and advertising campaign based on emotion, indulgence, and luxury. It has a high media profile and recently hired a branding agency in London.

KEY EXAMPLES

Ganjam[1]

How did a traditional, century-old jewelry house become a contemporary, high-profile house with international presence? It has been a slow and steady process for this Bangalore-based company.

"The signature of the company from the time of the forefathers has always been high quality," explained joint managing director Umesh Ganjam. "We were a traditional south Indian jewelry company that specialized in diamonds and the colored stones popular in the south, set in 22 carat gold."

The company ventured into pure gold jewelry in the 1960s when the Government of India enforced the Gold Control order. But it was Umesh Ganjam's deep desire to walk a different road that made the first big change happen: "In 1996–97, we introduced a design studio, and began taking on designers to work out patterns and designs that were off the beaten track."

It was a definite breakaway. Today, the company has 15 designers on board, not counting Sri Devi, the design team head, and Kazuo Ogawa, the Japanese designer, who also creates lines exclusive to Ganjam in India. The company worked steadily to position itself as a quality brand, by choosing only the best in material that came in from outside, and in sending out only the best in design and quality as finished goods. "We are trying to reach world-class standards," Umesh Ganjam added, "but have yet to get there."

As part of the process of "getting there" Ganjam has restricted its diamond imports to only the F color (third highest color grade a diamond can achieve) and the VVS (very-very small inclusions) grade of stones, something that few companies have done. Ganjam sees it as the first major step to reaching the benchmark set by international jewelry houses such as Cartier, Bvlgari, and Harry Winston. The other steps would include finding new highs in the art of enameling and engraving, which are important aspects of the jewelry of India.

Ganjam has won a handful of design competitions, including those of the Diamond Trading Corporation (DTC) and the World Gold Council, among others. When it came to exhibiting the winning piece, Ganjam broke the rules and put together an exhibition of all the winning pieces, though it meant exhibiting the work of his competitors. This surprised many people in the industry, but Umesh Ganjam says, "I felt we were only doing the industry a favor by exhibiting the talent that the Indian talent pool had created."

This brought about an important change in perspective and clients began to realize that design was an important element in jewelry beyond the mere investment value.

"In fact, the real change happened in our lives," Umesh Ganjam says. "We realized that contrary to our thinking, the consumer was far ahead of us, and had not just a keen eye for good designs, but was open to investing in them." Encouraged by the response, Ganjam went on to win the Virtuosi Award in 1998 and the international design award in 2002. Design had become the focus of the company's work.

With the design element in place, Ganjam decided the time was right to take the company to the next level of visibility and positioning. "We realized that though India is one of the biggest producers and consumers of gold jewelry, we had no say in the international pricing or other matters. Hallmarked gold was being brought in from Switzerland, and the price was being fixed in London. India was not seen as important enough in the raw material scenario to have an opinion let alone a role in the process. I realized as a

Ganjam headpiece

country, our marketing of us was not right, and decided to change things at Ganjam at least."

He himself had an IT hardware background, and had, over the years, interacted with Fortune 500 companies such as Motorola, which had given him an understanding of how they functioned. To become a luxury brand, Ganjam realized the company had to be strong in three respects: design, quality, and marketing.

Umesh persuaded Hindusthan Thomson Ltd. (HTA) to open an office in Bangalore, and work on promoting his brand. The image of the brand changed substantially when fashion photographer Prabuddha Dasgupta was brought in to shoot a series of black-and-white images that spoke of high fashion and showed the product in a fashion context. This was a huge statement coming from an Indian company, and the images were used in the *World Graphic Book* as an indication of the successful makeover of a very traditional heritage company into a contemporary one. The title spoke of the "New Emotion of India."

Perhaps one of the biggest moves in the internalization of Ganjam was the linkup with Kazuo Ogawa. This collaboration came about as a result of Ganjam's desire to attain international class through studying the creations of the biggest international jewelry houses. He noted that most of the diamond and stone settings were in platinum, and this coincided with a Platinum Guild of India (PGI) survey of India as a potential market. Ganjam, the PGI discovered, was the only Indian company working with platinum but, by its own admission, had little knowledge of working with platinum and was looking for an experienced designer.

PGI was only too happy to help, and brought in the well-known Japanese designer to share his inputs. The interaction proved fruitful. Impressed by some of Ganjam's designs, Ogawa took jewelry back with him to market in Japan. Ganjam's first international footprint was thus made in the year 2000.

Ganjam trod new ground by taking part in a festival of India organized to showcase designer Tarun Tahiliani's collection at the

Milan Fashion Week in 2003. It was a good experience in more ways than one. "I was walking into our exhibition area when I noticed a small shop near it, displaying our brochures," Umesh Ganjam recounted. "I was intrigued and walked in to ask about it. Franco Ricci, the owner of the shop, which made and sold handmade books, said he had taken a fancy to the lovely jewelry by an Indian firm that was displaying next door, and had placed the brochures so passers-by could take a look at them. We were introduced, and Ricci invited us to showcase in Italy the following year. Thus Milan continued."

The exhibition caught the eye of *Vogue Italy*, which has subsequently covered Ganjam in several editions. Umesh also had the honor of being asked to hold a showing at Madame Tussaud's in London, which led to further invitations to exhibit at Citibank and other shows at other "India places" in London. Although sales were minimal, the exposure gave Ganjam a better understanding of the foreign buyer.

Although the collaboration with HTA worked wonderfully in India, in 2004 Umesh Ganjam turned to PGI to help him find an overseas partner to further his brand outside India and to propel it into the luxury segment. London-based brand communications agency Large Smith Walford (LSW), which handled, among others, some of the Louis Vuitton brands, stepped in. LSW spent six to eight months studying India and the brand, and by 2006 Ganjam had moved into top gear.

When it was discovered that the Royal Windsor Polo Club in England was looking for a sponsor for the Jaipur Cup Polo matches that led up to the finals, which were sponsored by Cartier, Ganjam was quick to take up the sponsorship. This was an excellent opportunity to show fine jewelry to the very segment of the British who would best appreciate it.

The following year, Ganjam knew it had arrived. PGI pitched for and won the brand the honor of making the exhibition piece of platinum to be unveiled at the Watch Fair in Basel, Switzerland. Ganjam is one of the few companies in the world that still makes all

Ganjam drop necklace advert

its pieces by hand, and PGI knew that this exhibit would help put India on the world jewelry map.

Iraja, as the piece was called, is a flowing water-inspired neck-and-shoulder adornment that is intricately fitted and sparkles with the movement of its many moveable pieces. It has been displayed since at the Jaipur Cup and in Mumbai, and will soon take off on a world tour.

Upholding the industry standards in design, quality, and marketing, Ganjam has earned the distinction of being one of India's true, branded luxury companies.

To a lesser extent, the company Hidesign has demonstrated its aspiration to be considered as a luxury brand.

Hidesign[2]

Though this Puducherry-based firm does not yet match the criteria to be considered a branded luxury goods firm, its 2007 joint venture with Louis Vuitton has started to give it a lift in that direction.

When founder Dilip Kapoor began in 1978 making handmade leather bags after a self-proclaimed "useless Ph.D." in international affairs from an American university, he realized that he was after a lifestyle more than anything else. His initial creations reflected the lifestyle he had known in the U.S., and his penchant for natural products gave him a more personalized appeal, albeit within a smaller community. Essentially, Kapoor extolled the virtues of not belonging to any big, uncaring group or organization. It is a little puzzling, then, that he would choose to align himself with the signature brand in a multinational group driven by profit margins and limitless ambition.

Kapoor's leather-tanning processes do not involve chemicals; he prefers eco-friendly natural vegetable dyes, which feed and nourish the leather and grain. Between 1990 and 2000, Kapoor built his business, beginning with a buyer from John Lewis, then extending to Selfridges and Australia's David Jones and Myer, before moving into

Hidesign leather bag advert

the U.S. Today Hidesign has 28 stores in India, seven stores in Russia, two in China, and retails in Europe and the U.S. too.

The road to the co-branding with Louis Vuitton has been long, but Hidesign had been seeking a partner capable of bringing it to the next level and helping it to grow into a global luxury brand.

"I realize now," Kapoor says, "how big a job we have ahead of us. We were so overconfident, we thought we could do it alone, but there is so much to be learned, so much hard work and concentration ahead. I can see how 150 years of hard work has helped build the LV brand into what it is; and it does have a huge heritage, a serious work culture and an organizational system that I can learn endlessly from.

"It is really hard work to create and sell a global brand, and the trick is to be yourself in what you create. It is so much easier to sell by just copying successful designs like some Indian brands do so well, but my challenge is to make my Indian brand a leader."

The new deal has a new store concept for Hidesign with eye-catching advertising from Paris-based photographer, Dinh. The 20% investment in the company by Louis Vuitton goes beyond the aesthetics. Essentially the agreement calls for there to be no mingling of the brands or selling of both companies' products in any one store, and for Hidesign to play a role in facilitating Louis Vuitton's integration into India, advising on such matters as human resources practices and factory setup. In exchange, Louis Vuitton will work with Hidesign in the brand-building aspects of its concept, including marketing and design. Particular emphasis will be placed on the reorientation of the brand towards women through such things as store design and new color schemes throughout the points of sale.

NOTES

1. This example is based on an extract from *DNA-Me*, "The Spirit of Luxury", 2008, vol. 2(2), pp. 78–83.
2. ibid., pp. 137–42.

PART III
MARKET POTENTIAL

CHAPTER 7
MAPPING FASHION AND LUXURY BRANDS IN INDIA

THE EMERGING MARKET FOR BRANDED LUXURY AND FASHION COMPANIES

The considerable potential for the international branded luxury and fashion companies is now increasingly evident, even though this segment is in its nascent stage. The current luxury market in India is estimated to be worth between 15 and 20 billion rupees (up to $400 million) and has the potential to register an annual growth of 15–20% over the next five years.[1] The global brands that have yet to register a presence are becoming abundantly aware that they are already lagging behind those who paved the way. Having the right partnership is tantamount to ensuring success and thus of primary importance.

The market for these goods covers a wide spectrum, and has evolved to encompass categories such as jewelry, watches, apparel, accessories, fragrance, gourmet foods, wines, and spirits. The number is increasing as those companies that had previously adopted a wait-and-see approach are now responding to the "India is the next China" adage they have been hearing since 2006. Lessons can now be learned from the likes of Montblanc, Ermenegildo Zegna, Louis Vuitton, Bvlgari, Cartier, Girard-Perregaux, Hugo Boss, and Burberry, who were among the first to seize the opportunities presented by the Indian market.

Beyond the luxury brands, the market is seeing an increased presence of other brand categories, which Uché Okonkwo, the Paris-based luxury branding consultant, categorizes as follows:

> Luxury and Prestige brands represent the highest form of craftsmanship and product quality and command a staunch consumer loyalty base that

is not affected by trend. These brands create and set the seasonal fashion trends and have the ability to retail an item for €20,000 and another for €300 to different consumer groups. They are an epitome of prestige and are capable of pulling all of their consumers with them wherever they are located. Brands in this group include Bvlgari and Hermès, among others. The luxury and prestige brands do not utilize mass-market strategies in order to become mass-market brands. Rather, they have recognized the changes in the luxury marketplace and are attuning their strategies accordingly, without sacrificing their core heritage and brand essence.

Premium brands are those brands that aspire to become luxury and prestige brands but their marketing mix strategies are more attuned to a mass market, albeit a luxury mass market. The brands in this group are also sometimes referred to as mass-premium brands, aspirational brands, mass-luxury brands, designer brands, or simply high-end brands. The group of premium brand has a broad scope, which makes narrowing them down challenging.

The premium fashion brands segment has arguably witnessed the greatest changes in the consumer market. They are also facing aggressive competition from the higher-priced luxury and prestige brands and the lower prices mass-fashion brands.

Mass-fashion brands on the other hand are those that dress the masses. A recent evolution brought about by competition has also created a significant change in the way this category is viewed. Although brands in this group include supermarket ranges such as Wal-Mart, Carrefour, Tesco, and Asda; and other brands like the U.K.'s Primark and France's Tati, these brands are effectively implementing differentiation and are currently developing strategies to elevate their offerings.

The difference between luxury brands and fashion brands is not only in the marketing mix aspects of products quality and pricing. It also applies to availability and exclusivity of the products. Fashion brands are for the mass-market, whether the products are of high quality or not. Luxury brands remain for a distinct market although this market has broadened. They are defined by high quality, differentiation, and precision in product design and manufacture.

A brand is either a luxury brand or it is not. There is no in-between. If a brand does not set out to target the high-end market, then it would be difficult for it to become a luxury brand.[2]

This categorization is useful because in India the consumer mindset rarely makes the distinction between luxury and premium. The "mallification of India" created a new class of premium brands, whereas luxury brands established their presence in the corridors of five-star hotels, attempting to educate the market without sounding preachy on their brand values. For example, Bvlgari had a great challenge selling bespoke jewelry in a market where women wear made-to-order jewels that rival a Cartier or Bvlgari brand.

Western luxury returns: Montblanc and Swiss watches

Elsewhere, other enterprising businessmen were assessing the potential of the nascent market. The growing awareness of designer ready-to-wear, and the large number of designers in the marketplace who set up stores of their own or worked with diverse outlets created a setting that augured a greater scale. It was not long before the luxury market that had watched the changing scenario from outside began to find itself welcomed in India.

Today, Delhi continues to be considered as the biggest market for the conspicuous consumption of high-end products, and is the first city to begin realizing the Indian buying potential in the areas of watches, fashion, accessories, or even wines and spirits. This is primarily due to the Delhi mindset, "flash for cash," which looks for the latest, the best, and the rare. Brands opened in 2008 were Hermès at the Oberoi Delhi, Cartier (which closed its first boutique in 2002), Dolce & Gabbana, Giorgio Armani, Tiffany, Paul Smith, Kenzo, Marc by Marc, and Tod's at the Emporio in Delhi.

In the late 1990s, cricketer Dilip Doshi set up Felicitous, a gift store in the Taj Palace in Mumbai. He followed it with an outlet for Montblanc, which was successful enough to warrant moving to a bigger space in the Taj. He then added Girard-Perregaux watches to his offerings, and took on Anna Bredemeyer in Mumbai to manage development and PR. Montblanc thus set an example for the others.

The 1990s also saw a renewed interest in exclusive wristwatches, and Swiss watchmakers were beginning to recover from the inroads made into their realm by the Japanese manufacturers. Rauf Ansari, a distributor with strong links with Switzerland, set up Regent at the Taj in Mumbai. In Delhi, Kapoor Watch Company and a host of others brought in Swiss wristwatches. Sensing the market potential, other brands were quick to bring in jewelry, accessories, luggage, and a host of other lifestyle products.

Cosmetics brands: affordable luxury

When, in 1986, cosmetics brands were allowed to be sold legally in the market for the first time in recent Indian history, the House of Baccarose, headed by Himanshu Kotecha, brought in three trusted and well-known fragrance labels—Nina Ricci, Burberry, and the Bogart group, which proved to be the forerunners of many more by the middle of the decade.

Capturing the public imagination with a range of fragrances was a clever way of breaking into a market where traditional, age-old home remedies were preferred to what were perceived to be chemical-loaded cosmetics. In conjunction with their Indian partners, the brands followed this up by introducing makeup and, finally, skincare products. The cost factor proved to be a challenge for the international brands but the luxury ambience—the feeling of being pampered at select outlets by trained staff—soon swept away the initial barriers to acceptance.

Within a few years, brands such as Dior, Elizabeth Arden, and Tommy Hilfiger, as well as the lesser-known Shishedo and La Prairie, had found their niche buyers. This success prompted fashion and luxury goods brands to look at India with anticipation.

The entry of international brands has greatly accelerated since 2005. India's luxury-loving royalty and the current status-conscious generation have both the money and the inclination to spend. India is now a compelling market because of the increasing tendency among the rich to spend on luxury brands. And the number who can afford to do so is, as we have seen, increasing rapidly.

Luxury influx

While it was not, as is commonly believed, the first luxury brand to open shop in India, Louis Vuitton was certainly in the vanguard. As did Ermenegildo Zegna before it, Louis Vuitton made its entry by using a silent partner. A reconnaissance mission in 1999 by the company's marketing guru at that time, Jean-Marc Loubier, resulted in an internal memorandum, which today shows startling clarity and sagacity. He mapped the Indian market's lack of branded fashion and luxury, and outlined the development potential for the Louis Vuitton brand. His incisive perspective on the market provided a blueprint for the ideal means of building the business in India through key relationships, and was the cornerstone of the brand's success in India today.

Louis Vuitton has had singular success. Its new launches are eagerly awaited, and, despite the price tags on its bags and shoes, sales are brisk in Delhi and Mumbai. Cashing in on the Indian preference for exclusivity in clothes and accessories, the company promoted a customized special-orders service. In 2006, Louis Vuitton India's Prasanna Bhaskar aimed at reaching one million lifestyle consumers in India, and offering them what she called a "superior Louis Vuitton experience" that would increase the contribution of Indians to the LV share worldwide.

Prasanna was not far off the mark. Today, more Louis Vuitton bags are bought than any other brand, although other luxury brands are equally visible across economic segments, in the metros at least. Young people think nothing of spending the equivalent of a month's salary for a middle-class family on a handbag or a pair of shoes.

The Salvatore Ferragamo store at the Grand Hyatt in Mumbai does brisk business in shoes and bags, as does Montblanc with its watches, wallets, belts, and pens. Wallets costing upward of 35,000 rupees, and earrings with a six-figure price tag have replaced the usual gifts that the jetset in Delhi, Bangalore, Chennai, Kolkata, and Mumbai bought on special occasions. Hugo Boss, Ermenegildo Zegna, Burberry, Canali, Chanel, Escada, and Valentino have also opened stores, though with varying degrees of success.

Current market scenario

The coming decade will present a more conducive growth environ-ment for luxury goods as the numbers of upmarket malls, world-class retail outlets, mono-boutiques, and retail chains increase. The continuing relaxation of restrictions on foreign direct investment in retail, though very slow, will also contribute substantially to the growth of India's luxury retail market.

Recent moves by the Ministry of Commerce to reduce taxation, to look at introducing a uniform tax regime across the country, and to allow multibrand retail by foreign investors will permit brands such as Sephora and Saks to set up shop.

India's middle class will continue to balloon—far beyond the esti-mated 50 million of the past decade—and the number of super-rich will grow sharply as well. After decades of socialist deprivation, when consumer goods were so limited that refrigerators were given pride of place in living rooms, there are now so many more ways to spend this new wealth—cell phones, air-conditioners, and washing machines; Botox, sushi, and Louis Vuitton bags; and, perhaps the biggest status symbol of all, cars. However, questions still remain on India's future role as a luxury destination. For example, Rahul Mehta, managing director of Creative Outerwear Ltd., one of India's foremost export companies (supplying to Giorgio Armani, Morgan, and Diesel, among others), in an interview with the authors expressed his belief that:

> The number of people who can buy luxury goods or are interested in the brands is small. Even among those who do aspire to the luxury brands, there is a snob value in buying it abroad. For one, it is a conversation

starter, and for another, the gray market is suspect, so even a Head & Shoulders shampoo is bought abroad. The counterfeiters are, however, quick to catch on to buying trends: recently a reputable department store in Breach Candy in South Bombay was caught selling fake Louis Vuitton bags! More important, the perception is that luxury brands send their cast-off, old stock to India and other Asian countries, and though this may no longer be true, it has yet to filter into the buyers' minds. Besides, the import duties make it cheaper to buy abroad; in India, duties make an expensive item even more prohibitive. However, aggressive advertising, brand building, and imaging have helped build up a market for luxury watches and accessories such as eyewear. In the apparel market though, ladies ethnic wear still rules for the big spend. Mass luxury shows more signs of being acceptable in India. There is an automatic escalation of mass brands into mass luxury because it is imported. This is as much a factor of price as perception. Thus, Levi's, though a mass brand in the U.S., becomes a mass luxury brand in India, notches above Dollar and Jealous jeans that are locally made. And by the same yardstick CK and FCUK become classed in Indian minds as luxury. Or pretty close to it. Armani Exchange too falls into the same category, while Armani might not even be considered seriously as worthy of the spending it demands.

Current mapping

There are several ways of mapping the brands currently in India. The face of retail is ever changing, as the market evolution continues at an unprecedented rate. For the purposes of clarity, we have organized the brands into groupings by sector and by distribution.

Essentially, international brands have limited choices in how they enter and develop their presence in India. They may opt for mono-brand retail stores or shop-in-shops for these brands, in which case they have two alternatives:

- *Joint ventures*—the distribution company will enter into joint venture with the international parent companies to represent exclusively one or more brands in their portfolio in India. The shareholding may vary in each case.
- *Distribution agreements*—a distribution license agreement might come into play in cases where a joint venture is not possible

or desirable for the international brand. The agreement would give the distribution company the right to retail the brand in India on an exclusive basis (through franchising, for example). These agreements might also include the right to manufacture the brand products in India.

The mapping of the brands in tables 7.1 to 7.5 shows the local partnership and distribution arrangements in place at the time of writing. For purposes of focus and clarity, we have excluded beauty (fragrance and cosmetics) and wines and spirits. The breakdown is organized into the following industries: apparel and accessories, jewelry and watches, home décor, tableware, and leisure.

Table 7.1 Apparel and accessories

Brand name	Distribution company	Info on stores, retailers, and corners
Alberta Ferretti	TSG International Marketing Ltd.	One store in New Delhi
Aldo	Major Brands Group	
Alexander McQueen	TSG International Marketing Ltd.	One store at Emporio, New Delhi
Alfred Dunhill	Brandhouse Retail	One store at The Shangri-La in New Delhi, and opening store at UB City, Bangalore
Argentovivo	Marigold Group and Xess	
Bally	Apparel Group (Dubai based)	One store at Grand Hyatt Plaza
Belmonte	Brandhouse Retail	
Bottega Veneta	Genesis Colors	One store at Galleria Mumbai and one at Emporio
Brioni	BadaSaab Designs Pvt. Ltd.	One store at the New Delhi Oberoi Hotel, one store at the Mumbai Oberoi Hotel
Burberry		One store at UB City, Bangalore, one store at Emporio, New Delhi
Calvin Klein Jeans	Genesis Colors and SSIPL	Two stores
Canali	Genesis Colors and SSIPL	One store at UB City, Bangalore, one store at Emporio, New Delhi

Table 7.1 (*Continued*)

Brand name	Distribution company	Info on stores, retailers, and corners
Carmichael House	Brandhouse Retail	
Chanel	Chanel India Pvt. Ltd.	One store at the Imperial Hotel New Delhi
Christian Dior	Christian Dior India Pvt. Ltd.	One store at The Oberoi New Delhi
Christies	Marigold Group and Xess	
Diesel	Reliance Brands Ltd.	Opening in New Delhi and Mumbai, possibly later in Bangalore, Hyderabad, and Chandigarh
Dior	Dior India Pvt. Ltd.	One store at The Oberoi New Delhi, one store at Emporio, New Delhi
Dolce & Gabbana	DLF Universal Fun Fashions and Chordia Group	One store at Emporio, New Delhi Thanks multibrand store
Ebel	Sunglass Palace	
Ermenegildo Zegna	Zegna India Pvt. Ltd.	Taj in Mumbai, Emporio in New Delhi, and one store UB City, Bangalore
Escada	Brandhouse Retail	Two stores in Mumbai
Esprit	Madura Garments	Ten stores in Mumbai, New Delhi, Chandigarh, and Pune
Etienne Aigner	Genesis Colors and SSIPL	Three stores
Etro	Fun Fashions and Chordia Group	Thanks multibrand store, one store at UB City, Bangalore
Giorgio Armani	DLF Universal	One store at Emporio, New Delhi, and one store at UB City, Bangalore
Gucci	Genesis Colors and SSIPL	Two stores in Mumbai and New Delhi, with flagship at The Oberoi Trident Towers The Galleria; third store opened at Emporio
Hermes	Khanna Retail	One store at The Oberoi New Delhi, opening store in Mumbai
Hugo Boss	Bin Hendi	One store at Emporio, New Delhi

(*Continued*)

Table 7.1   (*Continued*)

Brand name	Distribution company	Info on stores, retailers, and corners
Jean Paul Gaultier	TSG International Marketing Ltd.	One store at UB City, Bangalore
Jimmy Choo	Genesis Colors Delhi	One store at Genesis Colors at Emporio
Judith Leiber	Marigold Group and Xess	
Kenzo	Genesis Colors and SSIPL	One store at Emporio, New Delhi
Kimaya	Kimaya Fashions	One store at UB City, Bangalore, one store at Emporio, New Delhi
La Perla	Reliance Brands Ltd.	Opening in Mumbai, one store at UB City, Bangalore, one store at Emporio, New Delhi
Lanvin	TSG International Marketing Ltd.	One store at UB City, Bangalore
Louis Vuitton	LV India Pvt. Ltd.	Exclusively in Louis Vuitton stores: four in 2008: two in New Delhi, one in Mumbai, and one in Bangalore
Manzoni	Raymonds	Available at Manzoni exclusive stores at select Raymond Shops, and also at King's, Options, Prestige
Max Mara	Kimaya Fashions	Opening in Mumbai
Montblanc	Entrack International Trading	Montblanc stores
Moschino	TSG International Marketing Ltd.	One store at Taj Mumbai, store opening at UB City, Bangalore
Movado	Sunglass Palace	
Nine West	Major Brands Group	
Oviesse	Brandhouse Retail	Bangalore, Mumbai, New Delhi year end 2009
Paul Smith	Genesis Colors and SSPIL	One store at Emporio, New Delhi, one store at UB City, Bangalore
Pollini	TSG International Marketing Ltd.	
Promod	Major Brands Group	
Reid&Taylor	Brandhouse Retail	
Salvatore Ferragamo	DLF Universal	Stores in Mumbai, Delhi and Bangalore; opening of up to 10 stores at Grand Hyatt in India planned by 2013

Table 7.1   (*Continued*)

Brand name	Distribution company	Info on stores, retailers, and corners
Shanghai Tang	Modi Group	Opening in New Delhi
Stella McCartney	TSG International Marketing Ltd.	One store at UB City, Bangalore
Stephens Brothers	Brandhouse Retail	Two stores
Stuart Weitzman	Apparel Group (Dubai based)	
Tods	Bukhanvala Holdings	Stores at The Galleria/ The Oberoi Hotel in Mumbai, one store at Emporio, New Delhi, and one store at UB City, Bangalore
Tommy Hilfiger	Arvind Brands	Stores in Ahmedabad, Bangalore, Chandigarh, Chennai, Gurgaon, Hyderabad, Kolkatta, Mumbai, Pune
Vertu	Matrix Distributors	Rodeo Drive, Helvetica, Fone Time Machine, Popley La Classique, Johnson Watch Company, Prime Watch World, Ethos. Retailed in Bangalore, Chennai, Hyderabad, Mumbai, New Delhi, Kolkata, Ludhiana, Chandigarh
VF Corporation	Arvind Brands Ltd.	Distribution of Lee, Wrangler, and Arrow
Xess Couture	Marigold Group and Xess	

Table 7.2   Jewelry and watches

Brand name	Distribution company	Info on stores, retailers, and corners
Anmol Jewelers	Anmol India Pvt. Ltd.	Anmol stores, one store at Emporio, New Delhi
Antonio Bernini	Rose Group Mumbai, Delhi, Kolkata, Ahmedabad, Surat	Rose, Plush, Watches and More, Just in Vogue, Watches of Switzerland, Swiss Paradise, Johnson Watch Co., RAM's, Golden Time I, Golden Time II, The Golden Time III

(Continued)

Table 7.2   (*Continued*)

Brand name	Distribution company	Info on stores, retailers, and corners
Audemars Piguet	Audemars Piguet Singapore Pvt. Ltd. Chennai, New Delhi, Mumbai	The Helvetica, Kapoor Watch Co., The Regent Watch & Jewellery Co., The Rose International, Time Avenue
Baume & Mercier	Jot Impex Pvt. Ltd. Ahmedabad, Bangalore, Chandigarh, Chennai, Hyderabad, Kolkata, Mumbai, New Delhi	The Golden Time, Rodeo Drive, Ethos, Zimson Watch Boutique, Talwar Jewellery House, Helvetica, Beyond Luxury, Fɪ Time Machine, Exclusive Lines, Time Avenue, Watches of Switzerland, Swiss Gallery, Swiss Paradise, Johnson & Co., Johnson Watch Co., Kapoor Watch Co.
Hugo Boss	Titan Industries	
Breguet	Swatch Group India	Ethos Luxury Boutique, The Helvetica, Johnson & Co., Johnson Watch Co.
Breitling	Various distributors	The Helvetica, Exclusive Lines, Times of Lord, Kapoor Watch
Bvlgari	Mohit Diamonds	Two stores
Cartier	Navratna Bharat Retail Pvt. Ltd.	Opened at Emporio, New Delhi, possibly in Mumbai, Bangalore, and Chennai
Cerruti 1881	Various distributors	Rose, Plush, Watches and More, Johnson Watch Co., Swiss Paradise, Lifestyle, NAC Jewellers, Kapoor Watch Co., Watches of Switzerland, Just in Vogue
Chopard	Mohit Diamonds	The Chopard Boutique (Mumbai), Time Avenue, DiA, Johnson & Co., Johnson Watch Co., Kapoor Watch Co., The Helvetica, B.C. Sen Jewellers, Prime Watch World, Talwar Jewellery House, Meena Jewellers, Rodeo Drive, The Golden Time, one store at Emporio, New Delhi
Corum	Various distributors	Johnson & Co., Beyond Luxury, Kapoor Watch Co., Time Avenue, Rose, Swiss Boulevard, The Helvetica, Rodeo Drive, Exclusive Lines, Swiss International

Table 7.2　*(Continued)*

Brand name	Distribution company	Info on stores, retailers, and corners
DiA Diamonds	Mohit Diamonds	Two DiA stores, one store at Emporio, New Delhi
DIT Group	Gitanjali Group	One Stephan Hafner store in Mumbai
Ebel	Sunglasses Palace Pvt. Ltd.	Johnson Watch Co., Beyond Luxury, Watches of Switzerland, Swiss Gallery
Ferrari	Various distributors	Time Avenue, Johnson & Co.
Ganjam	Ganjam India Pvt. Ltd.	Ganjam stores, one store at Emporio, New Delhi
Girard Perregaux	Entrack Online	Two exclusive stores
IWC Schaffhausen	Various distributors	Johnson Watch Co., Johnson & Co., Ethos, The Helvetica
Jaeger-LeCoultre	Jot Impex Pvt. Ltd.	One store at Emporio, New Delhi. Retailed in Ahmedabad, Bangalore, Chandigarh, Chennai, Hyderabad, Kolkata, Mumbai, New Delhi
Jaquet Droz	Various distributors	Ethos Luxury store, The Helvetica, Prime Watch World
Leiber	Marigold Group	XESS store
Mariella Burani Group	Gitanjali Group	Opening soon
Minawala	Minawala	Three stores in Mumbai and one store at UB City, Bangalore
Mirari	Mirari Indian Jewels	One Mirari store, one store at Emporio, New Delhi
Montblanc	Entrack International Trading	One store at UB City, Bangalore
Montres Auguste Reymond	Montres Auguste Reymond India	One store
Omega	Various distributors	One store at UB City, Bangalore
Piaget	Mohit Diamonds	Piaget store (Mumbai), Time Avenue, Johnson & Co., Johnson Watch Co., Kapoor Watch Co., B.C. Sen Jewelers, Prime Watch World, The Helvetica, Talwar Jewellery House, one store at Emporio, New Delhi

(Continued)

Table 7.2   (*Continued*)

Brand name	Distribution company	Info on stores, retailers, and corners
Raymond Weil		Kapoor Watch Company, Popley La Classique, Swiss Gallery, Swiss Paradise, Watches of Switzerland, Ethos, The Helvetica, The Golden Time, Ethos. Retailed in New Delhi, Kolkata, Mumbai, Gurgaon, Chennai, Bangalore, Ahmedabad, Chandigarh, Ludhiana, Pune
Rolex	Rolex India Watch Co. Pvt. Ltd. (Mumbai)	Opening store at UB City, Bangalore
Rose	Rose Group Mumbai	Rose, one store at Emporio, New Delhi
Tag Heuer	LVMH Watch and Jewellry	Tag Heuer stores LV Watches and Jewellery, store at UB City, Bangalore, one store at Emporio, New Delhi
Tiffany & Co.		One store at UB City, Bangalore
Tudor	Rolex Watch Co. Pvt. Ltd.	Official Rolex retailers
Ulysse & Jardin	Beyond Luxury	Beyond Luxury
Vacheron Constantin	Mohit Diamonds	DiA, Time Avenue, Johnson & Co., Johnson Watch Co., The Helvetica, one store at Emporio, New Delhi
Van Cleef & Arpels	Fun Fashions and Chordia Group	Thanks
Varuna D Jani	Popley India	Popley Eternal (by appointment only)
Versace	Various distributors	Just in Vogue, Swiss Boulevard, Watches of Switzerland, Swiss Paradise, Versace Boutique (Mumbai), Johnson Watch Co., RAM's, Golden Time I, Golden Time II, The Golden Time

Table 7.3   Home décor

Brand name	Distribution company	Info on stores, retailers, and corners
Belmonte	Brand House Retail	Four stores
Carmichael House	Brand House Retail	Two stores
Lladro	The Spa Group	Eight stores, and one store at UB City, Bangalore
Raro	House of Raro	One store

Table 7.4   Tableware

Brand name	Distribution company	Info on stores, retailers, and corners
Bo Concept	The Spa Group	Opening
Christofle	The Spa Group	Store at UB City, Bangalore
Daum	Ganga Creations Pvt. Ltd.	Store at UB City, Bangalore
Good Earth	Eicher Group	Store at UB City, Bangalore; opening seven other stores in Mumbai, Chennai, and Delhi
Rosenthal	The Spa Group	One store at UB City, Bangalore
Villeroy and Boch	The Spa Group	Three stores, of which one at UB City in Bangalore
WMF	The Spa Group	Opening

Table 7.5   Leisure

Brand Name	Distribution company
NetJets	Fun Fashions and Chordia Group
Porsche	Fun Fashions and Chordia Group
Tumi	Murjani Group

Examples of key distribution companies based in India are:

- *Arvind Brands Ltd.:* Nautica, Tommy Hilfiger, VF Corp. (Lee, Wrangler, and Arrow)
- *Bird Group:* Cranchi
- *Brandhouse Retail Ltd.* (BHRL): Dunhill, Escada, Stephens Brothers, Reid & Taylor, Belmonte, Oviesse
- *DLF Universal:* Giorgio Armani, Emporio Armani, Salvatore Ferragamo
- *Entrack International Trading:* Montblanc, Girard-Perregaux
- *Genesis Colors:* Genesis Luxury (Etienne Aigner, Paul Smith, Canali, Kenzo) and Genesis Colors (Bottega Veneta, Satya Paul, Deepike Gehani)

- *Gitanjali Lifestyle:* Valente, Roberto and Just Cavalli, Nina Ricci, Calgaro, Philip Sector, Strefan Hafner, Morellato, Facco, and Campo Marzio
- *Madura Garments:* Esprit
- *Murjani Group:* Gloria Vanderbilt, Tumi, and Build a Bear
- *Popley Group:* CK Watches, Breguet, Blancpain, Hamilton, and Glasshütte
- *Reliance Brands Ltd.:* Diesel, La Perla, and Paul & Shark
- *Raymonds:* Manzoni
- *TSG International Marketing Pvt. Ltd.:* Aeffe Group: Moschino, Alberta Ferretti, Jean Paul Gaultier, Stella McCartney, Lanvin, Alexander McQueen, Diane Von Furstenburg, Pollini, Marc Jacobs, and Marc by Marc
- *The Spa Group:* Lladro, Villeroy & Boch, Rosenthal, WMF, Christofle, and BoConcept
- *Wadia Group:* Furla

Some India distributors based in the Middle East are:

- *Apparel (Dubai-based):* Stuart Weitzman, Bally, Mango (five stores), Nine West, Kenneth Cole, The Athlete's Foot, La Senza, Alain Manoukian, and Tommy Hilfiger (Gulf region only)
- *Bin Hendi (Dubai-based):* Hugo Boss (currently negotiating with DLF and Madura Garments)
- *E.L. Rothschild (Dubai-based):* Burberry
- *Jashanmal (Kuwait-based):* Burberry

DISTRIBUTOR CASE STUDIES

DLF Universal

DLF was founded by K.P. Singh in the early 1960s, and is managed by family members Pia Singh, Rajiv Singh, and Timmy Sarna. In addition to real-estate development projects such as Emporio in

New Delhi, the company is in joint ventures with several luxury brands, including Salvatore Ferragamo.

The Armani Group waited for what it deemed to be the right moment on a variety of levels to make its entry into India, in mid-year 2008. Hopeful that the regulatory environment would be liberalized, it mulled over the optimal strategy for entry: franchising, partnership, or joint venture. Unlike in China, where it opted to move forward with a mix of direct control and a franchise retail network, in India, the company established a joint venture in which it is the majority shareholder, and opened both a Giorgio Armani and an Emporio Armani in New Delhi's Emporio in October 2008, followed by one of each in UB City. It is currently studying the opportunities for retail expansion of its various collections in cities such as Hyderabad, Chennai, Pune, and Ludhiana. The company's policy when entering a new market is to a launch a Giorgio Armani boutique first to set the overall tone for the brand. It has invested in a seasonal media plan, which will grow in line with its forecasted retail and wholesale expansion.

Salvatore Ferragamo opened its first own-branded Indian store in 2006 at the Grand Hyatt Plaza Hotel in Mumbai. The Florence-based company has a 51% holding in the joint venture with DLF, and plans to open up to ten new stores in India by 2013. It already has stores at UB City, Emporio Mall, and The Oberoi in Mumbai.

Dolce & Gabbana also signed an agreement with DLF to open its first boutique in the Emporio Mall.

The Murjani Group

Founded in Shanghai in 1930 by B.D. Murjani, the group moved to retailing in Hong Kong in 1952. Under the direction of B.D.'s son Mohan, the company became one of the more visible entities in the Mumbai luxury scene. Now the chairman, Mohan's perspective is simply stated: "Building brands is not only our strength, it is our passion." From his collaboration with Gloria Vanderbilt for the first designer jeans in the 1970s, to his close ties with Tommy Hilfiger in the 1980s, Mohan Murjani broadened the company's mission by creating a multibrand retail platform and having his son Vijay manage the initiative when the latter moved to India in 2001.

By April 2004, Murjani had opened multiple freestanding Tommy Hilfiger stores across several cities. From 2005 onwards, during the following stage of development, the group then secured relations with brands such as Jimmy Choo, Calvin Klein, French Connection (FCUK), Gucci, and Bottega Veneta. Aiming for the same level of customer experience for Indian consumers as the international clientele, the group built what they refer to as the first luxury mall, "The Galleria" in Mumbai, where several global luxury brands are housed.

In early 2008, Murjani raised US$20 million through a private equity firm, Matrix Partners, to further its ambitious plans to acquire brand franchisees and joint ventures.

However, effective 2009, the Murjani platform witnessed an unraveling of some relations, notably with Gucci, Bottega Veneta, and Jimmy Choo. The financial credibility of the company has come into question as the business model for these brands does not seem to result in a profitable outcome.

Reliance Brands Ltd. (RBL)

Headquartered in Mumbai, RBL has an ambitious objective to become the leader in premium lifestyle space in India. Darshan Mehta, as CEO managing director, is focusing on the premium and luxury segments (apparel, footwear, and accessories), and RBL operates with three distinct business models.

International brands   RBL will bring international brands into India through joint ventures or long-term distribution and licensing tie-ups. RBL will endeavor to take a meaningful or minority stake in like-minded brands based on the potential that these brands offer in the Indian lifestyle market.

In September 2008, RBL acquired the lingerie brand La Perla, formerly distributed in India by the Murjani Group.

In October 2008, RBL signed a joint venture with Diesel, the world-famous Italy-based lifestyle brand, in which Diesel holds 51%. The venture is aimed at combining the distribution strengths of RBL and Diesel's experience in moving ahead of fashion trends, and predominantly targets avant-garde Indian consumers looking for fashion and individualism. A launch is planned sometime in 2009 in Mumbai and Delhi, while the venture is keeping a keen eye on fast upcoming markets such as Bangalore, Hyderabad, and Chandigarh.

It recently completed its joint venture with Paul & Shark and should be opening a store before the end of 2009 in Delhi.

Own brands   RBL plans to introduce its own brands based on perceived gaps in the lifestyle market, with the intellectual property embedded into these brands owned by RBL. These brands could be developed from scratch by RBL, which may choose to use an Indian celebrity, whose name will give the brand a jump-start in the market. In return for allowing his or her name to be used in conjunction with the brand, the celebrity will be paid a royalty. Alternatively, it may engage an Indian designer, using the designer's label to launch RBL's own brand. In this case too, RBL will have a perpetual license on the designer's name. The sales channels for these brands would be monobrand retail stores (which will be run by RBL); large-format lifestyle stores; and multibrand outlets (both of which will be run by third parties).

Entrack International Trading

Formed by Dilip Doshi, the company was the first to introduce the modern version of a joint venture in India for a global luxury brand. In 1993, Montblanc made its entry into India with Entrack, and has set the standard for a successful development program across the country (see chapter 14).

Raymonds

Formed by Gautam Singhania, Raymonds is a name associated with premium products. The group extended its presence into the luxury space by introducing Manzoni as a ready-to-wear brand to cater for the bespoke suits market at the end of 2007.

Arvind Brands Ltd.

Arvind Brands, a wholly owned subsidiary of Arvind Mills Ltd., is a force to reckon with in the textile industry. The company is one of the top three producers of denim worldwide. Some of Arvind's shirt fabrics sell at a premium in international markets. Its knits and denim division serves some of the best brands in the world.

Arvind has facilities in Bangalore in the south, and caters to some of the best names in the ready-made garments industry through a group company which, in addition to its own brands (Flying Machine, Newport, Excalibur, and Ruf & Tuf), manages the Indian licenses for leading international brands such as Arrow, Lee, and Wrangler. Along with Murjani, it operates branded denim with Tommy Hilfiger.

With the Indian economy poised for rapid growth, Arvind has its sights set on becoming the largest apparel brand company in India. The Lalbhai family, which runs Arvind Mills, has recently undergone management change to face global branding challenges.

Its May 2007 joint venture with Diesel made a lot of sense. However, with the departure of Darshan Mehta and his senior team to Reliance, the luxury denim and fashion brand from Italy hit some rough patches. Time will tell whether the joint venture will last, or if Diesel will look elsewhere for opportunities to develop its market share in India.

TSG International Marketing Pvt. Ltd.

Formed in 1966, The Sachdev Group (TSG) is a family business with a vision to provide world-class products and services. Initially, manufacturing and exporting women's and children's garments, accessories and home textiles, it later moved into the automotive industry, with authorized dealerships with Ford, followed by Hyundai, Toyota, and Volvo. The group dovetailed its activities with insurance in 2002. In 2005, TSG International Marketing Pvt. Ltd. was created, and became the exclusive franchise partner of Moschino, Jean Paul Gaultier, and Alberta Ferretti for India. In 2008, the partnerships broadened to include Lanvin, Stella McCartney, Alexander McQueen, Marc Jacobs, Marc by Marc Jacobs, and Diane Von Furstenburg. Headed by Ms. Charu Sachdev, TSG International was conceptualized and formed to introduce and manage brands in India.

Wadia Group

The Wadia Group's foray into luxury began with its vision to establish Neville House at Ballard estate as the next destination for luxury brands after the Taj Mahal Palace Mumbai corridor. It set up talks with Furla, an Italian luxury brand for accessories such as bags, jewelry, belts, watches, and scarves; however, at the time of writing, this franchise arrangement has yet to bear fruit.

The Wadia Group claims that it will pursue its luxury path through Retail Initiative Business, a wholly owned subsidiary of Bombay Dyeing, which is managed by Ness Wadia, founder Nusli Wadia's younger son. Ness Wadia is overseeing the textile company's diversification into real-estate development and retailing. Bombay Dyeing is known for its franchise-driven model to promote its flagship textiles brand in India. Nusli Wadia is reported as saying that the company is "exploring opportunities with other luxury brands as well. To cater to a wider audience, we will also tie up with premium as well as mass brands."

However, these ambitious plans are still awaiting approval from various governmental bodies. Nevertheless, we believe that an opening date for Neville House has been set for September 2009.

The Spa Group

The Spa Group was founded by Amar Agrawal in Chennai in 1998 as a special-purpose vehicle to launch Swarovski in India through a distributorship agreement. In 2001, Swarovski opened its own subsidiary in India and took direct control of operations. Subsequently, The Spa Group diversified into two fields of business: cubic zirconias and gemstones, and luxury retail and luxury brand management. In the first, they launched "Sprankel" to compete with Swarovski's synthetic stones brand, Signity.

In the luxury retail category, since 2001, it has concentrated on the home segment, with brands such as Lladro, Villeroy & Boch, Christofle, and BoConcept. Its growth strategy is driven by the expansion of the number of boutiques and its brand portfolio. In 2008, the group operates about 14 boutiques, and has another 17 boutiques under construction and for completion by early 2009.

Brandhouse Retail Ltd. (BHRL)[3]

Brandhouse was set up as the retail arm of India's foremost textile and apparel major, SKNL. Subsequently, after a period of sizeable growth, Brandhouse also became the exclusive India franchisee for international luxury brands such as Dunhill and Escada. Thereafter, it was demerged into a separate company, and was listed on the Bombay Stock Exchange in March 2009.

Brandhouse has been involved in the setting up and managing of exclusive brand outlets (monobrand stores) for various brands across India with a special focus on fashion and lifestyle. Brandhouse plans to dot the country's retail landscape with luxury, super-premium, premium, and midprice brands.

With a successful network of more than 600 monobrand stores, Brandhouse has set its sights on a new retail conquest to expand its total network of stores to more than 1,200 by March 2010.

The company provides a sustainable competitive advantage by translating core values combining products, image, and reputation into a coherent retail brand strategy. Domestic brands such as Reid & Taylor, Belmonte, and Carmichael House, and international brands such as Dunhill, Escada, and Stephens Brothers form an integral part of Brandhouse. The company forged a joint venture with Oviesse, the Italian apparel brand, in early 2009. Stores are to open in Delhi, Bangalore, and Mumbai by year end.

"Retailing luxury brands is for people with long term plans," believes Brandhouse. "India's luxury retail market will touch approximately Rs15,000 crore in the next five years and now is the time to enter it, for there is a boom waiting to happen."

Escada has been in India since 2007, and offers a range of women's apparel, accessories, eyewear, and fragrance. It operates in Mumbai at Turner Road, Bandra, as well as at the Shangri-La Hotel in Delhi.

Dunhill was also introduced into Delhi at the Shangri-La Hotel in May 2007, followed by the launch of two Alfred Dunhill flagship stores in the country at UB City and Emporio Mall during 2008. The brand offers an extensive range in formal and casual menswear to handcrafted leather goods, ties, watches, pens, lighters, shoes, and fragrances.

Gitanjali Group

The Rs4,000 crore Gitanjali Group has ambitious plans but is yet to gain acceptance, despite chairman Mehul Choksi's reported investment of US$15 million to US$20 million, adding fine jewelry from the Mariella Burani Fashion Group (MBFG), through which allied brands such as Rosato, Calgaro, and Valente are available. As licensee for the DIT Group, Gitanjali has made brands such as Stefan Hafner and Io Si available to Indian consumers. Other brands being distributed are Nina Ricci and St. Honore watches and Greggio silverware.

At the end of 2007, Gitanjali signed a joint venture with Morellato and subsequently created in May 2008 Morellato India to import and distribute the following watch brands: Morellato, Sector, Roberto Cavalli, Just Cavalli, Miss Sixty, Philip Watch, and Pirelli. All the watch brands of Gitanjali's portfolio are distributed in existing high-end jewelry and watch stores in India, and naturally in the newly launched group watch store concept called Bezel, "the temple of time." Today, there are already five Bezel stores across India, and Gitanjali should develop the concept through the franchise route. The chairman's aggressive push to gain entry into luxury circles has yet to be matched by the reach and opening of stores.

Bird Group

The Bird Group, one of India's diversified groups in the aviation, travel, and IT sector, in conjunction with European luxury yacht manufacturer Cantiere Nautico Cranchi, has formed a company called Bird Marine to represent Cranchi as well as other brands. The company also has plans to develop a marina on India's west coast.

Popley Group

CK Watches   Rajiv Popley, director of the Popley Group, brought Calvin Klein designer watches (for both men and women) into the Indian market. The collection, produced through a licensing agreement with the Swatch Group AG, the world's largest producer of finished watches, is available at Diatime (a Popley retail format in Mumbai, Bangalore, Kolkata, and New Delhi).

Breguet   Breguet, one of the world's oldest surviving watchmaking establishments, was established in Switzerland in 1775, and is currently part of the Swatch Group. Breguet watches, which are distinctive for their coin-edge cases, fine dials, and blue pomme hands (often referred to as "Breguet hands"), are available at Popley La Classique in Mumbai.

Blancpain   Blancpain was launched in Mumbai by the Popley Group in February 2007, and is available at Popley La Classique. One of the world's oldest and most distinguished Swiss watchmakers, Blancpain's crafts people are steeped in the tradition and history of Swiss watchmaking. They have also advanced it, bringing watch design to the digital age with computer modeling and testing ultra-slim watch designs with components no more than 0.5 mm.

Hamilton   Available at Diatime (a Popley retail format present in Shoppers Stop, Globus, Pantaloon and the like), Hamilton has been sold in India since February 2007. It is best known for the crown logo with the stylized "H" raised on the end of the crown.

Glashütte   Brought in by Popley Group, Glashütte has been available at Popley La Classique since February 2007. Glashütte is one of the few watchmakers worldwide whose movements are crafted exclusively in the manufactory. This results in functional movements with the classical design features of Glashütte watchmaking, which embody "German virtues" such as quality, precision, and reliability at their best.

Madura Garments

This division of Aditya Birla Nuvo is one of India's well-known apparel and retail companies. The group enjoys market leadership in home-grown lifestyle brands such as Louis Philippe, Van Heusen,

Allen Solly, and Peter England. The company entered into a distribution agreement with international brand Esprit. To bolster its presence in the retail apparel sector, the company started retailing its lifestyle brand and affordable popular brands through two subsidiaries: Madura Garments Life Style Retail Co. Ltd. and Peter England Fashions and Retail Ltd.

Genesis Colors

Genesis Colors, the owner of the Satya Paul brand, forged a luxury retail joint venture with Sports Station International (SSIPL). The joint venture—Genesis Luxury—established a franchise arrangement across India dedicated to luxury brands such as Etienne Aigner. Though details have yet to be finalized, it appears that Genesis will be a majority shareholder in the venture. Genesis Luxury established a franchisee arrangement for Kenzo, Canali, and Paul Smith, with a few stores opened at Emporio.

Kenzo is all set to bring its apparel, accessories, eyewear, and fragrance collections to India. At the writing of this book, a partnership has not yet been formalized. Genesis Colors (which also manages Satya Paul, Deepike Gehani, and so on) has been in talks with it to bring the brand to Mumbai and Delhi.

In 2009, Genesis Luxury took over from Murjani the Jimmy Choo and Bottega Veneta business in Delhi.

Bin Hendi

Bin Hendi Enterprises, based in the United Arab Emirates, has been involved in international products and fashion brands for the past three decades, and currently operates 29 highly successful fashion, jewelry, accessories, and food retail outlets. Bin Hendi ventured into the Indian luxury market with the launch of Hugo Boss stores in Mumbai and Delhi.

Jashanmal

This Kuwaiti group opened its first Burberry store in March 2006 at the Taj Mahal Hotel in Mumbai. The Jashanmal retail division operates a chain of seven department stores and standalone international franchises.

E.L. Rothschild

Promoted by Lady Lynn Forrester de Rothschild, E.L. Rothschild divested its stake in Field Fresh to Bharti Enterprises. The recent foray into luxury brands in India is under wraps, with market speculation on a possible future relationship with Burberry.

SUMMARY

Early entrants in the Indian market had first-in advantage as they paved the way for others. The loosening of restrictions on the entry of foreign single brands in 2006 gave this market a new allure.

Currently, the first choice for any international luxury brand is to set up a partnership with an Indian company, in which the brand may hold up to a 51% share. This gives it more say in the Indian partner's activities. At the same time, the Indian partner benefits from the brand's expertise in marketing and merchandising. The distribution companies and joint venture arrangements mapped in this chapter are making a significant contribution towards opening up the next phase of luxury retail—multibrand retail, which will enable companies such as Saks Fifth Avenue and Sephora to operate.

However, the results of these franchisee-run operations, in a country where everyone from Bollywood to industrialists want to own cricket teams and luxury brands, remain to be seen. This phenomenon is actually healthy for the growth and development of the market, despite real-estate issues and lack of adequate local expertise to run international brands. Discerning brands will choose their franchisees or joint venture partners carefully rather than simply on the basis of their social connections. Retail and distribution issues remain a major challenge, and it would seem that in this current economic climate, more and more distributors are focusing on developing private labels.

NOTES

1. *The Asia Pacific Post* 2006, "Luxury Goods Hit Last Frontier", Tuesday, June 27.
2. Uché Okonkwo 2007, *Luxury Fashion Branding*, Palgrave Macmillan, p. 42.
3. Deepti Chaudhary 2008, "Brandhouse Retails to Launch Multi-brand Discount outlets", *LiveMint*, February 7, <www.livemint.com/2008/02/06232401/Brandhouse-Retails-to-launch-m.html>.

CHAPTER 8
Retail and Distribution Issues

RETAIL IN INDIA

Like the Britain of yesteryear, India is stuck with the label of a nation of shopkeepers. From the humble roadside *kirana* (neighborhood store) with its rice and lentils, to the more developed shopping mall concept, which provides the setting for Indian brands such as Raymonds, a rising consumerism and a rapidly globalizing economy have changed the face of Indian retailing. Indeed, *kiranas* have evolved into supermarkets, traditional fabric markets have become branded department stores, and department stores have become malls.

The retail revolution in India has just begun and still has a long way to go. Indian retailers are experimenting with modern retailing formats, and are under pressure to provide efficient services as consumers look to alternatives such as mail order and out-of-town shopping.

According to the annual Global Retail Development Index (GRDI),[1] some retailers are entering countries such as India, China, and Russia through smaller second- and third-tier cities where consumers are ready to embrace Western-style retail concepts and products thanks to the influence of television, movies, and the Internet. In 2007, Russia and India occupied the top two spots of the GRDI, as they had for the previous three years. China vaulted past Vietnam and Ukraine into third place, largely on the strength of continued growth in consumer spending, and retailers moving into smaller markets. In 2008, India and Russia are respectively in second and third place, having left the top spot for Vietnam as it draws in more and more interest from large regional retailers. India has witnessed growth in modern retail formats and in particular of organized retail of 25% in 2008.

As reported by Julia Hanna[2] in April 2004, in a panel discussion at Harvard in 1994, Kishore Biyani, founder and CEO of Pantaloon Retail (India) Ltd., the country's first ready-made trouser brand, commented that: "Ordinary people are buying what the rich can afford," and that a surprising number of consumers have accepted private-label brands in a country where small, individual stores selling no-name goods had been the rule for decades. But success does not arrive overnight. Among the factors cited by Biyani to be considered by anyone contemplating launching a retail operation in India are:

- Foreign investment is restricted.
- India's culture favors saving, not spending.
- Real-estate costs are high.
- The taxation and legislation system is complex and difficult to navigate.

The luxury brand retail scene is but a drop in the Indian retail industry bucket. The retail industry is the second-largest employer (after agriculture), with sales of US$205 billion, of which US$6.2 billion was from organized retail. All in all, India remains an attractive retail market, as the GRDI results clearly indicate, and has the world's highest number of retail outlets in excess of 12 million stores.

The very small organized retail penetration rate—only 3% of the Indian retail market (but forecast to grow to 8% by 2010), leaving at least 80% of outlets run by small family businesses using household labor—has led to India being one of the least-saturated retail markets, with low barriers to entry and low competition. The rising tide of consumerism discussed earlier will continue to fuel the growth in both the commercial and retail sectors in the future. But the reality is, though, that only 4% of retailers currently have space larger than 50 m² (538 sq. ft.). Indeed, formal retailing currently comprises only 2.8% of the total industry.

India's foreign direct investment (FDI) rules make it difficult for foreign companies to own businesses in the country. Thus, although the 100% FDI rules for cash-and-carry trading have allowed the German chain Metro to enter, Marks & Spencer has taken the franchise route, while Mango has opted for a strategic alliance with the Piramyd retail group. As we saw earlier, joint ventures allow foreigners to enter with a degree of confidence that their local partner has some expertise in this new market. Mothercare, for example, has opted for this route with Shoppers Stop.

Although there are challenges to the future of the Indian retail industry, the growth potential is vast because India is among the least-saturated global markets. There are many strong potential regional and national players across different categories and most of these have undertaken thorough research and completed their respective learning curves on the Indian market.

Shopping-mall concepts are only in the first phase of the evolution of mall-based retail, and many developers are bleeding money as a result of poor planning and excessive real-estate costs. Increasingly, real-estate developers are capable of providing a qualitative environment for consumers, and the evolution will go from investing mainly in real estate versus creating a shopping mall concept.

There is a growing trend among brands, retailers, franchisees, investors, and malls to form partnerships, hoping that a gradual improvement in infrastructure and industry best practice will help ensure future success. Such arrangements are especially advantageous for setting up freestanding stores and luxury malls developments, as opposed to the traditional point of entry through five-star hotels.

RETAIL BOOM

The years since 2000 have seen a spurt in the number of designer shops opened across the country. Designers either float their own flagship stores or sell from a series of multi-designer stores in both the metros and smaller cities such as Hyderabad, Bangalore, Ludhiana, Chandigarh, and even the rather conventional-minded Chennai. Nagpur, Indore, Pune, and Nashik have also found buyers of fashion creations, which would have been unthinkable a decade ago.

Bringing fashion to the middle class is one step that will have an impact on luxury branding, as the experience of Pantaloon illustrates. The brainchild of Kishore Biyani, Pantaloon started off selling pants and shirts in its stores, and has since grown into a fashion store. Hoping to catch the imagination and the wallet of the young, Pantaloon signed on Bipasha Basu and Zayed Khan, two of the icons of India's hip generation, as brand ambassadors, and follows the modus operandi of international stores by offering collections that are in tune with the trend of the moment. In-house creations and the work of other Indian designers hang side by side with the work of designers from Dubai. The collections change every week— a first in Indian retail selling. Spanning the spectrum of needs, the clothes range from sportswear to partywear to nightwear, in both ethnic and Western styles. If the idea works and Pantaloon lures the cautious spender who prefers the big buck savings of Big Bazaar into the fashion segment, a new frontier will be opened in fashion selling.

RETAIL AND DISTRIBUTION OF FASHION AND LUXURY BRANDS

The decisions of some high-profile brands entering India are being driven as much by the ambitions and expectations of local joint venture or license partners as they are by the brand owners themselves.

However, problems arise from so few potential partners having any real experience of the luxury retail sector. The data they produce in support of their proposals are invariably compelling and supported by volumes of independent analysis; yet, in many instances, the prospective licensee or partner overstates the obvious and understates the more complex and less definable aspects of a proposed business strategy.

The challenges of a restrictive regulatory environment, the cost and availability of appropriate infrastructure, the lack of brand awareness, and the very limited media outlets for marketing combine to make establishing a successful luxury brand business model considerably more challenging than it might first seem. Added to this, the price consciousness of an emerging consumer class brings into question the widely held assumption that India is about to embark on a branded luxury goods spending spree. Before analyzing some of the specific issues relating to the retail and distribution challenges for luxury, some of the broader aspects of the industry context need to be put into perspective.

The Indian government recognizes the speed of change, the size of opportunity, and the lack of strong domestic players in the retail industry. Through a combination of effective corporate lobbying and protectionist populism, it has put in place legislation aimed at giving existing Indian businesses time to establish a competitive platform, before the market is opened to the global powerhouses of retail such as Wal-Mart and Carrefour.

The significant aspect of the legislation restricted international multibrand retailers to operating through franchisees and licenses. Wal-Mart positioned itself for future liberalization through a "wholesale" and "logistics" joint venture with Bharti (India's leading mobile-phone operator), which paved the way for establishing what may be the only meaningful near-term competitor to India's Reliance Industries.

As single-brand retailers can own up to 51% of their businesses in India, this limited the preferred route of many international luxury brands and forced them into either a joint venture with a passive or active partner or, more commonly, a licensing or distribution agreement.

The second important aspect of the legislative environment in India is duty. Import duties range from 35% on apparel, to 45% on accessories such as handbags and sunglasses, and 60% on watches, shoes, and perfume. Value-added tax at 36% and octroi (an inter-state duty—8% in the case of Maharashtra) further increase the store price. Bearing in mind the inevitability that India will continue to be governed by ideologically broad-based coalitions, the likelihood of there being sufficient political will to reduce import duties on luxury goods seems remote in the short term.

As important as the legislative environment are the less tangible but hugely important operating environment issues that currently exist. The first of these is the availability of the necessary infra-structure to support a commercially viable development strategy for a luxury brand. Apart from isolated examples of investment, such as Emporio in Delhi and UB City in Bangalore, there is no retail infrastructure for luxury in India that can be compared to developments in other fast-emerging markets in Asia, the Middle East, or Russia, let alone Europe and the U.S. Ravi Thakran, LVMH's group director, Southeast Asia, described the position succinctly during an interview:

> There is a great euphoria about Indian retail today. But I think we need to look beyond the euphoria at what is lacking. Retail should not, like tour-ism, become a great opportunity unexploited. Indian fashion consumption is fantastic today, and so is the consumption for luxury, as the attitudes of people change from a saving nature to spending nature, from basics to lifestyle. They are spending more on luxury items, design and quality have acquired great significance, and women are really coming out of the closet.
>
> With so many factors driving retail, and luxury retail in particular, why is it that the industry overall, the global industry, is still not investing in India? Many people say that it's a question of retail infrastructure. We

haven't had retail infrastructure, and that's why brands could not come in. I'll give you one example of how India has *had* one of the best retail infrastructures anywhere in Asia–Pacific for the past 50 years. There was no market in Asia that looked better or grander than Connaught Place in Delhi, with almost 1,800 beautiful boutiques in one place. Great boulevards, great places all around—we have had this most beautiful retail space in Asia for the past 50 years. And what have we done with it? Today, if you go around Connaught Place, it just sucks! It's not just about creating retail infrastructure; a Connaught Place is very difficult to create and very easy to spoil.

With the exception of the major luxury groups such as LVMH and Richemont, which have the critical mass to drive a largely independent positional strategy, international luxury brands have traditionally opted to locate themselves in India's premier hotels in the absence of any viable alternative.

The problem with this has proven to be twofold. First, there is a very finite number of luxury hotels that can support the luxury positioning required by international brands. In addition, the location and clientele of these hotels do little to increase sales projections. For example, Brioni opened in the essentially business-oriented Oberoi Hotel in South Mumbai, a very long drive from the affluent, conspicuous-consumption suburbs of Bandra and Juhu. Brioni took over the space that had previously been occupied by Hugo Boss and Tiffany, which had occupied the same space for less than two years. However, an overseas visitor on a business trip to India is unlikely to pay a substantial premium for a Brioni suit, which he could probably buy cheaper in New York or Milan.

Second, the cost of retail space in Indian luxury hotels is prohibitive, both in absolute terms and as percentage of sales.

This cost sensitivity is overlooked by many strategic forecasters of growth in disposable income and luxury brand purchases. While there will be a growing number of people willing to pay a 100% premium for an imported luxury car, for many other retail categories, the alternative of purchasing in New York, Dubai, Singapore, or

London is compelling. Not only does online price discovery enable comparative analysis, the newly affluent (with the possible exception of the Punjabi community) have a "value" perception that is probably considerably stronger than that of the comparable target market in Russia or China. The cost benefit of buying the same product internationally, the status value of shopping on Bond Street or Fifth Avenue, and the greater product range available overseas do not mean that there won't be a dramatic growth in the consumption of luxury brands: there will be growth but it won't necessarily be in India.

By not being dependent on the execution capabilities and commitment of an active local partner or licensee, the international brands can position and control a long-term brand-building strategy, rather than be driven by the shorter-term economic requirements of a local partner. The jury is out on whether joint ventures will turn out to be the most viable scenario in India, and it is probable that as a consequence of the highly specialized nature of luxury retail, joint ventures, and license agreements will face substantial challenges. At the heart of those challenges will be the misalignment of economic expectation between the local partner and the luxury brand. Luxury brands may well view their entry into India as a long-term strategy to establish and build brand awareness. In China, it has taken more than five years for many brands to establish a profitable local business. Bearing in mind the infrastructure and regulatory constraints in India, and the challenges of marketing, it is reasonable to assume that this time frame will be even longer. It is unlikely that most local partners or licensees in India are taking a five-to-10-year view on generating a positive return on their investment.

For the owner of a luxury brand, the economic risk of early entry into India with respect to the profit and loss (P&L) is worth taking. For the license holder, the risks have proven to be greater. The costs involved in license acquisition, real estate, fitout, inventory, duties, and salaries are committed largely in advance. In addition to budgeted costs for the local partner or license holder being largely quantifiable, the budgeted sales are only forecasted by guesswork, because there is not sufficient precedent to do otherwise. So projections tend to be overly optimistic. Misjudging sales may be less problematic for the owner than for the license holder, for which the only area of control in P&L is the variable component of cost: marketing and brand development.

The consequence of a probable scenario where local partners and license holders underinvest in brand development (irrespective of covenants in license agreements) is that international luxury brands will compromise both their development in India and the high-profile positioning they already have in the eyes of an affluent and sophisticated Indian consumer. The most pertinent example of this is Ermenegildo Zegna, which has learned through experience.

The mistake many brands are making is to hedge their bets on the market by giving away absolute control of their brand positioning. Ermenegildo Zegna had the advantage of being able to adjust its positioning once it realized it was compromising what it was trying to establish. While the higher cost it will incur through developing with greater control will slow down the profitability of its local operation, it will benefit substantially from the commitment it is making. This will be explored in greater detail in chapter 14.

The lesson for others is either to commit fully and build for the long term, or to spend a fraction of the money on advertising campaigns that build awareness among a sophisticated and increasingly affluent cosmopolitan Indian population without actually entering the market at all.

FRANCHISE MODEL

Franchising is undergoing close scrutiny in India. Many luxury brands were lured into fast-tracking their entry into India by opting for a franchised operation, ostensibly offering minimum risk and maximum "guaranteed brand equity." Among those that bought into the concept are Dolce & Gabbana, Fendi, Burberry, Ermenegildo Zegna, Escada, Valentino, Salvatore Ferragamo, Hugo Boss, and Chanel, and the list is growing.

Whereas in other countries franchising has been a viable and successful business-development option, there is one significant barrier specific to India that may spell trouble of this model for luxury retail: import tariffs. Franchising cannot flourish unless it is implemented in low-tariff markets. Following is a typical scenario on how such deals are structured and why they are problematic.

Stage 1

1. An Indian investor approaches a luxury brand with supporting financials and enough consumer knowledge to impress the principals into considering a relationship.
2. The brand proposes to open only in premium locations, huge capital expenditure (capex) package for shop-fit and millwork from approved suppliers (in Europe or Asia), a minimum storage area of 350 m² (3,767 sq. ft.), in the range of $1,800 per square meter ($167 per square foot), with fit-out costs of $2,500 per m² ($232 per square foot).
3. In his or her eagerness to procure the luxury brand, the Indian investor agrees to all the terms, focusing primarily on the prestige value of representing the brand. With little or no retail knowledge, the investor believes in the adage "If you build it, they will come."
4. The brand proposes a minimum open-to-buy per season, to which the investor readily agrees.
5. The store location is agreed (more than likely a lease in a premium hotel at astronomical fixed and recurring costs). The boutique is built and with great fanfare and much social ado, opens with insufficiently trained sales staff.

6. Once the initial week of friends, family, and high-profile shopping has subsided, the grim realities surface in the shape of the P&L, inventory management, and gross margins.

7. With high tariffs and the franchisee markup, this model is inherently flawed in that the cost of goods shoots up to levels that price the merchandise out of the market. Let's say the product costs 90 units FOB, to which are added CIF (cost insurance freight) costs of 10, to give a landed cost of 100 units. To this, add duties at 35%, multiply it by two for the franchisee markup, and you have a product selling for 270 units. Now repeat this exercise, eliminating the franchisee in a directly operated store, only omitting the last step and now multiplying the landed costs by 1.5 instead of two. Now you have a product selling for 202 units. You cannot cater to a demographic that predominantly shops overseas and is not ignorant of the pricing differences.

Stage 2

8. The Indian investor gets a full-price sell-through at an optimistic 35%. The brand is ready to ship the next season, while 65% of the previous season is still on the floor. To ship, the Indian promoter must open an on-sight letter of credit. So he or she does.

9. The co-op advertising arrangement has the franchisee reluctantly paying his contribution without fully grasping what impact the local marketing is having on his sales, nor how the synergies from the luxury brand headquarters are helping his business.

10. The second season of goods arrives very early in the season (December for Spring/Summer and July for Autumn/Winter), a merchandising phenomenon that does not work in India: who, after all, is buying winter clothes in 40°C (104°F) or summer clothes at 5°C (41°F) in New Delhi?

11. The old-season product goes to the stock room, as per the brand's best-practice directive. The same cycle is repeated.

12. By season three, the Indian partner's stock room is bursting at the seams. With no factory outlets (yet!) for leftover stock, an Indian promoter decides to put it all out on the floor, and sell as much as possible. This is the beginning of the end for the image of the luxury brand—major discounted goods—which may then result in bitterness and an eventual legal battle.

RETAIL SPACE

A major impediment to the luxury brands taking the country by storm is there being no real space where they can create the right ambience for their outlets. Cartier, for example, set up shop at the Oberoi in Mumbai, only to pull out because it wanted a more definite presence and its own branding away from the bigger branding of the hotel it nestled in. Though the brand has found a place in the new high-end luxury mall in Delhi, the success of the Mumbai shop is still in doubt because there seems to be no suitable space for it. Even if the brand was to pay the rentals that the city demands for prime locations, the ideal location seems unavailable.

Up until November 2008, when terrorists stormed Mumbai's Taj and Oberoi Hotels, the five-star hotels seemed to be the safest bet for most high-end brands. From Chanel (which opened shop in the Imperial in Delhi, a luxurious, period hotel, which, however, does not quite get the traffic required) to Canali, Burberry, and Moschino, most fashion brands sit side by side with accessory brands in one of the hotels. Similarly, Omega and other brands from the Swatch Group make good neighbors for the shops at the Grand Hyatt in suburban Mumbai.

According to Kishore Biyani of Pantaloon, "Distribution and retailing is the future of the industry that can take you to the top, and not manufacturing. There is space for 50–100 new retail formats for the masses." He said he is open to synergies and can help companies that can complement Pantaloon. "We have an appetite for growth and I believe in strategic investments in the early stage of a company." Biyani urged the domestic fashion industry to think big: "Make the best use of the opportunities available in the market today—before global players come in and take it away from us."

A typical flagship store in Shanghai covers a greater area than nearly every luxury store space available and in use in India at present. New malls are coming up to counter the problem, but whether they make the grade by international standards remains to be seen. Catering still to the middle and upper-middle class, most malls are not sufficiently tempting to the high-end luxury brands; but the mall ownership and management are cautiously booking their spaces despite this. A sure indicator, that though the market might not be ready to provide the right backdrop as yet, the public is more than ready.

FASHION

In the 1990s, the fashion sector influenced investors and retailers to reinvent their retail space and introduce large format stores either for monobrand or multibrand purposes. Building stores with anything up to 70,000 sq. ft., the new stores attracted more customer traffic away from the smaller stores, resulting in a period of retail concentration. Stores opened throughout India and the precursors were the likes of Shopper's Stop (Mumbai), Kemp Fort (Bangalore), Ebony (New Delhi), and Pantaloon (present in several cities). Large corporate houses, such as Tatas or Landmark, followed the movement, along with the multinational corporations into the fashion retail business, changing the whole mapping of the marketplace. With more players in the market, the competition was tougher, and consumer loyalty became the principal stake for success.

Therefore, it was more and more important to concentrate on consumer relations management and loyalty programs.

Larger format stores were pushed further as department stores and large space requirements encouraged real estate developers to build international-style malls such as Crossroads (Mumbai) or Spencer Plaza (Chennai). This retail expansion has generated a fabulous opportunity for Indian entrepreneurs to partner with world-class contemporary brands with low investments. This new development has forced independent retailers to modernize their space, products and services, consequently redefining the Indian retail activity. They have had to find ways to increase their attraction to customers, and also to expand existing stores or create larger ones in new locations.

In the following, we outline some chosen key players in retailing.

KEY PLAYERS IN RETAILING[3]

Shopper's Stop

This is a growing shopping chain that has expanded from only 4,000 sq. ft. of retail space in the early 1990s to more than 740,000 sq. ft. today and now has nearly 20 stores. It is recognized by the market as having one of the most efficient loyalty membership programs called "First Citizens" that has a 3+ lakh member base, receiving the Images Retail Destination of the Year label in September 2007.

Westside

One of India's largest and fastest-growing retail chains, it has 22 outlets throughout India, mainly in Mumbai, New Delhi, Bangalore, and Kolkata, thus representing a gross leased area (GLA) of more than 3.25 lakh sq. ft. It allocates its staff to the product categories (clothing, accessories, jewelry, and cosmetics) according to the sales generated from them; clothing being the most important category in terms of sales. To ensure customer loyalty and boost sales, Westside has several promotional campaigns per year, which coincide with national holidays (Diwali, Christmas, New Year, and Summer Carnival). It has also developed in-store labels such as SRC, 2Fast4U, Gia Richmond, Urban Angels, and Street Blues. In 2006, Westside relaunched its men's fashion department and its new brand Ascot. It has since partnered with India designers such as Narendra Kumar, Vivek Karunakaran, and Vivek Kumar for a special classy, affordable womens' wear and menswear range. In 2007, Westside also launched its Kidwest program, under which the retail chain organizes special workshops and activities for children so they have an opportunity to shop, learn, and play while having fun.

Piramyd

Part of India Bulls Retail Services, Piramyd has majorly expanded in recent years. First opening stores in the north and west, and more recently in the south and east, there are approximately 30 stores today. Following the large store concept, it opened a 78,000 sq. ft. megastore in the capital in 2008. It is likely to have a portfolio of 30 department stores, 16 entertainment centers, and 125 large, medium, and small supermarkets very soon.

Globus

Part of the Rajan Raheja Group, this retail chain had 24 outlets in several cities (Chennai, Bangalore, Mumbai, Indore, New Delhi, Pune, Kanpur, and Hyderabad among others) by 2008. With an average GLA of 25,000 sq. ft. per store, some stores have staff strengths of more than 125 to cope with the customer flow. These outlets focus on fashion apparel for youth because the clothing category represents approximately 80% of total sales each year, whereas the cosmetics and perfumes and jewelry represent the other 20%, so store space is allocated proportionally to the profit generated by each category. The chain has developed its own in-store labels: Globus (all categories) and F21 (accessible high-end casualwear and clubwear) to attract more customers and increase sales profits. It also holds several promotional campaigns throughout the year, which have been known at times to generate an extra 45% in sales.

Lifestyle

This chain of specialty stores has turnover of more than Rs650 crore and more than 14 malls throughout India, the largest of which has a GLA of 55,000 sq. ft. at the InOrbit Mall. At least four promotional campaigns are held each year in each mall (Great Toonage Fest, Style Vroom, Shop for a Surprise, and Well-O-Fortune).

Ebony

Ebony has retail space, concept stores, and an online shopping portal offering men's, women's, and children's apparel and designerwear, cosmetics, jewelry, luggage, and music and books. It has a customer loyalty program representing a base of more than 40,000 customers. There are plans to add 20 mid-sized stores to the existing seven by 2010 in places such as Gurgaon, Mumbai, Chennai, Pune, Bangalore, Kolkata, Chandigarh, Ahmedabad, and Hyderabad.

Pantaloon

Pantaloon Retail Ltd. sells fashion through four main formats: Pantaloon (chain of fashion outlets), Big Bazaar (hypermarkets), Food Bazaar, and Central (chain of malls). It also distributes through 10 other formats: Depot, Shoe Factory, Brand Factory, Blue Sky, Fashion Station, aLL, Top 10, mBazaar, Star, and Sitara.

Big Bazaar promises a wider range of products than most hypermarkets and at lower market price. It couples this with a shopping experience under the catch line "Is Se Sasta Aur Acha Kahin Nahin!" ("You cannot find it as cheap or as good anywhere else"). Sales and operating income increased by nearly 60% between 2006 and 2007, with store growth of 10–12% for the same period.

Sohum Shoppe

Opening its doors in 2000 in northeast India, Sohum Shoppe was one of the first retailers to bring lifestyle brands to that part of India. Once again like others, its key sales are generated by the clothing category, its focus area. The number of staff allocated to each of its stores is once again proportional to sales generated by each product category.

Sohum Shoppe also has three shop-in-shops that have been slowly growing in recent years: Gili, Provogue, and Watches & More. In terms of sales, Watches & More is ahead of Provogue and Gili, respectively. However, in terms of floor space, Provogue has more.

Dhiraj Sons

From the Gujarat textile city of Surat, Dhiraj Sons Fashion World has several outlets with a maximum GLA of 40,000 sq. ft. The clothing category is more profitable than the others (footwear, jewelry, gifts, and toys). They traditionally organize promotional offers three times a year lasting between two and five weeks: a watch *mela*, Diwali and a family special.

Dhiraj Sons also has ten shop-in-shops: Ruff, Napoleon, Blackberrys, Sunny, BKK, Tiny Girl, zeal, CHN, Allen Solly, and Gini & Jony. Space allocations range between 150 and 300 sq. ft. and Ruff generates the highest sales.

Emporio

The architect Mohit Gujral designed the 320,000 sq. ft. luxury mall with Italian marble and brass details, which is spread over five floors. The opening of the mall was often delayed, postponed, and reprogramed, and it finally opened in late 2008 after several years of business management that has came under scrutiny. Promising to be "the" retail space of India, many fashion and luxury brands demonstrated their interest in this project because it is the only space to unite more than 130 brands, with 70 international brands alongside more than 30 top Indian designers. It also features fine dining areas, a spa, and a salon, and has a members' club that aim to make shopping at Emporio a whole retail experience for the customer. However, footfall is a problem and there is a segregation of India brands relegated to a separate floor, not exactly a promising sign for those local brands looking to be held in the same esteem as their foreign counterparts. Whereas this may have been imposed by the very foreign brands seeking entry into the luxury space, the message is one of "we/they" and not so subtle: luxury brands have "their" space, the Indian designers seem to have not been deigned as worthy.

Crossroads

Part of Piramal Holdings Ltd., Crossroads was the first shopping mall in Mumbai, and opened its doors in 1999. Highly prestigious and successful in its early days, most of its tenants have since abandoned their retail space, with the exception of McDonald's. There have, however, been talks in recent times of foreign brands acquiring this space, but this has yet to happen.

UB City Mall

The operational luxury mall UB City Mall opened in 2008, and is owned by Vijay Mallya. It houses many renowned luxury brands in jewelry, leather goods and luggage, apparel, and footwear (such as Louis Vuitton, Montblanc, Tiffany's, Dunhill, Salvatore Ferragamo, and Tod's). With a luxury positioning, image and exposure, the mall's luxury retail space is backed up by a seven-star hotel, luxury serviced apartments, offices and fine dining restaurants where the customer can effectively have a luxury experience through and through.

SUMMARY

Retail and distribution in India is evolving and expanding to cater for a new type of clientele and to make luxury brands, both international and local, more accessible to Indian customers. The scene is complex, and infrastructure barriers are constantly being redefined. Greater lease space seems to be the road to development of international luxury brand presence in India both through franchising and joint ventures. In addition, coupling retail space and hotels seems to be an interesting lead to developing customer service where prestige and quality are a major concern for all involved. It would seem that design and retail concepts will also be key differentiators for retail success.

NOTES

1. A study of retail investment attractiveness among 30 emerging markets conducted by management consulting firm A.T. Kearney (2007, *Emerging Opportunities for Global Retailers*; 2008, *The 2008 A.T.Kearney Global Retail Development Index*).
2. J. Hanna 2004, "Ground-Floor Opportunities for Retail in India", *Working Knowledge*, April 19.
3. *Research Fashion Retail Business India,* <www.imagefashion.com>.

CHAPTER 9
Human Resources Issues and Practices

CURRENT POSITION

Human resources management and development in India's growing luxury and fashion category is still in its nascent stages. The most critical areas requiring attention today are how to attract, retain, and motivate the talent required to develop the sector. Within this spectrum are key issues that relate to the recruitment of industry-specific talent, the transfer of luxury and fashion experience to future teams, training and executive education, coaching, and having competitive compensation and benefits that reflect the influx of non-Indian residents. Retaining and motivating employees and developing leadership skills will become key challenges given the expected increase in demand for, and the limited supply of, suitable talent.

As the international brands arrive on the scene and as more local companies become more competitive, the supply of experienced local leaders has become extremely restricted. The result is that most companies will soon be faced with the choice of developing their own, expatriating (or repatriating) specific individuals, or recruiting individuals with appropriate skills from other sectors such as services or fast-moving consumer goods.

One of the immediate realities of the market is that many Indian companies feel they are unprepared to respond to global competition in real time. Human resources professionals within a local company faced with expansion need to meet the needs of their own people while also competing with international brands seeking to poach their resources. The lines have been drawn in what will become an escalating war for talent.

One of the few favorable aspects of this situation is the impact it is having on the executive education programs, coaching activity, and executive search firms. This increasing market may be short-lived, however. No sooner are talented individuals being recruited with one company than they being headhunted by another, and there is a serious need for Indian firms to incorporate so-called talent processes into their DNA. Developing solutions to this leadership vacuum requires creative and systematic thinking as well as real expertise.

The consensus among human resources professionals is that all of this can be built, but will require time. With a few notable exceptions in the Indian diaspora, there are few individuals with the skill set required for luxury brand management.

India today is similar to the Western world of the 1960s, when engineers were predominant. Marketing really started in the 1970s with the intensification of competition, and branding approach and positioning. This was followed in the 1980s by the arrival of more sophisticated financial tools and new decision-making and business practices, with newcomers such as LVMH's Bernard Arnault. Many family businesses disappeared, acquired by financial tycoons with flair and vision. The 1990s was a period of valorization and profitability for the industry at large, leading to today's situation as mapped out earlier.

When Europe was confronted by the scarcity of talent that India faces today it took crucial steps to tackle the problem. These included:

- creating dedicated educational programs via schools and universities, such as in France (ESSEC, Sup de Luxe, and Sciences Po)
- reinforcing professional representation through the likes of the Comité Colbert in France

- organizing forums for open exchanges with business schools on the need for an industry talent pool to address industry-specific needs. For example, in February 1999, France's prestigious HEC (*Ecole des Hautes Etudes Commerciales*) hosted an event with LVMH, the Comité Colbert, and an executive search firm, as well as the *International Herald Tribune* and WWD annual conferences
- organizing support from trade bodies and governments to support and protect the sector
- poaching talent with the required marketing and merchandising competencies
- appointing suitably qualified and dynamic individuals to lead the management and design teams in branded companies
- encouraging mergers and acquisitions and the formation of specialized groups in luxury and fashion brands.

Similar developments occurred in the U.S. during this same period. These included:

- developing a sizeable high-end retailing segment
- introducing greater professionalism into the industry and upscaling department stores
- developing merchants as a specialized practice that would feed into future leaders of luxury brands
- introducing the systematic use of marketing, packaging, and media
- developing and giving greater recognition to the role of the designer.

From Europe and the U.S., these developments spread to Japan, China, and Russia and a key driver during these years of significant growth in all of these countries was a determination to succeed.

Then what of India? Who will be the future leaders of luxury and fashion? Where are those individuals with the vision, the means, and the willpower to see their ambitions become reality?

One possibility is the designers who have proven their capacity to grow their companies locally, and possess the potential to build their brands internationally. But do Indian designers really want to develop their businesses beyond a market as vast as India? Why consider the rest of the world when they can live (and live well) with a local clientele? This has been the reality for many Indian designers until the recent arrival of fierce competition in the form of the global luxury and fashion brands. They have realized that they are in a comparable position to that of their European counterparts during the 1970s and 1980s. Many have yet to find their "other half" to finance and manage their development à la Yves Saint Laurent and Pierre Bergé, or Tom Ford and Domenico Di Sole.

Whichever path they choose, however, they will need sound HR management to be able to attract, retain, and motivate the talent they will need to grow their businesses and people in an intelligent manner.

ATTRACTING TALENT

Hiring is a major challenge in India. The poaching of talent within the industry is not uncommon, and in such a burgeoning sector there is a potential bonanza awaiting executive-search firms. Firms such as Egon Zehnder, Korn Ferry, and Heidrick & Struggles have established themselves over the past decade, and have been joined more recently by Spencer Stuart and Russell Reynolds. It should be noted, though, that none of these specializes yet in luxury and fashion. While they have crossed over into this new territory, they are still recruiting talent from their more usual area of expertise, the consumer-goods sector, in the hopes that the talent can adapt and learn quickly, but this is not sufficient.

In addition to the international executive search firms, Indian players such as ABC Consultants combine recruitment with strategic consulting. As in other emerging economies, there is an increasing number of midmarket recruitment firms and an even bigger presence in the ads recruiting market.

Outside India, there are other specialist recruiters in the luxury and fashion sector, Sterling International being one of them. From offices in Europe and the U.S., they are able to recruit top-level talent from the sector who are willing to make the move. Not having an office in Delhi or Mumbai has not prevented the likes of Sterling from recruiting talent for and from the local market.

With both authors having backgrounds in the executive search industry, we are sensitive to ethical practices in recruitment. We have seen the major search firms with a generalist mindset turn, over the years, towards sector specialization, into what we call "practice" areas. We understand the importance of offering clients knowledge and experience specific to the needs of the luxury and fashion market. There is a premium to using experts from the industry: in our experience, clients are most satisfied when dealing with those most familiar with the industry and, particularly, within specific segments of the business. However, today in India's global perspective, the tendency is still to dilute specialization, but we believe that one best anticipates and understands sector-specific trends by having a specific focus.

"The battle for the best talent is extremely fierce," according to Deepak Gupta, managing director of India's Korn Ferry International. Compensation levels in India have risen dramatically in the past couple of years. Salaries of US$500,000 were the high two years ago, but US$1 million is increasingly less rare. Gupta feels that salaries of top professionals have been rising even faster than the annual increases of 16–17% in the general market.

In addition, for expatriates (or even repatriates) top jobs can include generous perks such as furnished luxury accommodation, chauffeur-driven transportation, and house servants. Most firms pay for children's education at international schools. Stock options and guaranteed bonuses are also *de rigueur*.

So acute is the recruitment challenge that many executive-search specialists report that supply is sufficient only to fill one in three vacant top-level slots. The average time taken to fill senior positions has doubled to more than 120 days. Fortunately, while working-age populations in the U.S. and China are shrinking, India's is growing. By 2020, a report done by the executive search firm Boyden[1] predicts that nearly half of all Indians will be between the ages of 15 and 59, and, as Kamal Nath writes: "India has time on its side. 40% of India—a full 440 million people—is under 18. This is the India demographic dividend: the century will be driven by the energy, risk-taking ability, open thinking, and innovation of youth."[2]

According to an interview with the executive recruiter Gauri Padmanabhan at Heidrick & Struggles India, in the 1980s and 1990s the market was focusing on lower-priced products. In the past five years, however, the growth in disposable incomes among professionals has fueled the expansion of luxury and fashion to the point where it is now becoming the fastest-growing sector. Yet there are still too few top professionals to set the tone and develop this new consumer base to the fullest extent.

Talent is undoubtedly available, however, in the following areas:

- *The multinationals:* The multinational companies in India are very professionalized, and are, in many respects, on a par with their colleagues in the West. However, the Indians themselves often do not believe this. It should be noted, too, that Indians are much less rigid than their Western counterparts in the distinction they make between work and nonwork. For example, they don't hesitate to work on a weekend if the job requires it or if it can help others to do their jobs. The same eagerness is harder to find in Western countries.
- *Family businesses:* These can be divided into three types: the "big ones" such as Tata or Godrej, which tend to behave more like the multinationals, even if the family concern remains alive, says

Visty Banaji, executive director and president group corporate affairs, Godrej Industries Ltd.; those like Wipro, where the original has stepped back to allow the organization to be run by professionals; and those like Reliance, with an owner-driven culture driven by first-generation entrepreneurs.

- *Women:* This population is in transition, and there are differences between sectors and functions. According to Visty Banaji women "are underused at a systemic level, and this is one of the problems India faces." Today, many women want to return to the workforce after having their children, but this attitude is differently perceived according to the specific social milieu. In addition, there is still the expectation that it is for a woman to give up her job if her husband relocates elsewhere when he changes jobs. Differences can be found between sectors: in the newer industries such as investment banking, telecommunications, IT, and so on, there are fewer stereotypes than in the more traditional sectors of textiles or manufacturing. There are differences, too, between the functional areas: there is a higher proportion of women in human resources than in sales or manufacturing.

Other potential sources that can be mined for the future talent requirements of the luxury and fashion sector are within the organizations themselves. For many years, there has been sustained underinvestment in leadership development—both in organizations and the education system. The focus has been almost exclusively on using the current asset base; that is, on producing the technical abilities required mostly by the BPO sector, rather than working to achieve sustainable competitive advantage in the knowledge arena.

As in Europe, there could well be an increasing mismatch between job requirements and levels of education. This is as much a matter of overqualification as it is of the opposite. Overqualification can be a recipe for frustration, as we have seen with so many MBAs working in BPOs.

Kamal Nath sees India having "a stock of 85 to 90 million graduates in the 2020s—20 million more than the entire population in France."[3] That may well be true, but today there are nowhere near enough to fill the demand. There has long been a tradition of the best and brightest of Indians from the top schools abroad being lured by the salaries and perks offered by the multinationals.

The challenge for India as a country then becomes how to evolve from only 10% of the workforce, mainly urban workers, being concerned by these disparities to obtain higher figures? How to reduce the huge disparities between rural and urban India? Organizations need talents throughout the ladder. In addition, they need to attract not only urban high-level individuals but also those coming from rural areas.

One road to explore in ensuring that there is a balanced supply of qualified individuals for the luxury and fashion industry is to set up partnerships with specific schools to identify talent in advance, making sure that those identified are properly trained, and offering selected students traineeships with jobs waiting when they complete their studies. Creating long-term relationships will help to attract and retain people with potential. The retail industry in India has shown what can be done in creating dedicated channels of business through links with universities and giving companies a competitive advantage in this real war for talent.

The luxury and fashion companies in India will need to develop an understanding of precisely what a brand is, both at the individual level and, perhaps more importantly, at the team level. There is an aesthetic in this sector that cannot be acquired outside and there will be a real need to educate a "fresh" team on all these issues, establishing specific behavior patterns, customizing the way they should work within the specialist organization.

Coaching will help to create such teams, as well as enabling individuals to better understand the brand's home culture (French, Italian, British, or whatever it is). Those who come to India to work will need to receive a thorough briefing on the specificities of the Indian market.

Clear leadership sets the tone, and, at present, there is a definite need to import the best practices from more mature markets.

One element that works in favor of the local labor market is that it is no longer a foregone conclusion that Indians will leap at the offer of a role abroad, as used to be the case. *The Hindu*[4] newspaper identified five out of 20 overseas offers by leading investment banks being rejected in favor of jobs in domestic private equity firms. Increasing numbers of Indians now working abroad are seriously thinking of coming back to participate in the country's development. This trend is being encouraged by the government's dual-passport approach, which enables Indians to maintain both full Indian citizenship and their "overseas" nationality. Examples of those who have worked or completed their studies abroad include Dhruv Singh of Yatra.com, one of Asia's leading travel websites, who spent six years with Arthur Andersen in Delhi before moving abroad and completing his MBA at INSEAD. Binita Cooper is another example, who worked with L'Oréal in Europe for many years before repatriating to India with the company to head L'Oréal's luxury division there, prior to joining De Beers to manage the Indian entity.

The process of persuading talented individuals to remain at home, rather than decamp to greener pastures at the earliest opportunity is a slow one, but one that offers hope to the luxury and fashion sector.

Ananth Iyer, director of the executive search firm Shilputsi Consultants, says that the overall attraction of a growing economy, a vibrant financial market, increased mergers and acquisitions activity, and the expansion of Indian operations by multinationals are significant reasons for the reverse flow of people.[5]

Executive search firms say that some companies in India have begun to look globally for leadership-level candidates who combine Western experience with knowledge of operating in India. Umesh Ramakrishnan, vice chairman of New York executive recruiter CT Partners, says that some companies are "throwing serious dollars at the right folks." The net is being cast wide, he says, to catch not just overseas executives of Indian origin, but also Americans and Europeans with an India connection who want to come to India "because they feel this is where all the action is."[6]

Many industries are expanding rapidly, new companies are starting up, and multinationals are establishing themselves in the country. Though India is billed as a talent powerhouse with the largest working-age population in the world, the top executives in the country are being wooed from all directions as annual economic growth has averaged more than 8% in the past three years. Some local executives are being hired by Western companies for assignments outside India, further depleting the local talent bank. According to Nanu Pradhan, president and managing director, Red Hat, leading provider of open source solutions to enterprises, "The global executive from India is moving into senior regional and global roles, leaving behind a void in the local market."

To fill this void, local companies are hiring executives from overseas. Gibson G. Vedamani, CEO of the Retailers Association of India (RAI), explained the situation to us this way:

> Some new businesses in India such as retail and home electronics have realized the need for hiring expatriate consultants or employing individuals at the senior levels. These expatriates are employed as CEOs or as functional heads so that they bring best practices into the organization. The mode of employment is usually on a contract basis in the capacity of a consultant or a short-term contract employee, usually for two or three years. Often these contracts extend for longer periods based on the performance of the individual and the value addition he or she can bring into the organization. Often there is a probationary period of six months.

Some companies have found that foreign executives can have a tough time adapting to the local business culture. That puts even more of a premium on the most "global" of local candidates.

"The whole country is on a dizzy growth trajectory, and talented people are the most crucial factor in this rush," said Kishore Biyani, chief executive of Future Group and MD at Pantaloon (part of the

Future Group), a retailing conglomerate, which has hired professionals from South Africa, the U.S., and Britain. "There is a dire mismatch in the demand and availability of top people." In something of a twist, he says, top Indian executives are often the most expensive to hire: "I have been able to draw foreigners to some of my top positions at half the salaries."

The Indian retailing sector is largely fragmented. It is also hampered by a lack of adequately developed real estate, a shortage of trained and specialized human capital, weak labor laws, and frail logistics and supply-chain systems. While most of these challenges are gradually being met, the talent issue remains serious across all levels. The gap between supply and demand is resulting in high levels of attrition, skewed salaries, and increased costs of doing business for the industry.

The retail industry can no longer afford the luxury of looking the other way. Opening up the FDI will bring in established global retailing chains. To compete effectively with them, Indian companies will need experienced leaders at senior levels and the right talent on the shopfloor. Attracting talent from international markets is an option that can be exercised at the senior level, but cannot be a solution for the longer term.

The more viable option is to hire talent from other industries: consumer products, telecommunications, and the like. "We have worked with some of our retail clients to attract talent from other industries by crafting a value proposition that appeals to high-quality executives employed by multinationals," says Sonny Iqbal from Egon Zehnder. "These executives," he adds, "have been attracted by the entrepreneurial challenge, the freedom to make quick and sometimes risky decisions, direct access to the board of directors, and wealth-creation opportunities. Many of them have succeeded in transferring their skills, and have brought managerial breadth, as well as processes and systems into an environment of intense growth and flux at our clients."

Gauri Padmanabhan from Heidrick & Struggles explains the current situation this way:

> One common stop-gap measure adopted has been to import knowledge and processes by seeding the "human value chain" from overseas or through strategic alliances and joint ventures. Expatriate leaderships need to be brought up to speed very quickly in terms of cultural, workplace and market sensitivities. With Indian retail still at a nascent stage, many standard processes typically lack the maturity and sophistication of developed markets and expatriate leadership needs support to navigate these areas. Shadowing these key executives with a strong local second line achieves this and also addresses succession planning and knowledge transfer. To combat high attrition rates, innovative strategic human resource schemes and strong training aimed at improving retention need to also be firmly in place.

RETAINING TALENT

However, this strategy will bring with it another set of challenges as the industry matures. Experience tells us that within three to four years, these executives will be looking closely at the career path their company has to offer them. The sooner the industry takes cognizance of this and puts an action plan in place to deal with these future challenges, the better.

As mentioned in previous chapters, one of the characteristics of a luxury brand is its internationalization. Now more than ever, leadership in the sector requires a truly global mindset. In a complex international market environment, effective leaders are able to think systematically, understand how business operates in other parts of the world, and use differences in national and cultural backgrounds.

One of the key issues in retaining talent is to understand the DNA required of the talent. In research done by the consulting company Gateway 2 India,[7] entrepreneurship is all important. In India, there is a natural and cultural inclination toward entrepreneurship, reflected in such networks as the Indus Entrepreneurs and the National Entrepreneurship Networks, which have helped harness talent globally. Indeed, to quote Dinesh Mirchandani, head of Boyden India, "India's entrepreneurship is particularly fascinating in that it does not take a single form. It has not solely been learned, or acquired, or brought in. It is like a DNA strand running through the population—thicker here, thinner there, more scientific here, but a constant in India's story." This observation is confirmed by Kamal Nath:

> A street-smart nation, poor in cash perhaps but never poor in ideas and never afraid to multitask... [with] a greater sense of self-belief and a confidence in home-grown enterprise... respecting competition and saluting pioneers... The apparent entrepreneurial instinct of Indians is in no way in conflict with the country's long spiritual tradition, which has been society's anchor for centuries. The two are complementary resources that have given the average Indian a sense of timelessness and infinite patience.[8]

This more entrepreneurial approach will require a less established system, and one allowing for longer reins. At the same time, and this may seem contradictory, Indians are inclined to follow orders, while Westerners are challenging at all levels, and want to be allowed to exercise initiative.

Other general points of comparison between Indian and European cultures that may be useful to keep in mind when attracting talents, or trying to retain them, are that:

- Indian society is family oriented with attendant social obligations to the extended family network.
- Religion is very much part of everyday life, whereas in Europe, religion is waning and more personal.
- Indians typically speak three or four languages, including English, the language of business and urban India. While English is also widely used in Europe, there are different working languages in different countries.
- Indians have an ability to think laterally, at different levels at the same time, and a limited infrastructure has encouraged levels of

resourcefulness in Indians. A cultural emphasis on respect and hierarchy, together with a relaxed philosophical approach to life, render them good corporate employees. Compare this with the Western tendency to overreact and complain.

- In India, recognition, status, and titles are important. (Giving more formal and prestigious titles may well help in facilitating retention of staff.)

A typical organizational structure in India may be described as follows: employees are called officers and then executives, while a fresh, just-out-of-school MBA will enter as assistant manager, and based on the Indian Institute of Management (IIM) he or she has attended will get an offer. There are presently three IIMs: Kolkata, which was the first created, considered number three today; Bangalore, which was the third created and considered number two today; and Ahmedabad, seen as being the best today. More IIMs are under creation, as we will see in chapter 10.

Managing director is the most important title. He or she may be called CEO, but this would be more an Anglo-Saxon approach. In a listed company, the title of "director" can only be given to someone who sits on the board. One may then have an MD heading a company, with CEOs reporting to him or her as head of businesses. One can also find a president with a CEO reporting to him or her. If the company is not listed, one can give a director title; vice president and director titles are mostly alike. General managers could report to a CEO or even a senior vice president.

COMPENSATION

The difficulties of attracting the best talents create a spiral. When a sector grows at 15% a year, the compensation gap is getting bridged with the rest of the developed world; however, it will probably take 10–12 years to see this arbitrage difference vanish definitively.

To attract the right talent to compete internationally, it is necessary for Indian companies to bridge the gap between Indian salaries and those offered by their Western counterparts, even if this is costly for the organization. This is particularly true for professional services firms and investment banks, and at CEO and other senior-level positions. Even in the IT and BPO sectors, where competition is fierce, the necessary adjustments have to be made.

It is easier for a new company to align itself with international practices than for one that has operated for many years, when it is quite a challenge to revisit common practices.

One key point to underline is that it is scale, rather than market value, that defines the level of compensation. A marketing director can be recruited with a pay level of US$60,000–80,000 in a small startup operation in India, even if it is one of the best names in the luxury world. Where the scale is bigger, the salary can be between US$110,000–150,000. One of the common mistakes made by companies in India is to seek out young talent and offer them "bargain pay." The companies may feel that they are getting value for money, not realizing that this relative lack of expertise, maturity, and sophistication will create major opportunity costs and result in lower overall performance levels. Companies that have a leader mindset and vision will recruit talent and pay it its real worth based upon what it will bring to the company.

Expatriate salary components

Expatriate salaries are usually competitive with international standards. At the top levels, salaries are usually designed as a package known as the annual total employment cost or annual cost to company. This includes the components of monthly salary, annual payables, and performance-linked incentives. Monthly salaries would include remuneration, accommodation allowance, and local conveyance (cost of car divided over three years, fuel expenses, and driver's salary), while annual payouts would include medical insurance (including dental) and an annual-leave travel allowance (which includes the return airfare to the incumbent's former resident base for the whole family). Performance-linked incentive payments of up to 20% of the base salary are applicable in most organizations.

Though salaries and remuneration may vary according to an organization's size and the scale of its operations, the RAI's Gibson Vedamani says that the total package for an expatriate CEO in retail is in the range of US$400,000–500,000 per annum; for functional heads (visual merchandising, merchandising and buying, supply chain, store operations, and so on) this figure may vary from US$200,000 to US$400,000 (see figure 9.1).

If an expatriate comes with the necessary skills, relevant experience, and expertise, many Indian firms are willing to meet the applicant's needs. However, only a few organizations (mainly multinationals operating in India) pay sign-on bonuses, and these are generally restricted to very senior-level appointments.

If the rate of growth is not very high, there is a tendency to limit overseas recruitment to first- or second-generation Indians currently abroad.

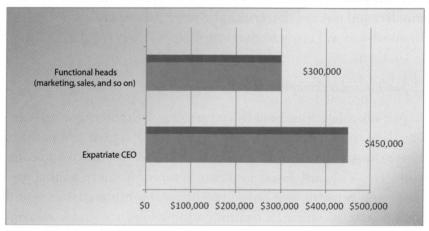

Figure 9.1: Indicative salaries

Employees of Indian companies usually work a 48-hour week, spread over five-and-a-half or six days. Leave entitlement is usually 30 days per annum, which is fewer paid vacation days than offered by most European companies. Being more precise, one can get 30 calendar days or 22 to 25 working days as leave allowance plus a few days for sick leave, when in other places that are "more relaxed," one can have 30 days privileged leave actually paid, seven to 10 casual leave, and 10–12 sick leave. Leave can be accumulated for up to 180 days (as opposed to 60 in Europe), and, if not taken, can be converted to cash.

India is context driven, whereas Westerners are content driven. According to one leading Indian writer, "The country [has] survived centuries of invading influences, absorbing the best of alien features into its own culture…India's capacity to assimilate, synthesize and modernize is infinite—that, in fact, is the nation's genius."[9]

To retain Indian talents, one has to understand the idea of working with others, rather than for others, that will result in retention within the company.

This has led some organizations to be very active in people issues. Some are even considered to be role models for the country. India's family traditions and social responsibilities have always been active, but probably, in the long term, the Indian corporation has to create an employer brand if it has to attract serious talent from foreign markets at reasonable benchmarked compensation. One road open to the Western world and in line with its psyche would be a developed and organized approach of mentoring. A dedicated mentoring approach, a will to transmit from the grey-haired to the young talented generation, could indeed be an interesting approach for the luxury and fashion market: creating a bridge between the Old Europe experience and understanding of the luxury and fashion market, would create a win–win approach between India, an emerging country, and our old ones; the dividend being a better understanding from both sides of the business and thus potentially creating value in less than a generation.

Today, executives from the developed world seriously consider working in Asia, and India, for reasons already described (language, culture, and so on), is therefore becoming a preferred destination. It is now observed that: "As a result, entire chunks of the Western economic system may be eroding at a faster pace than few believed possible only a few years or even months ago. In brief, this is the unexpected, flipside of 'globalization.' … Giants like India and China not only 'pull' Western jobs from much stronger foundations than before, but are building up systemic dependencies on continuing to do so."[10]

MOTIVATING TALENT

"It's the mindset above all which has changed in India", says Anand Mahindra (vice chairman and managing director, Mahindra & Mahindra).[11]

Having a respect for their culture and an appreciation of their inner spirituality, making an effort to understand their history—these can provide firm foundations for motivating staff within a company. This point is well illustrated by what is occurring within two of India's leading companies: Infosys and Tata.

Infosys may be a family business with a first-generation entrepreneur at the helm, but it is run as a global organization. It has been a front runner in creating employee partnerships in business through employee stock option plan (ESOP), and many organizations in other sectors have followed its strategies. Infosys instituted annual awards for excellence to motivate employees toward the achievement of excellence within their work teams. The awards are part of the company's efforts to achieve best practice in helping every individual employee excel in the workplace.

The company believes that the success of economies will depend on how adept they are at attracting, nurturing, and retaining talent.

In the knowledge economy, countries must focus on education to develop a skilled labor force. Infosys believes that world-class talent knows no geographical boundaries, and believes in tapping into the global pool of talent to empower the talented to realize their potential.

Infosys is a people-oriented organization, which introduced to the growing corporate sector in India the value of long-term employee retention by the effective use of ESOP. According to CEO Nandan Nilekani, "Infosys is symbolic of this moment of possibility for India. We have sixty-six thousand employees and the average age is twenty-seven. It's about building a global brand. It's about achieving on merit. It's a company about the future, not about the past."[12]

Another best-practice company is the Tata Group, which, since its foundation in 1904, has established itself as a pioneer and a thought leader in developing managerial talent at senior levels. TAS (formerly known as the Tata Administrative Service) was conceived in the 1950s by J.R.D. Tata, then chairman of the group. His dream was to select and groom some of the best young Indians, provide them with opportunities for professional growth, and use that pool of talent as a group resource—one that could be tapped by companies across the Tata organization. TAS, which is essentially a training program, is perhaps the only employment brand in Indian business that consciously recruits for lifelong mobility, across companies, industries, and functions, to impart that macro view of business, which is critical in preparing young professionals for general management.

Models designed to attract and retain talent, which may have proven successful elsewhere, can be applied to the Indian scenario only if they take account of India's unique circumstances. As the psychoanalyst and writer Catherine Clement, who lived in India for many years, observed: "One cannot understand what people see in India without reading, without observation, without deduction."[13] When all these things have been done to gain a thorough understanding of India's specific needs, the task of attracting and retaining suitable talent in the luxury and fashion industry will be that much easier.

NOTES

1. Boyden Report 2007, *The Sun Rises on the Indian Executive*, September.
2. Kamal Nath 2007, *India's Century: The Age of Entrepreneurship in the World's Biggest Democracy*, McGraw-Hill.
3. ibid., p. 185.
4. *The Hindu Business Line* 2007, "Thinking Beyond Salaries & Overseas Allure", March 13.
5. Rajeshwari Sharma 2008, "Rising Job Refusals Put Headhunters in a Bind", *LiveMint*, February 11, <www.livemint.com/Articles/PrintArticle.aspx?artid=76357DAA-D8CF-11DC-8FD6-000B5DABF636>.
6. Saritha Rai 2006, "Search for Top Talent Gets Fierce in India", *The International Herald Tribune*, December 5.
7. Jacques-Etienne de T'Serclaes & Sanjeev Rao 2006, *Gateway 2 India Market Report*, November.
8. Nath, op. cit., pp. 7, 8, 24.
9. Ashutosh Sheshabalaya 2004, *Rising Elephant: The Growing Clash with India Over White Collar Jobs and Its Challenge to America and the World*, Common Courage Press, Introduction.
10. ibid.
11. Quoted in Mira Kamdar 2007, *Planet India*, Scribner, p. 92.
12. ibid., p.9.
13. Catherine Clement & Tobie Nathan 2002, *Le Divan et le Grigri*, Odile Jacob, p. 42.

CHAPTER 10
Fashion Education in India

If fashion is seen in the broader sense of the term, and includes everything to do with personal style and the Indian way of life, then it is possible to see glimpses of how fashion was a part of education over the years. The adjacent towns of Sriniketan and Santiniketan in West Bengal are closely associated with the Nobel Prize-winning poet Rabindranath Tagore and the Vishva-Bharati University. Here art, music, and dance were taught, and Sriniketan, which was at heart a rural reconstruction center, revived craft-based traditions such as embroidery, weaving, metalware, leather goods, and terracotta pottery.

From the 1920s, Santiniketan and Sriniketan brought teachers from all over the world to train students in a variety of disciplines. Crafts and clothes were an intrinsic part of the syllabus. Tie-and-die processes such as *batik* and *ikat* and the weaving of different kinds of cotton and patterns into saris and fabric lengths were some of the path-breaking endeavors taught there. Some of these teachings filtered into the mainstream of daily wear; *batik*, for example, enjoyed resurgence in the 1950s and 1960s, with housewives creating saris, *kurta*[1] pieces, and wall hangings with batik designs. *Ikat*, from Thailand, and *shiburo*, from Japan, remain part of the fashion vocabulary of designers even today, and have shown up in mainstream daily wear through the years. Other teachers in self-contained institutions also branched out into creating what would later become fashion statements.

In Tamil Nadu in the south, Kalakshetra, an institution started by the formidable Rukhmini Arundale in 1936, gave the Bharat Natyam dance form respectability, and ingrained the intricacies of its costumes and jewelry into the social fabric of the time. Her insistence on understanding textiles and her mission to revive some of the temple sari traditions that the advent of synthetic fabrics had relegated into the background resulted in a line of resplendent saris woven with temple borders in contrasting colors. These Adayar border saris (named after the institution's location) became the fashion statement of the ladies who lunch and those who professed to be art conscious. Today, they have even been absorbed into the style statements of mass brands such as Nallis of Madras, which sells a thousand saris a day.

THE NATIONAL INSTITUTE OF FASHION TECHNOLOGY

One of the biggest impacts on the contemporary Indian fashion scene was the arrival of the National Institute of Fashion Technology (NIFT) in 1986 under the umbrella of the Ministry of Textiles. Though it was meant to educate and produce professionals for the fashion world, it has been more successful in creating fashion designers. Today, it has centers in New Delhi, Bangalore, Chennai, Gandhinagar, Hyderabad, Kolkata, Mumbai, and Raebareli.

In 2006, NIFT was accorded degree-awarding status, putting it on a par with the Indian Institutes of Technology and Indian Institutes of Management. The list of NIFT alumni who have gone on to establish themselves in the fashion scene is long and impressive, boasting among its numbers the likes of Rajesh Pratap, Ashish Pandey, Narendra Kumar Ahmed, Puja Nayyar, Manish Arora, J.J. Valaya, Ranna Gill, Sabyaschi Mukherjee, Shantanu Goenka, and Ramesh Nair. Ritu Kumar, a founding member of the Fashion Design Council of India, was nominated to NIFT's board of governors in 2000, and helped organize the first ever India Fashion Week in Delhi that same year.

A look at the evolution of NIFT graduates shows very clearly the definite shift in the focus of its students. Reports of the NIFT

Alumni Association show that unlike in the past where almost every graduating student wished to go out on their own and don the mantle of designer, many are now happy to work in big manufacturing houses, export firms, and retail houses. The more enterprising of them form groups that offer consultancy.

OTHER FASHION SCHOOLS

The other big influence on today's fashion scene is the National Institute of Design (NID), an autonomous national institution for research, service, and training in industrial design and visual communication set up in 1961 based on the recommendations of Charles and Ray Eames as set out in *The India Report*. This renowned design team had been invited by the government to recommend a design program that would serve as an aid to small industry in coming to terms with the rapid changes that were being introduced with new technologies and production processes.

The NID provides a multidisciplinary approach to design education, training, and practice. Today, it is internationally recognized for the quality of its programs, which have introduced changes in kind, rather than merely in degree.

Its courses have given rise to designer labels such Abraham & Thakore, and, in 2007, Nachiket Barve, a young postgraduate of NID, Ahmedabad, launched his eponymous label at Lakme Fashion Week to great acclaim.

NID and Bocconi University, Altagamma and Confidustria (the Trade Association for Italian Industry and the Confederation of Italian Industry, respectively) in Italy launched a collaborative certificate program, "Managing Fashion & Design Companies Successfully" in 2006.

The popularity of NIFT and NID have given rise to other design institutes, such as the Pearl Academy in Delhi, and to courses such

National Institute of Design

as SNDT University's fashion designing course and the Sophia Polytechnic's design course in Mumbai. The curriculum covers all aspects of fashion but, not surprisingly, the majority of students aspire to become designers, with creative lines and labels of their own. However, export houses have begun to recruit graduates from NIFT and the privately run design schools (for both the creative and marketing wings) to meet the demands of a growing overseas clientele.

WESTERN-TRAINED DESIGNERS

The constant growth in India's national GNP has given the younger generation a lot of spending power. Almost as though answering a need, the younger line of designers is creating clothes that appeal to both the spirit and the pocket of the upwardly mobile. Not surprisingly, many of these young designers have worked or studied abroad, imbibing the aesthetics and technological expertise of the West, adding a global perspective to their interpretation of fashion.

Raghavendra Rathore, of the royal family of Jodhpur, for example, studied at the Parsons School of Design, New York, and followed this with an apprenticeship at DKNY and Oscar de la Renta. His label, Rathore Jodhpur, launched almost a decade ago, has been quietly successful with both men and women, with little drama and a clear signature. His men's line aspires to create a fashion statement for the urban professional male, and combines Indian and Western touches with deftness.

Other designers who have had some training abroad include Sabyasachi Mukherjee, who won a British Council scholarship to work in London. This experience, though brief, "changed me completely," he says. Sonali Mansinka studied at the London College of Fashion and at the London Center for Fashion Studies and now creates hip clothes for the women with a touch of daring. Nandita Basu followed up a six-year assistantship with Suneet Varma with a course at Central Saint Martin's School of Art and Design in London. Not surprisingly, the vision and aesthetics of these designers from the younger school influence how the IT generation clothes itself.

FASHION JOURNALISM

As recently as 2000, there was very little concept of fashion writing in India. Journalism and communication students were taught a range of subjects including news reporting and feature writing—"serious" journalism—but fashion occupied very little space in the curriculum of colleges across the country. With the fashion industry growing steadily, and the increasing numbers of international brands entering the country, some knowledge of fashion became a prerequisite for any journalist covering a fashion show or a launch. Fashion TV (FTV) provided one window into the importance of understanding trends and the fashion industry.

NIFT was one of the first colleges to run courses in fashion journalism. The idea was to give its students an extra string to their bow, using their knowledge of design and manufacture as a basis for a potential career in fashion journalism.

This was a significant step away from the fashion writing that characterized the color supplements of newspapers, where fashion industry news revolved more around which designers got whom to sit in the front-row seats, and general gossip about models, makeup, and men. Magazines, on the other hand, delved deeper, endeavoring to educate their readers on putting clothes together, talking about design philosophies, and explaining the difference between a textile expert and a designer. *Femina* was among the first magazines to do this, attempting in the process to guide its readers into evolving style statements of their own.

Elle, India's first domestic version of an international fashion magazine franchise, showed inventive combinations of designer wear in evocative shoots, and picked mix-and-match ensembles and accessories to create a communication on fashion that was way beyond what had been done by any Indian magazine until that time.

In the 1980s, the two premier women's magazines were *Eve's Weekly* and *Femina*. Both carried much of what they thought interested women of that time, and the contents included a smattering of craft and fashion. Fashion was more often than not contained in two color pages (out of a total of eight color pages editorially), and would feature a woman (who might or not be a professional model) wearing a sari or a *salwar kameez*. The film magazine *Filmfare* also carried fashion of sorts, showing a heroine of the day in the clothes she wore in her work and play.

In the early 1990s, *Femina* became full color, and the time was right to focus on the nascent fashion industry. A decision was made to devote eight pages of each issue to designer fashion, with eight more on regular fashion. These could be sponsored by some of the ready-to-wear and sari brands in the national market. The first issue proved to be a challenge because there was no designer focus or high-end fashion. The very next issue, though, had six pages of fashion by Rohit Khosla, a pioneer of the Indian fashion industry, and he was featured on the cover surrounded by three of his favorite models. It also carried an article with him talking about his fashion philosophy, his muses, and his clothes. This marked the formal beginning of fashion communication through magazines in India. As *Femina* gained strength, tripling its circulation in a very short period, other magazines, including the then dying *Eve's Weekly*, began to devote more pages to fashion.

In the late 1990s, government rules allowed international magazines such as *Elle* and *Cosmopolitan* to publish in India, and this prompted *Femina* and other local publications to undergo a major facelift, improving paper quality, increasing the number of pages, and linking fashion and beauty to give the reader a holistic understanding of both. *Femina* also started bringing out books on beauty and fashion and weddings to educate readers interested in the subjects. Its first book on fashion (which sold 40,000 copies at a price of 150 rupees) listed all the designers of the day, categorizing them into their style statements, with a page dedicated to each outlining their background and design philosophy. The book ended up in many college libraries and is still referred to by students from the U.S. and U.K. working on Indian fashion.

Elle and *Cosmopolitan* were among the first to devote entire sections to fashion, and made *Femina* look staid in comparison. They aggressively dictated looks and forecast trends, raising the bar for magazine design and styling.

Today, fashion has become an inherent part of almost every magazine, including those in the vernacular. Even magazines for men and the family devote segments to the subject, even if superficial.

Fashion writing still has to come of age, but the younger set of professionals in magazine journalism generally hail from backgrounds that understand and wear brands, and the change is bound to come. Fashion journalism also invaded newspaper space, with color supplements and tabloids commenting on fashion shows. This current surge of interest has seen NIFT alumni taking up writing and styling for magazines and newspapers, which is a great step in explaining fashion to a country that has little knowledge beyond basic styles.

In 1996, Anuradha Mahindra launched what must be considered the first Indian magazine dedicated solely to fashion: *Verve*. Flush with the success of the home and lifestyle quarterly *Interiors* (launched in 1992), she felt conditions were ripe for a publication which would reflect the changing face of women in India. "I grew up in the 1970s, and saw history unfold before my eyes," she explained. "Time was when you could not get imported goods, could not travel, or call abroad easily. Suddenly changes were taking place everywhere: women in the workplace, women studying, and women changing." *Verve* was the first upmarket publication, priced at 200 rupees, and had the look of a coffee-table book. Printed in Singapore on high-quality glossy paper, the magazine is now a monthly. After the first issue, *Verve* was contacted by the agency handling Cartier to book the back cover. Since then there has been no looking back. For example, the first issue of *Vogue* had no fewer than 63 overseas luxury brands advertising within its covers. In the early days of *Verve*'s existence, selected teams would come over to have previews "by invitation only," and would make audiovisual presentations to prospective buyers. The brands were making their presence felt. Recently, when Lancôme was about to launch in India, the teams were met by the press before the launch. Similarly, *Verve* did an introductory feature on Guerlain.

It was inevitable that the communication for luxury brands would take the route of celebrity endorsements. The market offered major brands a better foot in the door if they used established Indian stars. While luxury communication in Europe and America is built on the exclusive nature of the products and services and the persons who use them, it needed to be more inclusive and inspirational in India.

The Indian luxury context, while evolving rapidly, still had its own codes, its own implications. Celebrity endorsements and ambassadors from Bollywood (Shah Rukh Khan for Tag Heuer, Aishwarya Rai for Longines, for example) created brand awareness, but the mass appeal of these stars also contributed to a diffusion and dilution of the brand. The more available a brand is perceived to be, the greater the risk of compromising its promise and of tarnishing its luster.

The endorsements of Bollywood stars or cricketing idols still hold the key to many markets. Amitabh Bachchan has endorsed all manner of products, from pens to Pepsi. He and Shah Rukh Khan have endorsed bank services as well, a far cry from the glamor of the movie industry. It is that appeal that the luxury brands are tapping into.

The sophisticated wealthy class, who are accustomed to refinement, may well be the cornerstone of the market for luxury brands, but it is the growing middle class who aspire to own luxury brands and it is they who drive demand. The Indian consumer had been ready and waiting for the "right" magazines in this category. Her awareness of fashion, beauty, and some of the luxury brands showed a steady evolution, and she was looking for a little help to celebrate her personal style.

The relaxation of the rules on international ownership enabled publishing companies to set up wholly-owned subsidiaries in India and opened the way for a completely new dynamic.

In 2007, France's Groupe Marie Claire launched *Marie Claire* India. The magazine is published in 13 languages across the world, and sells more than four million copies. The Indian version marks the twenty-sixth edition for the magazine, which positions itself as the "thinking women's fashion magazine." *Marie Claire India*, which has the tagline of "let me be me," began a campaign against moral policing from the word go, and gave Indian readers an editorial mix of serious journalism and glamor, transposed and adapted for an Indian audience by an Indian editorial team. Targeted at women between 25 and 35, the magazine had an exceedingly low entry price (50 rupees).

In September 2007, to much fanfare, Condé Nast Publications launched its flagship brand, *Vogue*. *Vogue India* was the next big step in the fashion communication industry, and was the seventeenth edition of the unparalleled style bible. Condé Nast India has a dynamic team, and brings the best of Indian and international fashion to the reader by presenting a holistic vision of what fashion means to India and to the world at large.

The magazine was launched in 39 cities across India, covering all traditional outlets (4,500 stores) and non-traditional outlets (700 stores). Targeted at women between 25 and 40 with an average household income of US$100,000 or dual car ownership, at 100 rupees the entry price was double that of *Marie Claire India*. Both magazines have since increased their pricing, and the stage is set for increased competition, fueled by the increasing number of international fashion and luxury brands coming into India. These companies will become major advertisers in both magazines, something the latter are counting on as the key factor in the success of their business models.

To continue with the growing trend in Indian fashion journalism, February 2009 saw the launch of the twenty-ninth edition of *Harper's Bazaar*. Its mission, according to the editor-in-chief, Arone Purie, is "to partner and grow the fashion industry in India." The magazine is to reflect the Indian woman's style and identify embodying "an easy, seamless blend of the best of Indian and international fashion, style and values," as introduced by Sujata Assomull, the editor.

Though online fashion has not yet taken hold in a major way in India, this is set to change as the influence of foreign designers increases.

NOTE

1. This is a loose overshirt worn by men.

PART IV
THE INDIAN DESIGNER

CHAPTER 11
DESIGNER MARKET STRUCTURES

THE FIRST INDIAN FASHION DESIGNERS
AND FASHION SHOWS

There is no real explanation for the fact that the 1970s witnessed the rising of young men and women who were strongly motivated to create clothes very different from what most people were wearing at that time. But there is no denying that James Ferreira, Bina Ramani, Rohit Khosla, Hemant Trevedi, and Xerxes Bhatena were the forerunners of what today is a bustling creative space. Each of these people made very definite contributions to bringing a

James Ferreira

design sensibility back to Indian clothes and, in turn, inspired future generations to take up design as a full-time vocation.

A series of fashion showings for the Clothing Manufacturer's Association of India and companies that wished to showcase their products in the Middle Eastern markets caught the eye of foreign buyers. Sometime during the mid-1970s, foreign buyers, particularly of cotton-based products in the ready-to-wear segment in search of low-cost suppliers, descended on India, as well. This led to a mini-revolution of sorts in the apparel sector, and not just for the big companies. The small town of Tirupur in Karnataka, for example, began doing piecework for the bigger exporters based in Mumbai and Delhi, but is now a direct supplier to some of the hottest names in global fashion.

At another level, Ritu Kumar, Munira Chudasama, Parmeshwar Godrej, Pallavi Jaikishen, and Bhanu Athaiya were also making very definite contributions to creating a fashion consciousness. One common thread that seems to have bound these diverse talents together, even in their diversity, is that they reveled in the luxury of fabric, in the lines cloth could take, in the voluminous flow of a garment or the sheer minimalist sweep of fabric curving along the body.

In the 1980s, another concept to catch the eye of well-heeled Indian women (including the then Prime Minister Indira Gandhi and her daughter-in-law Sonia) was the originality and quality of the printed fabrics being produced by the Satya Paul Design Studio. The studio later became Genesis Colors, which grew into one of the few professionally run designer brands.

The increased interest in clothes and a growing fashion sensibility, evident in the work of these and other trailblazing designers, persuaded many women's magazines to devote more pages to fashion.

In the early 1980s, Mrs. Gandhi, through her drastic curtailing of civil rights at the end of the 1970s, gave impetus to two of the premier women's magazines at that time, *Femina* and *Eve's Weekly*, to do their bit to discuss women's rights and project the Indian textile and fashion industry into the limelight. Subsequently, fashion took to the ramp in a serious manner, with fashion shows being taken across the country to at least five cities, where they formed a backdrop for the Miss India Contests. Vimla Patil, Shanti Chopra, and Jeanie Naoroji were among those who staged fashion shows, backed, first, by the government and the handloom sector, and later by the mills that created cloth for the middle class.

"There was no real knowledge of how to do a show", says Shanti Chopra of those days. "We would rehearse for 10 days; the models had to be taught every move. [They] were nothing like the shows we see today. There were no rules: we made the rules." She cites an instance of a model falling ill the day before a show and being replaced by someone much smaller in stature. The clothes were obviously too large, and the new model's hands were hidden by the cuffs, but the show went on nevertheless.

As *Business Today* reported some years ago, "Their small and medium enterprises success has not come easy, though. Most of the tier-two companies, which typically were exporters of private labels, have spent considerable time, energy and money on product quality, reading the market trend."[1]

In the early 1990s, as market conditions in India eased, many of these exporters decided to tap the potential of the apparel industry domestically. During the 1990s, more than 125 apparel brands were launched in India, most by local small and medium-sized companies. And today many of India's high-street premium brands are at par with their global counterparts.

As India grew as a supply base in the 1980s, so did the number of homegrown buyers for foreign labels. Sunil Sethi, for example, started out almost 20 years ago selling cotton ties to May Department Stores and Lord & Taylor in America. In the process of selling almost 50,000 ties, he realized that design and quality had to be foremost if India was to succeed in the export market. He became a buying expert, and then a buying agent. Using his experience of foreign buyers' requirements, he set about helping them find what they wanted in India. According to Sethi, this was no easy task; even as recently as five years ago, designers whom he approached had no idea what was required: "They were mainly creators working in some haphazard manner. They would take their goods as samples in suitcases and travel abroad to sell; they had no knowledge of export needs, rules, restrictions, and the protocol."

In 1988, Sethi set up his own company, Alliance Merchandising, and offered a full range of services under one roof—merchandising, design, product development, quality control, and logistics. It specialized in apparel by Indian fashion designers, fashion accessories, and lifestyle products in textile and handicrafts. Over the years, he has represented some of the most reputable names in the U.S., Canada, the U.K., Italy, Belgium, France, Malaysia, and Japan, and worked on designs by international designers such as Manolo Blahnik, Aldo Cibic, Sir Terence Conran, Paola Navone, Tom Dixon, Eileen Fischer, and Nate Berkus. In early 2008, Sethi sold his company to global sourcing giant Li & Fung, but continues his association with the company as senior VP in charge of Indian operations—a classic case of having your cake and eating it too.

Some of India's fashion designers, too, have honed their skills making clothes for top-drawer designers such as Valentino, Ralph Lauren, Galliano, DKNY, and Tommy Hilfiger. Rohit Bal has made shirts for Paul Smith; Pooja Nayyar developed fabrics for British designer Alexander McQueen's menswear collections; and Varun Bahl makes garments for Armani, Kenzo, Christian Lacroix, Versus, and Zara.

How far has India come, though, as a manufacturing base? There is an interesting story in the designer team, Lecoanet and Hemant.

Didier Lecoanet grew up in eastern France. After studying fine arts, he did a stint in advertising before enrolling to train in fashion design at the Ecoles de la Chambre Syndicale de la Haute Couture in Paris. Hemant Sagar, the son of a German mother and an Indian

Design by Sunil Sethi

Lecoanet and Hemant

father, spent his childhood in Delhi, studied design and dressmaking in Germany, learned the ropes of the ready-to-wear business with a major German firm and then went to learn fashion design in Paris, where he met Lecoanet in 1978.

With shared interests and passions, they set up a tiny workshop on the rue du Faubourg Saint Honoré in 1981 and developed it first into a salon, then into a boutique and finally into a fully fledged fashion house. In 1984, they were joined by Roy Gonzales, who had worked with Pierre Cardin and Jean Patou, and Juliette Cambursano, who had worked at Cristobal Balenciaga and Mila Schön. From then on, they came into their own, putting out *haute couture* and ready-to-wear collections every season. In 1988, they introduced a line of accessories in Japan, and in 1991 moved to smart new premises at the Hotel d'Argenson in the Heart of the Marais. In 1994, they enjoyed their crowning success, the Golden Thimble fashion award.

When the costs of running a *couture* boutique in the Paris of the 1990s became prohibitive, they moved their manufacturing base to India in 2001. Hemant says they were aware of the contradictions inherent in India's social fabric ("How could we be so pretentious to think a new blouse could be more important than a road, or electricity, or water?"); nevertheless they continued "in the hope that one day the one billion-plus consumers will have an opinion and will make this novelty-based industry into a reality, and that is when even we will be able to boast an international style that comes from India, just like many other countries before. We already have the resources, the knowhow and the hands to do it for worldwide audiences, but do not seem to realize the capital it represents."

He brought his European production team with him to train the local workers, which they did and still are doing today, from "the basics (setting up bank accounts for each) of hygiene (washing

Hemant bag

hands before work, no spitting) and punctuality, saying good morning and goodbye to each other ... that was the beginning of my work here. In fact, what I realized only later was that a vast majority of certainly capable workers never even get to work properly, because they never get a fixed employment: many get an amount of cash in the hand in the evening, and are looking for a job the next morning again."

Lecoanet and Hemant have transformed their Franco-Indian fashion house into a fully fledged Indian fashion house with the opening of their worldwide headquarters in Gurgaon in 2008.

FASHION DESIGN COUNCIL OF INDIA

As the industry started spreading in scope, and the glamor attached to the designers gave it greater visibility and acceptance, something was needed to draw the various strands together and to nurture its development further. The Fashion Design Council of India (FDCI) was established in 1998 to perform this role.

The aim of the FDCI was to set up links between its members and government bodies, and between retailers and manufacturers to help ensure a smooth supply chain. The council also planned and proclaimed to conceptualize market trends and coordinate with manufacturers and retailers for the development of fabrics, prints, and so on.

Furthermore, as a cohesive body, the FDCI would work toward promoting the interests of India as a country, and market the individual designers, supporting their endeavors to enter mainstream fashion. Through workshops, trend-forecasting seminars, and other interactions, the FDCI did what it could bring cohesion to the fashion industry.

Perhaps the most significant step taken by the council was to initiate India Fashion Week, in Delhi in 2000, amid skirmishing egos, confusion, and delays. The idea behind the concept was to increase the interaction between designer and client, which had been minimal up to that stage. Such interactions were restricted to weddings or other special events, when orders were placed and executed. However, the client base seemed almost static, despite a burgeoning middle class with much greater purchasing power.

To overcome this, Fashion Week aimed to encourage designers to move away from *couture* and bridal creations and expand into the world of ready-to-wear. The idea was that affordability and style—backed by the social cachet and brand values that the designers now carried—would increase the customer base, to the benefit of the industry as a whole.

By its second year, Fashion Week was stable enough to encourage the organizers to move it to Mumbai. Attempts were made to put it on the fashion map that took buyers and journalists from New York, to Milan, Paris, London, and south to Australia. Though India Fashion Week had yet to achieve anything like the stature of the events in the fashion capitals, that Indian fabrics were a treasure-house for designers from across the world created a certain interest.

By 2003, the foreign press had begun to take an interest, and there was sporadic coverage in publications in the West. It was a beginning, but one that had a greater impact on Indian clients more than it did on the fashion scene in the West.

Two Fashion Weeks, Two Cities

In 2005, India Fashion Week's contract with IMG Fashion, the New York-based international fashion and designer fashion event management company hired by the FDCI to organize the show, expired. This prompted IMG and Lakmé—the number one cosmetics and beauty company owned by Hindustan Levers and the original sponsor of Fashion Week—to start a rival event in Mumbai, the Lakmé Fashion Week, now held twice a year.

There was a great deal of media coverage and speculation regarding the choices and changing loyalties of various designers as they opted for one or other of the events. The fashion scene is divided over whether it owes its allegiance to the FDCI or to Lakmé; to Delhi or Mumbai. While this may not be entirely healthy, it does at least point to fashion having become big enough to be a sparring ground and it has opened up opportunities for more young designers to showcase their talent.

In the past three or four years, there has been increasing evidence of the emergence of a real interest in the business of fashion, as opposed to the glamor and gossip that have always surrounded it.

The number of aspiring models (and training academies), makeup artists, and photographers has grown remarkably; and if the business media that covers the shows is any indication, this interest is here to stay.

Mid-2008, the FDCI announced its support of the first Indian Couture Week, held in September of the same year. Designers for the event, held in Mumbai, were chosen by the real-estate company sponsoring the event. Though the names featured were impressive enough and included Anamika Khanna, Ashish Soni, J.J. Valaya, Manav Gangwani, Manish Malhotra, Pallavi Jaikishan, Ritu Kumar, Rohit Bal, Suneet Varma, Tarun Tahiliani, and Varun Bahl, the grounds for selection remained a mystery. The indication is now that perhaps fashion is to be played by sponsors' rules, rather than by public taste or creativity.

After Rathi Vinay Jha's transfer to a new position (at Work Travel Tourism Council), her deputy, Sumeet Nair, replaced her for several months in this function before creating his own *couture* and fashion week, which runs simultaneously to FDCI's Fashion Week.

Perhaps the third fashion week could create a scenario where the fashion fever in Delhi peaks in October, as the Wills India Fashion Week and the Sumeet Nair orchestrated event overlapped in October 2008. Staging the event at Emporio and shifting his focus beyond the usual-attendee Indian buyers to those from Malaysia, Australia, and Thailand, as well as the normally less attended-to Indian buyer, are Sumeet Nair's way of giving his event a new focus. The designers to the Emporio event will be invited to participate and selected by a yet-to-be-announced jury panel. Whether the luxury mall will take the fashion week to a higher level, making it an event that involves and interests more buyers who are looking at *couture* designers from India, remains to be seen. But fashion is definitely gaining more of a buzz.

Today, Sunil Sethi is the honorary president of FDCI; elsewhere he is heading the division of lifestyle and fashion at Alliance Merchandising, after signing a management outsourcing contract with Li & Fung, the largest sourcing agent in the world.

THE MULTIDESIGNER STORE CONCEPT

Perhaps the real credit for designers climbing down from their *couture*-lined ivory towers and coming to a level where the young urban fashion follower could access their creations goes to an enterprise with the name of BE.

Sadly, the catch-22 situation facing designers in the late 1990s was a tough one. The real money and breadth of sales were in the ready-to-wear market, but there was no financial support for designers to be able to manufacture a special fabric and produce a garment in quantities that would make sense. Most designers had poor marketing sense, so it was easier to stick to the narrow confines of the safe world of bridalwear and *couture*. The vision and business acumen of Gautam Singhania, heir to the House of Raymonds (which specialized in men's suits and semi-formal ready-mades), led him to launch the venture known as BE, which aimed at "corporatizing" designer ready-to-wear.

The enterprise took off among much fanfare, and signed up some of India's best-known names to float new lines with BE as a partner. Many designers saw it as a step toward establishing themselves as a brand that could become a household name. Keeping the Indian psyche in mind, BE offered a mix of "ethnic" and Western styles. Western wear made up 60% of the collection at any given time, with the balance comprising ladies' Indian wear (30%) and accessories (10%). Its menswear collection was largely Western, and soon proved to be the fastest-selling category; a surprising but telling comment on the new focus retail was to take. Afford-ability, accessibility, and acceptability formed BE's mantra for success.

The luxury hinted at in these ready-to-wear lines came through in the limited editions of the constantly changing collections. This was reinforced by the casual elegance of the BE stores, where the ambience conveyed the feeling that this was where those in the know shopped and could expect to find interpretations of their personality at prices that were more affordable than designerwear had ever been in the past. The bespoke mode was recreated, with the best cutters and tai-lors in the business working to create lines with highly prized labels. The fabrics ranged from knits to woven and cottons and linens to silk, with a spectrum of colors starting from earthy and aqua tones to bright colors. The prices ranged from 600 to 6,000 rupees.

Rajesh Pratap, Rathore, Rohit Bal, and Anshu Arora Sen were among the first batch of 18 designers who jumped on the BE band-wagon. Some fared better than others, depending on their knowl-edge of the market and their appeal to consumers.

Overall, however, BE failed to achieve the level of success expected of it, but the experiment showed that there was a mar-ket out there, if everything could be handled right. BE failed to overcome the basic lack of trust that prevailed between design-ers and corporate houses. Despite Lina Tipnis, a designer who had had considerable success in the ready-to-wear market, being employed as a consultant for the enterprise, a range of problems quickly surfaced: delivery dates were not met; goods were not of the same standard as samples; there was a quick turnover of buy-ers with different tastes; in-house production was slow to take off; and BE itself fell far short of its goal of opening 100 stores across the country within the first year. Only 13 stores opened, and there was no way the quantities ordered could help hold the price line.

Though the clothes were labeled "ready-to-wear," the prices were closer to those for diffusion wear. While BE still operates today, it now lacks vigor.

But a light had been ignited and other chain stores began to experiment in multidesigner selling. Shopper's Stop began to hold trunk shows over two or three days, creating a buzz that resulted in designers placing goods on consignment. Westside followed suit, and designers such as Wendell Rodricks, Anita Dongre, and Lina Tipnis found new buyers among those who had never ventured to buy designer labels earlier.

ROHIT KHOSLA

Persuading his family to let him go to the U.K. to train to be what it considered at the time to be nothing more than a common tailor, Rohit Khosla enrolled onto the fashion course at Kingston Polytechnic in 1979. His battles were far from over because he was the only Indian on the course, and, unlike his fellow students, had never held a needle or learnt to cut or sew, although he produced highly stylized fashion sketches of women's figures. Throughout the course, his charm and dedication gained him precious support and admiration from staff and colleagues, allowing him to find his strengths, and learn how to make the best of his Indian heritage.

During his career, Rohit Khosla overcame all the obstacles in his way, and consequently became to be regarded as the forerunner of fashion consciousness in India, the first Indian designer with international stature and the purveyor of a new fashion ethos that now characterizes Indian designers. He evolved as a key player in the fashion industry at a time when there were no specific support system and no stylists, makeup artists, or fashion photographers.

Rohit Khosla

Rohit Khosla design

In the 1980s, he sold his creations at Harrods in London, something that many current designers long for today. He worked with export houses that provided the impetus to keep his creativity afloat, although overseas clients sometimes thought that a Westerner was at the helm. Rohit therefore spent his personal time on creating other designs to express his real self, extending himself into fields where he could publicize his work. He became a one-man industry: styling his own creations, and choosing and directing the models, the photographers, the makeup artists, and the hairdressers himself.

After his studies at FIT in New York, he created entire collections and showcased them in such a way that it put him on a par with other better-known names. He created high drama out of his clothes, choreographed his shows to show them off in style, and introduced those real feelings and vital components of glamor and luxury into fashion. Using silk, cotton, rope, organza, wood, and pleated fabric, as well as embellishments and embroideries from India, Africa, Morocco, and Europe, Khosla created line after line of striking clothes. It made him the darling of the jetset, a "reference," and the one to lead the way into the future of fashion while evoking the regality and splendor of *couture*.

Indian fashion began to be visible in the 1980s, with women's magazines taking up the baton and extending color pages to the cause of educating their readers on new trends in clothes, and showcasing the creations of some of the new kids on the block.

FASHION STORES

Ensemble

In the 1980s, designer Tarun Tahiliani and his sister Tina started India's first fashion store. Ensemble, at Lion's Gate in Delhi, was a place where talented designers could display their wares without having to worry about overheads. It was a daring and surprisingly successful move, and proved that couture was stepping out of the trousseau closet and into all aspects of daily life again.

Under Tina Tahiliani Parekh's guidance, Ensemble acted as a trailblazer for the likes of Melange, Ogaan, and the countless other multidesigner stores that can be found in almost every city in India today. Tahiliani held wine and cheese events, at which designers mingled with their clients, and organized seasonal sales, which helped both store and designer offload stock to make room for new collections. The exquisite fit, colors, and lines ensured repeat visits.

Melange

When Sangeeta Singh Kathiawada set up Melange in 1993, she adopted a very different approach, placing the emphasis on the natural and the organic. The look and feel of the interiors

Ensemble: view of store interior

were very different from those of Ensemble and other competitors such as Ravissant and Glitterati. In a converted wine cellar, Sangeeta gave Melange an understated rustic look that appealed to many.

Working with the first batch of NIFT graduates, who shared her involvement and interest in textile innovation and offbeat design, Sangeeta opened the doors of her store to Sarah Eapan, Narendra Kumar, and Hidden Harmony, among others, and over the years has attracted some of the industry's brightest talent to her store.

Despite the rustic interiors having belied the price tags (Wendell, Sabyasachi, or even a revivalist such as Anuradha Vakil of Ahmedabad can sell for six-figure prices), the preview evenings, which combine sophistication with business, have worked wonderfully.

Kimaya

Businessman and exporter Pradeep Hirani started the business in 2003, with a single store in Mumbai. Today, Kimaya claims to be a leading fashion house that is home to Indian designers old and new. Hirani assumes the mantle of being a key player at India Fashion Weeks. Buying outright rather than relying on consignments, Hirani has inverted the demand–supply equation, and offers logistical support to the designers to produce the required volumes at a given price.

Representing a mix of 118 designers in its stores in Delhi, Mumbai, and Dubai, Kimaya now features some Western brands such as Max Mara and RED Valentino. Over the next few years, the company has ambitious plans to launch 48 stores in new markets such as Goa, Ludhiana, Chandigarh, Bangalore, Kolkata, and Hyderabad.

It is said in Indian industry circles that Hirani is keen to be a luxury brand franchisee. His first choice was to open Roberto Cavalli at The Taj Mahal and Palace in Mumbai. Over the past four years, Kimaya Fashions has consistently emerged as the single largest buyer at the Delhi and Mumbai Fashion Weeks, and has been visiting and working with international designers in Milan, London, and South Africa.

Santushti

When, in the mid 1980s, the Air Force Wives Welfare Association was given the opportunity to create a space for Indian designers as well as artisan stores of high quality, its response was to create Santushti, a small shopping center on a large plot in the heart of Delhi's diplomatic area.

This was Delhi's first taste of luxury, and it soon became an almost obligatory stop for most visitors to Delhi, and a regular haunt for those looking for something off the usual track.

Design houses such as Ogaan (which would grow into a multidesigner store chain); Ensemble's Delhi wing; Noorjehan, specializing in handcrafted Indian wear and stoles; and Tulsi, where Neeru Kumar offered fine fabrics created out of her innovations with weaving; and designers such as Rajesh Pratap were quick to seize the opportunity. Santushti was soon outpaced in popularity by 1 MG Road in Delhi, and The Courtyard in Mumbai.

Other stores of note include *Ogaan*, at The Hauz Khas Village and at Santushti in Delhi, and, more recently, in Mumbai. The brainchild of designer Kavita Bhartiya, the stores stock designs by Aki Narula and promising new names, alongside jewelry by Amrapali.

The Courtyard was conceived as Mumbai's own designer nook, within walking distance of The Taj Palace. It features such designers as Manish Arora, Narendra Kumar, Rajesh Pratap Singh, Tulsi, Abraham, and Thakore. Despite features such as an art gallery and a café, The Courtyard has fallen short of expectations regarding the traffic it hoped to attract.

When *Ffolio* was launched by Yashodra Shroff in Bangalore, it was a totally new concept. Designers at Ffolio were happy to find a new clientele, and fashion showings and invitee evenings kept the space vibrant and busy. At that time, Ffolio was the one-stop shop for any woman wanting an outfit for a special evening, and the shop was buzzing the night before the Miss World Contest that was held in the city in 1996 (the first Miss World to be held in India after Aishwarya Rai's crown as Miss World in 1994 and Sushmita Sen's crown as Miss Unverse the same year). Today Ffolio also has a wing in the Leela Palace Hotel's Galleria, where designs by Anamika Khanna, Meera Muzzafar Ali, A. D. Normal, and others are on offer.

Aza, in South Mumbai, features well-known designers Sabyasachi Mukherjee, Wendell Rodricks, Kiran Uttam Ghosh, Manish Malhotra, Narendra Kumar, Anamika Khanna, and Rohit Bal, as well as a clutch of new talent such as Dev R Nil, Anand Kabra, Abdul Haider, Varun Bahl, and A. D. Normal. Aza also stocks jewelry by Queenie Dhody and bags by Malaga (Meera Mahadevia), and holds regular soirees to promote new collections. A new Aza Men store offers men's lines by Rohit Bal, A. D. Normal, Narendra Kumar, and others.

Cinnamon in Bangalore is a classy and delightful space. Color-coded clothes—saris, Western wear and Indian wear by designers such as Sonam Dubal, Jason Cherian, and Sonya Khan—hang in quiet corners.

Aza: view of store interior

Amethyst was, when it started, a store that was streets ahead in concept and use of space. Kiran Rao transformed an old, beautiful home into a space where clothes by Kiran Uttam Ghosh, Sonam Dubal, Tulsi, Anamika, Tarun Tahiliani, Hidden Harmony from Bangalore, and most other designer brands from Delhi hang in their own nooks, and over the years, it has been the inspiration for other stores to follow suit.

Launched in Mumbai in late 2006 by Priya Kishore, *Bombay Electric* has become something of a fashion reference point, with Sonam Dubal, Gaurav Gupta, Rajesh Pratap Singh, and Nikasha as well as lesser-known and newer designers selling there. It is a careful blend of a gallery and shop atmosphere that represents "the harmonious culture clash that is Mumbai."[2]

Bombay Electric: store exterior

85 Landsdowne Road, commonly known as Kolkata's best space for fashion, is another old house that sells designerwear as well as art objects. Prominent Indian designers including Sabyasachi Mukherjee, Shantanu Goenka, Kiran Uttam Ghosh, Cue, and Anamika Khanna have built up a dedicated clientele from this store.

Garden of Five Senses on Qutab Road in Mumbai, is, like The Courtyard, a space with individual stores. Designers here include Rajesh Pratap, Manish Arora for Reebok, Anamika Khanna, and Amit Sikka, among others. It has yet to fulfill its early promise.

Square One Mall is a space holding designer lines such as Riti Kumar, Swapan and Seema, Jattin Kochchar, Ragini Singhania, and

Aza at the Crescent

others who are not from the top tier. Though Rohit Bal is also featured here, this is not a very successful venture.

The Crescent in Delhi has enjoyed success, and houses the likes of Cue, Payal Jain, Shantanu-Nikhil, Rohit Bal, Aza, Meera Muzaffer Ali, and others.

NOTES

1. Shaleish Dobhal 2001, "The Rise of Apparel's Also-Rans", *Business Today*, December 9.
2. Priya Kishore quoted in Dan Pinch 2008, "Bombay is Electric", *Dazed and Confused*, May 28.

CHAPTER 12
DESIGNERS

Although the Indian fashion scene has gained momentum in the recent past, there is still a group of tightly woven cliques, not dissimilar to the 1980s in Paris, London, and Milan, in which an old guard dominates the scene while a pool of new talent gradually settles in. Both the old and the new are eager to ride the wave of India's dynamic growth and increased consumer spending, and parlay their local stardom into something broader. Growing their businesses both within and outside India presents a challenge, not just in the choice of foreign markets but in the management of their businesses. By and large, they have only just begun to tap the export market potential for building their brands.

Many of these Indian designers have stores in the newly developing luxury malls, and their presence serves to lure in the consumers. Once inside, the consumers are also exposed to competing Western designer brands. Given the current predominant passion for local Indian-designed products this should present few risks to local designers, but this may well change in the longer term.

There is an abundance of Indian design talent using traditional art and craft techniques in new and modern ways. Detailing is already highly developed, but there is a need for greater focus on garment construction and cutting.

The vast majority of Indian designers are reliant on the domestic market. Few could be considered luxury brands, although some have luxury products. In India, high-end fashion implies bridalwear, although many local designers say that their interest lies in ready-to-wear and contemporary, or trendy creations, rather than elaborate ethnic clothing. It is widely felt that Indian designers cannot compete with international brands on quality, and that most consumers would not be willing to pay high prices for Western clothing designed by an Indian in India.

With a multitude of global players coming in, these designers realize that they are facing stiff competition, but feel that this will have the effect of raising industry standards in design, quality, and price.

It is worth noting that some of these designers are perfectly poised to be further developed as fashion brands in India, and have real potential to become international brands. Historically, there hasn't been a great deal of private-equity support either in India or outside. There are exceptions, of course, as was seen in 1985 when former bankers Sanjay Kapoor and Jyoti Narula acquired the Satya Paul Design Studio to create Genesis Colors. With 27 stores across the country, 50% of which operate on franchise, Genesis Colors is a clear leader in the branded Indian designer sari market. While saris are what the SP label is best known for, the brand also caters to the men's accessory segment, with ties and cufflinks, which can now be found in any premium department and multibrand store. Summer 2008 witnessed the launch of a new range of women's handbags.

While this might appear to be small beer when compared to global corporates, in Indian terms, Genesis Colors is taking big leaps. It has also acquired the Dipika Gehani label, set up a licensing agreement with designer J.J. Valaya for his Valaya Quantum diffusion line, and established Samsaara, a multibrand designer store chain.

Genesis Colors could be seen as being on the cusp of creating what just might be India's first fashion-based corporation. To fund expansion, Kapoor and Narula sold a small stake in their company to JM Financials, which has launched a private-equity fund for India, backed by New York-based hedge fund Old Lane Partners.

The speculation within the industry is that Genesis Colors has the funds to look for outright buyouts of fashion companies with the potential to become brands. The company has also created an international arm to retail foreign luxury brands in India. These already include Canali, Kenzo, Etienne Aigner, Jimmy Choo and Boltega Veneta, with more in the offing.

The time is ripe to provide the necessary financial and managerial support to the current crop of talented designers to ensure the optimization of resources and proper branding techniques.

Fern Mallis of IMG, a great supporter of Indian design talent and one of the most highly respected professionals in the fashion business, sees the current situation this way:

> Indian fashion is at a very exciting crossroads. I love the Indian fashion scene and have great respect and admiration for the designers in this amazing country. I frequently wear their clothes and enjoy being a fashion ambassador for India.
>
> It is because of this that I have great concerns for their future. As India is on the brink of a luxury invasion from France and Italy (and soon I suspect from the U.S.), India designers— who are among the most talented in the world— are going to be playing second fiddle in their own country. India is still a country where one can shop and buy things that *are* Indian...clothes, scarves and jewelry that are not available on every major shopping street and cool neighborhood in a predictable world-branded boutique.
>
> India's rich history, its textiles, its handcrafting techniques, its colors, its beads, precious stones, mirrors, and embellishments are a great resource for the world's leading designers. They come here to play, get inspired, interpret and export India back into their own collections.
>
> India's designers are in a constant quandary—one mostly fueled by inexperienced fashion journalists who continually judge them by their "international sales." At each of the fashion weeks, whether in Delhi or Mumbai, the biggest catch is the "international buyer" and the question du jour is always "What are you buying and how much are you spending?" Many come to see, experience and enjoy an underwritten

trip to India. Most of the designers are not prepared to sell and comply with the exacting standards, deadlines and deliveries imposed by department stores overseas. The sizing is not yet standard, the fiber content is not labeled, the delivery dates are erratic, and most frustrating (to me) is the lack of communication. Not responding to emails or faxes, having full mailboxes and full voicemails make it even more difficult to complete transactions. To do business around the world, one has to be in constant communication with the world. It is my hope that the financial community funding the explosion of European brands entering the Indian market shares some of those financial resources, infrastructure, marketing and advertising dollars with their brethren at home and helps build their brands and companies into world-class businesses. The time has come for Indian designers to be recognized as equals amongst their peers around the world, but they need help to make it happen.

On the other hand, India has a domestic market and demand that is worth millions to these designers. It is this market that everyone else is trying to reach, so why aren't the Indians showing more passion and working harder to own it? This market needs to be cultivated, romanced and supported with a strong business plan, smart business partners and financing. With these factors in place, India's creative talent can begin to take their rightful place amongst the leading designers of the world.[1]

From among the many designers present in India today, the following have been selected for the creativity and aesthetics of their collections as well as for the history or future growth potential of their businesses.

Table 12.1   Designer category list

Designer category	Trademarks	Examples of designers
Old Guard (Classical Indian)	• Use of traditional crafts, colors and embellishments on predominantly Indian silhouettes • Elaborate wedding clothes • Responsible for updating ethnic fashion • Influence from the Mughal period	Tarun Tahiliani Rohit Bal J.J.Vallaya Ritu Kumar Abujani and Sandeep Khosla

Table 12.1   Designer category list (*continued*)

Old Guard (Avant-Garde)	• Non-typical Indian designs, focused on fusion or Western wear, no embellishments • Asymmetrical cuts, surface texturing, drapes, pin-tucks and pleats • Influences from Belgium and Japan	Rajesh Pratap Singh Ashish N. Soni Abraham and Thakore Narendra Kumar Shahab Durazi Wendell Rodricks
Neo-Revivalists	• Reinvention of ethnic India by giving contemporary spins to very traditional handicrafts and appropriating Indian draps and silhouettes for Western clients • Influenced by Dries Van Noten and Marni	Sabyasachi Mukherjee Anamika Khanna Anupama Dayal
Modern India (Street Influence)	• Channeling street influences, multi-cultural mythologies, popular cinema (Bollywood), and changing identities • Freshness, innovation, and wit brought into their designs	Manish Arora Gaurav Gupta Aki Narula Nandita Basu
Modern India (Contemporary Indo-Western)	• Western designs with a modern Indian touch • Flexible silhouettes	Namrata Joshipura Rohit Gandhi and Rahul Kanna (CUE) Varun Bahl Sonam Dubal Anand Kabra Payal Jain Gauri and Nainika Karan Rina Dhaka Monisha Jaising Prashant Verma
Soft Fashion (and upcoming)	• Eco-friendly • Promotion of self-sustaining business of fashion • No superficial embellishments, designs rely on techniques developed to add quirky detailing or subtle surface texturing	Anshu Arora Kiran Uttam Ghosh Nachiket Barve Dev R. Nil Varun Sardana Samant Chauhan

THE OLD GUARD (CLASSICAL INDIAN)

These are Indian designers who have championed the cause of "Indian *couture*." Their trademark is the use of traditional crafts, colors, and embellishments on predominantly Indian silhouettes. They are particularly popular for their elaborate wedding clothes. They are seen as the pioneers of Indo-Western fusionwear, responsible for updating ethnic fashion and making it relevant to the changing times. Their strongest influence is the use of indigenous cuts and shapes, some going back to the Hindu and Muslim covert culture. All five designers have benefited tremendously from the wedding industry; they are very popular with brides-to-be across India.

Tarun Tahiliani[2]

Tahiliani's designs are Mughalesque, with Grecian/Indian draping, and have a fan following that spans generations. His digital-print collections of tees and kaftans are his all time bestsellers. His modernization of the Indian sari has made it the ensemble of choice at cocktail parties.

In 1987, Tahiliani, together with his sister, Tina, and fellow designer Rohit Khosla, opened India's first designer store, Ensemble in Mumbai. In 1990, he set up the Tarun Tahiliani Design Studio. Today, he sells from Amethyst in Chennai; Brisah in Hyderabad; Studio Ivory in Ludhiana, Chandigarh, and Delhi; Samsaara in Delhi, Ludhiana, and Chandigarh; and Ensemble in Delhi and Mumbai. He also operates his own flagship stores in Mumbai and Delhi.

After receiving a degree from the Fashion Institute of Technology, New York, in 1991, he held his first solo show in London in 1994. In 2000, he was one of the founder members of the Fashion Design Council of India. In 2003, he was invited by *Femina* magazine and the Indo-Italian Chamber of Commerce to show at Milan Fashion Week and then again in 2005.

Tarun Tahiliani creation

Tarun Tahiliani

Tarun Tahiliani creation

Tahiliani's collections range from ready-to-wear to *couture* and heavy bridal sets. The craftsmanship and color sensibility displayed in his clothes and accessories appeal to both Indian and Western tastes. His bridalwear has become a status symbol, the most celebrated of his brides being Jemima Khan. Other celebrities who have worn his work include the Duchess of Kent, actors Amir Khan, Aishwarya Rai, Elizabeth Hurley, and Goldie Hawn, and supermodel Naomi Campbell.

Rohit Bal[3]

Although Rohit Bal has something of a reputation as the "enfant terrible" of Indian fashion, *Time* magazine called him "India's Master of fabric and fantasy."[4] Bal is a designer ahead of his times and lives by his own rules; what he does to shock often becomes the norm years later.

An avid lover of Indian crafts (especially those from his Kashmiri roots), his daring, colorful creations have contributed to the resurrection of age-old or dying art forms and handicrafts.

In 1990, he created his first independent line of traditional designer clothes for men. Working with village craftsmen, he has used their expertise with the needle to transform his cuts and silhouettes into works of art. While reviving traditional Indian menswear, he has stayed on track with international design trends, his clothes ranging from the outrageous to the stunning.

In 1998, he was invited to create a showing for Omega with three top Indian models. In 2004, he received a three-year appointment with Titan Industries to design a line of watches and eyewear for the luxury segment of the domestic watch market.

His clientele includes Uma Thurman, Cindy Crawford, Pamela Anderson, and Naomi Campbell, and tennis star Anna Kournikova has modeled his clothes. At the wedding of Liz Hurley and Arun Nayyar in 2007, he dressed a host of celebrities as well as the bride and groom. He has held successful standalone fashion shows in New York, London, Paris, Dubai, Singapore, Mauritius, Sao Paolo, and all the major cities in India.

Rohit Bal

Rohit Bal creation

Bal has plans to achieve international status by setting up opera-tions overseas, and, closer to home, his ready-to-wear line and the line he provided to BE when it was first launched, and a few years later for the government-run Khadi Gramudyog Bhavan, proved his intention of making his otherwise very expensive clothes more acces-sible to the consumer.

J.J. Valaya[5]

One of India's senior most and best known designers, J.J. Valaya was born in the princely state of Rajasthan in India but spent most of his childhood travelling to different parts of the country due to his father's various postings in the army. The House of Valaya was founded in 1992 by brothers J.J. Valaya and T.J. Singh with the launch of its *couture* label. Valaya's creative vision regarding elegance and edgy grandeur, together with his brother's entrepreneurial abilities, has been the key factor for the success of Valaya as a luxury brand.

The brand today encompasses *couture*, diffusion, ready-to-wear, home, and a corporate social responsibility prerogative, the Valaya Magic Foundation. A larger than life approach to luxury fashion and lifestyle has been a signature of this "maverick maharajah." He believes that true style today is meant for those capable of carrying off both the whimsical and the bold, and that's precisely the ver-sion of sophistication found in the Nomadic Royal Valaya woman or man. It is the marriage of the uniqueness of India's craft and tradi-tion with the energy and the ever-changing nature of contemporary fashion that sets the pace for Valaya.

J.J. Valaya's success in the fashion industry has been recognized by a number of awards including the Prix d'Incitation at the young designers international competition held by the Concours Interna-tional des Jeunes Créateurs de Mode (Paris); the Elyxa Award (Delhi); the Thapar Dupont Medal (Delhi); and the KLM-NIFT Award for Best Designer (Mumbai). He was also the founder member of the

J.J Valaya

J.J. Valaya creation

governors of the Fashion Design Council of India (FDCI) and the first official brand ambassador for Swarovski India.

Ritu Kumar[6]

India's most successful designer brand, Ritu Kumar, is a household name that ranges from bridal *couture* to affordable, stylish ready-to-wear. She pioneered the use of Indian handicrafts in fashion. She has redefined traditional handwriting to meet the changing needs of the new generation. The inspiration for her designs comes from the basic Indian motifs, prints and embroideries but with the usage of a wide range of western silhouettes mingled with India styles.

Moving through various incarnations since its establishment in 1969, the business became a public company under the name Ritika Ltd. in 1996, and now has 23 outlets in 14 cities in India, a stand-alone store in the U.S., and franchise agreements in various countries worldwide.

Ritu Kumar studied Indian heritage and the history of Indian art at the Ashutosh Museum in Kolkata, which exposed her to the classical arts and folk art craftsmen in Bengal. Using this as a background, in the 1960s, she traveled extensively to rediscover the lost traditions of Indian crafts that were fast being replaced by plastic and printed synthetics.

In the mid-1970s, she was encouraged by the Craft and Handicrafts Board to make use of the block prints she had discovered in the villages of Uttar Pradesh to help ensure that the craft of the blockmakers and printers never died out. (Thanks to her efforts and those of other designers, the dwindling ranks of craftsmen have swollen to 16 million by the new millennium.)

Kumar's first shop was a joint venture with her aunt. Ritu's Boutique, situated on the ground floor of a tiny house in Delhi, sold ready-made clothes. It proved to be popular, although the boutique culture was little understood in those days.

Ritu Kumar

Ritu Kumar creation—in modern clothing

Ritu Kumar creation—in traditional clothing

Over the next few years, after a great deal of research, Ritu Kumar revived other traditional crafts such as *zardozi* (the art of gold, and sometimes, silver-thread embroidery on rich cloth) and *kashida* (a decorative technique using needle and thread), both of which are now widely used around the country.

In 1994, Ritu Kumar was a judge at the *Femina* Miss India Show in Goa and later went on to provide entire wardrobes for the winners of the contest.

In 2002, she launched "LABEL," a ready-to-wear line for the modern professional woman. Her bespoke bridalwear is very popular with brides in the U.K. and the U.S., who buy over the Internet. Her Paris lines, which, though trendy and contemporary, have the traditional touch that is the hallmark of all her work, and are also very popular.

Ritu Kumar has since developed her presence worldwide. She has designed personal collections for key celebrities in India such as Priyanka Chopra, Deepa Mehta as well as for various international beauty pageants. She was recently invited to showcase in New York for India's 60th Anniversary at Bryant Park.

Abu Jani and Sandeep Khosla[7]

Abu Jani and Sandeep Khosla are pioneers of the Indian fashion industry. Their 22-year-old partnership has seen them establish themselves as the premier luxury label in the country. Their creations are a unique blend of luxurious fabrics, exquisite embroideries and embellishments, and exceptional tailoring. India, with its unsurpassed craft legacy, is an eternal inspiration. They are best distinguished for their reinvention of *zardozi* and *chikankari* embroidery, having succeeded in lifting *chikan* from its middle-class or casual wear status to *couture*, red carpet, and bridalwear. Their sense of aesthetics is deeply grounded, and refuses to conform to transient trends. The onus is on impossibly intricate craftsmanship that

Abu Jani and Sandeep Khosla

Abu Jani creation

exudes elegance. The label is a favorite among icons in India and a growing number of fashionistas across the globe. They are the only Indian designers to have a standalone store in London, situated in Beauchamp Place, which is almost a decade old.

The duo launched their diffusion label, Abu Sandeep, in 2007 and will open a home label in Spring 2009. They have stores in Mumbai and New Delhi. The company is now committed to evolving to become India's first comprehensive luxury lifestyle label.

THE OLD GUARD (AVANT-GARDE)

Designers who veered away from typical Indian designs, and focused on fusion or Western wear without the usual Indian accoutrements of "bling" and "over-the-top" embellishments. They focused on asymmetrical cuts, surface texturing, drapes, pin tucks, and pleats to create radically different collections. Their biggest influences have come from Belgium and Japan.

Rajesh Pratap Singh[8]

Known as the Balenciaga of India, Singh is a great pattern cutter and discerningly chic. His clothes are simple and his use of embellishments minimal, relying instead on ruching, pleating, and pin tucks.

After graduating from NIFT in 1994, he worked in Italy and India to gain experience before starting working on his own lines, exporting mainly white cotton shirts. In 1998, he was invited to work with Amrita Singh of Amaya, and launched his first outlet, Pratap.

Today, he has three main lines: Rajesh Pratap Singh, his top-end line; RIP, for the younger, more casual set; and Pratap, which is a line of modern Indian clothes for men and women in strong colors and hardy cottons. Working with weavers from Varanasi on his unembellished silk saris, and with various government bodies to improve handspun hand-woven cotton and to create fine *pashmina* wool, he is striving to

Rajesh Pratap Singh

Rajesh Pratap Singh creation

help India become known internationally for world-class product. The brand has six stores in India and has recently opened one more at the Emporio Mall in New Delhi.

In Paris, his women's wear is sold from the renowned Colette, and his menswear from L'Eclaireur. He believes that cotton is a luxury in places like Paris, Tokyo, and in the U.K.

Ashish N. Soni[9]

Soni's debut at the New York Fashion Week in September 2005 was hailed as "one of New York's new discoveries."[10] His clothes are clean cut, stylish, and monochromatic. He has a unique signature all his own—its dissimilarity from any of his peers' work may be down to a childhood spent in Zambia and the Middle East. He is seen as a thinking woman's designer. His collections are consistently international, and his clothes remain definite style statements.

After graduating from the National Institute of Fashion Technology in 1991, he began an 18-month internship with Rohit Bal. He launched his own company, Ikos, in 1993, and for the first seven years, worked exclusively on men's collections under the "Ashish Soni" label. His first international success came in 2002 when he experienced a 98 percent sell-through in Selfridges in London.

Soni has clearly established himself among India's leading designers. Though simple, his signature lines add just a hint of embellishment to keep the Indian tone without sacrificing line and style.

In 2000, Ashish was chosen by the government to present an exclusive women's collection to commemorate the millennium celebrations of the temples at Khajuraho in Madhya Pradesh. In 2006, he was sponsored by the Indian government to represent the "Incredible India" campaign. He has interspersed his shows in India with a series of events abroad—international trade fairs such as Tranoi and London Fashion Week Exhibit, and has been showing at New York Fashion Week for the past three years.

Ashish N. Soni

Ashish N. Soni creation

His quest has been to always seek alternatives to the cold anonymity of mass production. The handmade feel and process are very important to him, and his fashion combines tradition and renewal. This experimentation with fabrics can be seen in his embroideries for the house of François Lesage in Paris.

Soni views luxury as "the country's cultural heritage. A growing number of affluent Indians are aspiring to luxury today that was earlier a privilege of a few."

In January 2008, he was appointed president of the Fashion Design Council of India.

Abraham and Thakore[11]

They are low-key designers, and don't do fashion weeks, but their inspiration and organic designs are undoubtedly influential. Among the first Indian designers to find success internationally, Abraham and Thakore are slowly finding buyers among Indians who have a highly developed sense of style. Their inspiration has always been Indian fabric in all of its infinite variety.

David Abraham and Rakesh Thakore met at NIT, and launched their Abraham & Thakore label in 1992. Their first success was to win an order from the Conran Shop in London and since then two-thirds of their creations have been sold overseas. This exposure to international markets has enabled them to keep pace with demands and changing tastes.

Their work has been exhibited at the Victoria & Albert Museum in London, at a British Council exhibition on contemporary Indian design, and at the Indira Gandhi National Center for the Arts in New Delhi. Each Abraham & Thakore collection has a modern voice, while simultaneously drawing on the rich traditional vocabulary of Indian design and craft. They also do furnishings that remain faithful to the influences and palettes of the main collection. Their work sells all across India, but their flagship stores are in Lodhi Colony (Delhi) and at The Courtyard (Bombay).

Abraham and Thakore

Abraham and Thakore creation

Narendra Kumar[12]

Understated almost to the point of reticence, Narendra Kumar's sense of style, clean lines, perfect finishing, and sculptural silhouettes have given him the status of a style guru, which is increased by his experience as fashion editor of *Elle* magazine.

After graduating from NIFT in 1988, he spent the next few years working with Tarun Tahiliani at Ensemble, cutting patterns for the store's Western range. In 1990, he started his own line of garments, which were heavily influenced in structure and tailoring by the styles of Thierry Mugler and Claude Montana.

Shahab Durazi[13]

The work of Shahab Durazi, commonly acknowledged as the Armani of India, is epitomized by careful attention to detail and understated classic features. Never one to pander to the media or to the demands of the fashion scene, he is another designer who does not do fashion weeks. Shahab lives by his own rules, and does everything himself, including cutting every garment in his collections.

As a student at the Fashion Institute of Technology in New York, Durazi won a number of awards for his designs. On his return to India in 1989, he began to create business suits, well-fitted jackets that would complement a woman's shape, and wearable Western lines. Renowned for the cut, style, and finish that have become his trademark, these sold in great numbers, and earned him the "Armani" appellation. Preferring to work with wool, linen, rayon, and crepe for his collections, Shahab believes that "luxury is defined by quality ... not only of the raw materials, but even of the thought process behind the design." Even though his work has undoubted mass appeal, he says, it is "truly targeted for a niche clientele with discerning tastes."

Narendra Kumar

Narendra Kumar creation

Shahab Durazi

Shahab Durazi creation

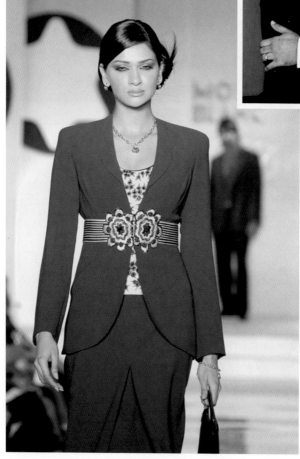

Wendell Rodricks[14]

Goan designer Wendell Rodricks, trained in Los Angeles and Paris, set a new minimalism style, which resulted in his "Guru of Minimalism" media tag. At a time when *couture* in India meant silk with embroidery, Rodricks led the way with his rural cotton weaves, eco dyes, and garment patterns favoring cut and color, never resorting to embroidery in his entire career.

Rodricks first came to pre-eminence through three shows in 1992, which earned him recognition as someone with creativity and talent. The following year, he created garments cutting ancient India's geometry. He moved the sarong and bikini to the mainstream, and created garments that set the first "resort style" in India way back in 1993.

Wendell Rodricks became the first Indian designer to be invited to the world's largent garment fair, IGEDO, in Dusseldorf in 1995. Since then, he has shown in Beijing, Dubai, New York, Paris, and many other cities worldwide, often representing the government of India.

Working out of a remote village in Goa, Rodricks has become a tour de force in India, and has firmly placed Goa on the fashion map. His clothes are worn by actresses (Ayesha Dharker, Rekha, Malaika Arora, Angelina Jolie, and Meg Ryan), supermodels (Helena Christensen, Iman, and India Hicks), writers (Sudhir Kakkar, Anil Dharker, Amitav Gosh, Bachi Karkaria, and Shobhaa De), and musicians (Shankar/Ehsan/Loy, Jose Feliciano, Remo, and Jean Luc Ponty).

NEO-REVIVALISTS

Younger designers who are reinventing ethnic India by giving contemporary spins to very traditional handicrafts, and appropriating Indian drapes and silhouettes for a Western audience. These talents have been influenced by Dries Van Noten and Marni.

Wendell Rodricks

Wendell Rodricks creation

Sabyasachi Mukherjee[15]

Sabyasachi Mukherjee is the blue-eyed boy of Indian fashion, the boy next door who made it big, both nationally and internationally. He showed his unique combination of Western and Indian silhouettes in New York for Fall/Winter and Spring/Summer 2008.

He graduated from NIFT, Kolkata, in 1999 with a clutch of awards, and launched his own label that same year. A stint with design houses in London courtesy of a *Femina*/British Council award gave him an insight into what he needed to become a global player. A 2001 internship with Georgina Von Etzdorf in England honed his international perspective, and in 2003 he won the grand award at the Mercedes New Asia Fashion Week in Singapore. In 2004, he participated at shows in Kuala Lumpur and Miami, and took his collection, *The Frog Princess*, to Milan Fashion Week, where London *Vogue* reportedly called his collection "the look of the season." Since 2004, Mukherjee has also designed for cinema.

Since early 2005, he has been very successful commercially, with Browns in London and a range of Indian stores including Carma and Ogaan in Delhi, Melange and Ensemble in Bombay, Espee and Intrigue in Kolkata, and Oorja and Origins in Hyderabad selling his creations. The success of his mainly vintage-look clothes internationally he attributes to "the nostalgia factor"—a need "to escape into a slower world, which is the ultimate luxury money can buy."

Anamika Khanna[16]

Anamika Khanna is a self-taught designer who came to prominence by winning the Damania Fashion Award in 1995. Her garments are understated, yet fashionable and classy. Trousseau wear is her area of specialization, and she creates her own fabric, a mix of sheer silk, georgette, and cotton to achieve a shimmering effect. The embellishments she uses are never overpowering, and her designs are earthy and eco-friendly.

Sabyasachi Mukherjee

Sabyasachi Mukherjee creation

Anamika Khanna

Anamika Khanna creation

She created her own label Ana-Mika in 2004 which is owned by the UK company Boho London. The label is now available in over 300 specialty stores in the UK, the US, Europe, and the Middle East. In India, she retails at Ensemble, Ogaan, and Ffolio amongst others.

She showed in Paris for Spring/Summer 2008, and has several major design awards and nominations under her belt.

Anupama Dayal[17]

Anupama Dayal's work includes vegetable dyes and layered and handicraft-oriented collections. Known primarily outside India (she sells from 26 stores across Europe, Australia, and Asia, and has only one store in the U.S. for the time being, but is working on a better presence in that market), her brand found Indian recognition only after she decided to participate at the Lakmé Fashion Week in Mumbai in March 2006.

Dayal is a graduate of the IIM, and has never felt that she required formal design training, having worked with her mother, a textile designer and artist. In 2004, she launched her own label (Anupamaa) of high-fashion women's wear, in which, she says, she sets out "to achieve an international look with an Indian soul." Indian colors are a very definite part of her color themes, and, through combining East and West, she manages to mix the modern with the forgotten. The mix of craft with print on sensuous silk in her 2007 collection, for example, made for some interesting clothes. Anupama is available in India at Melange, Ensemble, Ogaan, Ffolio, and Evoluzione. In April 2008, she participated in the Australian Fashion Week, where the response was overwhelming. Among others, Belinda Seper, Australia's leading fashion retailer for brands such as Lanvin, Stella McCartney, and Marni, fell in love with the line, and made an important order for her Belinda stores, present in several Australian cities.

Anupama Dayal

Anupama Dayal creation

MODERN INDIA: 1. STREET INFLUENCED; 2. CONTEMPORARY INDO-WESTERN

1. Channeling street influences, multicultural mythologies, popular cinema (Bollywood), and changing identities, these young designers bring freshness, innovation, and wit to their collections. It certainly helps that this group is not afraid to laugh at India "contradictions."
2. Using predominantly Western designs with a modern Indian touch. Silhouettes are flexible. For instance, an A-line tunic can be worn as a dress, or can also be worn with traditional Indian trousers to make it look entirely Indian.

MODERN INDIA (1)

Manish Arora[18]

Known as a maverick, Manish Arora draws inspiration from Indian music and the people around him. He has made color, texture, and form the subject matter of his expression in fashion.

After graduating from NIFT in 1994, he launched his eponymous label in 1997, and started retailing in India. In 2000, he represented India at the Hong Kong Fashion Week, and participated in the first Fashion Week in Delhi. The following year, he launched his Fish Fry label, and opened his first flagship store in Delhi at Lodhi Colony.

He had a successful debut at the London Fashion Week in September 2005, where he continued to show for four consecutive seasons. His label stocked at more than 75 stores internationally, including Harrods, Dover Street Market, Maria Luisa, and a franchise store in Villa Moda, Kuwait. Domestically, his label retails from five flagship stores in India—in Delhi and Bombay. The Fish Fry for Reebok line retails through select Reebok outlets and two Fish Fry for Reebok stores in the Garden of Five Senses and Select Citywalk, both in Delhi.

Manish Arora

Manish Arora creation

His aim, he says, "is to focus on Indian techniques, use traditional Indian embroidery, techniques, but with a twist...I am constantly looking to India for inspiration, and seeing it everywhere. I will never be sick of India."

Manish Arora's brand extensions are many and varied: high-end fashion shoes for Reebok; recently launched Manish Arora Eyewear; a signature makeup range for MAC cosmetics, and watches for Swatch; to name but a few. He has been showing on schedule at Paris Fashion Week since Spring/Summer 2008.

Gaurav Gupta[19]

His mirror image label (Gaurav Gupta/atpuG varuaG) says a lot about his ability to see things differently and to create impact.

Since graduating from NIFT, Delhi, in 2000 and Central Saint Martins College of Art & Design, London, in 2003, he has proved to be a designer who walks his own path. At the Rome *Couture* Fashion Week in 2003, he won the Award for Experimentation and Design. His experience includes working with well-known labels such as Hussein Chalayan, Stella McCartney, and Vivienne Westwood.

Gupta's designs question convention and the contradictions of existence. On returning to India in 2005, for example, his presence at Fashion Week in Delhi had the press proclaiming him the new hope of the Indian fashion scene. Experimentation with textiles, innovative pattern cutting, and sculptural draping are the signature features of his label.

Aki Narula[20]

Aki Narula has established himself as a young person's designer and found a dedicated clientele in Bollywood. His first show, with Mélange at the Opera House in Bombay, got him noticed, and by early 1997, his label was selling from diverse stores across India. Moving from Kolkata to Delhi, he set up a workshop with 25 staff, and by 2001, he was supplying Selfridges in London as part of its Bollywood selection. His participation in the 2002 Lakmé India

Gaurav Gupta

Gaurav Gupta creation

Aki Narula

Aki Narula creation

Fashion Week led to an assignment to design costumes for Mira Nair's film *Monsoon Wedding*, and he is now in constant demand to work on other such assignments.

Since 2002, Narula has been design director at the Sheetal Design Studio, which requires him to split his time between Mumbai and Delhi. His diverse lines for men and women sell from Ensemble (Delhi, Mumbai), the now defunct 1 MG Road, Grasshopper, Ogaan (Delhi, Kolkata), Mélange (Mumbai), Ffolio (Bangalore), Cinnamon (Bangalore), Sosas (Goa), Kali (Kolkata), and Zingra in Cannes and St. Tropez.

Nandita Basu[21]

At India Fashion Week in 2006, in conjunction with husband and fellow designer Abhishek Gupta, Nandita Basu launched Fightercock, a new casual streetwear brand. Their first signature store opened in New Delhi in February 2007.

As a designer, Basu believes in minimalism and subtlety, using traditional art and craft techniques in a modern manner. Her trademark techniques include 3D cutout textures, leather strips, and embroidery, with a focus lies on cutting and detailing.

Though generally reluctant to talk about her work, Basu has said that she is confident of being able to take on the increasing competition from international brands coming into India because she feels "we have a very good product, where we are giving the customer as much as they would get from a foreign brand."

MODERN INDIA (2)

Namrata Joshipura[22]

Graduating from NIFT, she launched her self-titled Namrata Joshipura label in 1996. Ensemble and Carma in Delhi and Zenon in Kolkata sold her creations through the early years, and she was selected

Nandita Basu

Nandita Basu creation

Namrata Joshipura

Namrata Joshipura creation

to represent India at the Hong Kong Fashion Week in 1999, where she won second prize at the Asia Pacific Young Designers Show.

The following year, she was the first Indian designer to be selected to participate in the World Young Designers' Award Ceremony at the London Fashion Week, and later presented her collection at the Indian Show in Sao Paolo, Brazil. Joshipura also designed the costumes for the award winning Indo-German film *Dance of the Wind*. In 2000, she moved to the U.S., where she now sells from well-known stores, including Neiman Marcus, Henri Bendel, and Anthropologie. She started showing at the Fashion Week in India in 2004, and currently sells to Evoluzione (Chennai), Elahe (Hyderabad), and Ensemble (Mumbai).

Her clothing line is also sold at high-end stores in Japan—Loveless and Beams to name a couple, Biffy in Italy, and H. Lorenzo in Los Angeles. She launched her flagship store at The Crescent in New Delhi in 2006, and opened her second store in Mumbai in June 2008. Her design philosophy is founded in a luxury minimalism, where the fabric functions as an important design element. She has a vision of an emerging global aesthetic, and her clothing translates easily across geographical boundaries.

Rohit Gandhi and Rahul Khanna of Cue[23]

Rohit Gandhi and Rahul Khanna began working as a team in 1995 and launched their H2O label for men's shirts in 1997. In 2000, they took part in the first India Fashion Week, where their ready-to-wear line gained considerable attention. They have now taken part in eight Fashion Weeks and were voted the best menswear designers for 2006. They also run a successful art gallery, Palette, which showcases established and young contemporary artists.

Their inspiration for their designs come from minimalism, linear structures, geometrical lines, mosaics, wallpaper, and even vibrant contemporary art, and their work is now available at five

Rohit and Rahul

Rohit and Rahul creation

standalone stores in Delhi, Mumbai, Bangalore, and Kolkata. Coconut, Aza (Mumbai), Evoluzione (Madras), CIMA (Kolkata), Ensemble (Mumbai, Delhi), Elahe (Hyderabad), Hot Pink (Jaipur), ITC Ltd., Kimaya (Delhi, Mumbai), Kali (Kolkata), and Chamomile (Delhi) also carry their work. Overseas retailers include Sun Motoyama (Japan), Sanskriti (Hong Kong), Flower for You (Germany), Indiva (Canada), Home Store (Turkey), and Moda In, Zinia (Dubai).

Varun Bahl[24]

Like most good designers who have succumbed to the passion, Varun Bahl too dreamed of making clothes as a child. His ability to put together a good look was so clear that, while still a toddler, he often took the liberty of choosing what his mother should wear. And more often than not, the look worked dramatically. When he grew old enough to be allowed to work with his family's export company, 17-year-old Varun, alongside his brothers, helped execute designs for brands such as Kenzo, Armani, Lacroix's Bazaar, and Jeans. At the same time, he completed an evening course at NIFT to gain a formal edge to his knowledge.

In 2003, he applied and procured a stall in Inside White, an exhibition that is a sideshow at Milan Fashion Week. Varun showcased his Spring/Summer 2003 collection at Inside White in Italy. Each season White, a select showcase of talented designers, introduces a select group of new designers to the international fashion fraternity. It was here that a tough jury of top 10 design stores of Italy such as Tessa Bit, Sugar, Penelope, and Luisa Via Roma, to name a few, voted Varun Bahl's collection the best of season from among 20 competing designers from different countries. By the end of the exhibition, on the third day, he had booked orders from 48 of Italy's top fashion stores as well as some from Spain. It was to get him to believe that

Varun Bahl

Varun Bahl creation

Italy was his ultimate Mecca, and he does admit that in a few years from now, he could relocate to that country.

Sonam Dubal[25]

Sonam Dubal's style is elegant and understated, and echoes his Sikkimese and Buddhist heritage. After graduating from NIFT in 1990, Dubal's early experience included a year working with Rohit Khosla. In 1999, he launched the Sanskar label, and began selling from Ogaan in Delhi.

His early creations depended on old brocades redyed and combined with silk textiles, cut into modern silhouettes that produced old-world charm. This brought him to international attention when an Oxford University academic used his work in her lectures on recycled textiles. In 2002, he took his collection based on Tibetan textiles to Fashion Week in Singapore, to great acclaim.

After his participation in the Lakmé India Fashion Week in 2003, his collection was picked up by L'Eclaireur of Paris. His pan-Asian styles also appealed to the English market and his collections were offered at Tashi in London in 2003, 2004, and 2005.

Dubal designs for an older, well-traveled woman, and his clothes have an appeal that transcends nationality or region. Since 2005, his work has broken into the notoriously difficult Japanese market, and continues to receive plaudits in Singapore. In 2006, he participated in the Australian Fashion Week, and this exposure led to orders from Naseema At Home in Melbourne. In both 2006 and 2007, he showed at Lakmé in Mumbai, and the diversity of perspective on local traditions and textiles resulted in buys from both Arida in Sydney and Les Nomades in Geneva.

By combining Eastern thought and sophistication with Western aesthetics through a play of Indian textiles, printing, and embroidery, he has managed to develop a unique individual style, both simple and universal in its appeal.

Sonam Dubal

Sonam Dubal creation

Anand Kabra[26]

Anand Kabra claims to be Hyderabad's only true young designer. Through his choice of color and fabric, there is a definite Indian sensibility, though his cuts are smart and Western.

Kabra was trained at the London School of Fashion, returning to India in 1996. The following year he launched his own label. Kabra designs for women who are not confined to a predictable style statement or trend, but who are products of a global world, where influences merge and blend.

His early forays into Bombay Fashion Week showed that he was capable of matching market needs while experimenting with art deco themes using home-grown organic fabrics and treatments. His move away from "traditional" revealed a free spirit willing to throw off the shackles of conventional craft techniques.

Anand Kabra currently sells from Aza (Mumbai), Ogaan (Delhi), and Maiah (Hyderabad).

Payal Jain[27]

A summa-cum-laude graduate from the Fashion Institute of Design and Merchandising in San Francisco, Payal Jain set up her eponymous studio in 1993. She has honed her skills working with *couturiers* in the U.S. and Europe.

A strong foundation of her designs is a neo-classical aesthetic coupled with an unparalleled standard of perfection in production. Her collections are soft and sophisticated, with a structured Western body and a strong Indian soul, reviving traditional Indian crafts and textiles in a contemporary context. Jain has shown at India Fashion Week since 2001, and has been showcased in New York, Moscow, Toronto, and many other cities.

In addition to her *couture* line, Jain has a diffusion line that she sells from several cities in India as well as exports to the U.S., the

Anand Kabra

Anand Kabra creation

Payal Jain

Payal Jain creation

U.K., Southeast Asia, the Middle East, and Europe from exclusive reputed stores and boutiques. She also designs ensembles for prestigious groups such as Hyatt, Shangri-La, Four Seasons, Aman resorts, Westin, and many more for their staff across the globe. She believes in working with social causes through her work, as a small effort to make the world a better place to live in.

Gauri and Nainika Karan[28]

Graduates of NIFT, New Delhi, the Karan sisters—Gauri and Nainika—grew up on a diet of their parents' favorite Broadway shows and old Hollywood movies, which may account for their fascination with fine-flowing lines. They made their debut at the India Fashion Week 2004, and are completely involved with their designer label, Magnetic Rag, which sells from designer stores across India, including Amara in Mumbai.

Rina Dhaka[29]

A graduate of NIFT, Rina Dhaka honed her skills with Intercraft and with designer Evan Grandhal. Her early work included designs for up-and-coming fashion houses such as Mutiny and Ensemble. She also clothed the contestants for a round of the Miss India contest, where her work caught the attention of Rohit Khosla. It was his appreciation that encouraged her to follow her ideas and style.

Dhaka believes that women should be able to dress as they wish, and offers them enough to choose from in Western wear, her forte. Her fabrics range from chiffons to silks, satins, and mesh lycra, and match the sensual picture she creates with her collections. Her clients include Indian society women with a dash of daring, as well as Naomi Campbell and Uma Thurman. Her work has been featured in international fashion magazines *Vogue* and *Elle*, and she believes that India doesn't lag in any respect. She maintains that

Gauri and Nainika Karan

Gauri and Nainika creation

Rina Dhaka

Rina Dhaka creation

Indian clothes are a tradition to be admired and carried forward into her Western lines. She doesn't employ assistants and creates each garment herself.

Monisha Jaising[30]

Monisha Jaising creates clothing for Indian women who are progressive and global, yet proud of their culture. Jaising started out as a designer-cum-exporter in 1989, and her clothes, though cut impeccably and international in appeal, have an element of "bling," which has earned her a reputation as the "princess of bohemian luxe."

Her collections are mainly for resortwear, and her signature style includes the *kurti*, which she claims has become an international garment, along with jeans and white shirts.

A student of fashion design in the London branch of the American College for Applied Arts, and of the history of art at the Royal College of Arts in London, Jaising calls herself a "garment manufacturer." For the moment, she too works without assistants, though this may change given the demand for her work, which sells from Scoop in New York, Harrod's in London, Mumbai Se in Singapore, Dubai, and Mauritius, Indiva in Toronto, and Tabla in Hong Kong.

Prashant Verma[31]

A series of training stints with the fashion houses of Alexander McQueen, John Galliano, Philip Treacy, and Christian Dior, and in the domestic market have only made Verma more determined to be his own man. Inspired by "great personalities in history—Jawaharlal Nehru, Martin Luther King, Alexander the Great...," Prashant Verma says that his aim is "to contribute to the treasure that their lives created."

To this end, this NIFT graduate imbues all of his creations with the fighting spirit embodied by his idols. His 2007 collection for

Monisha Jaising

Monisha Jaising creation

Prashant Verma

Prashant Verma creation

Fashion Week incorporated both Picasso and Marlene Dietrich, who challenged the rules of their respective artistic communities.

His collection in March 2008 centered round rage, as an expression of youth.

He sees himself as a brand veering toward luxury: "My products do not fit into the day-to-day struggles of life; they are part of the lives of the people whose presence makes the common man's life richer." His severely constructed, sharply body-contouring, dramatically voluminous creations sell from Ogaan, Maya, and Samsaara, as well as from his own flagship store in Delhi.

SOFT FASHION (AND UPCOMING)

Beyond handicraft and trends of the season, these designers worry a lot about the environment and ecology, promote self-sustaining business in fashion, and have eco-friendliness wound tightly in their design ideology. Their work is usually devoid of all superficial embellishments, and relies instead on techniques they themselves have developed to add quirky detailing or subtle surface texturing. They are great believers in the "imperfection of the human hand," which is an intrinsic part of all handmade embellishment and embroidery.

Anshu Arora[32]

Anshu Arora is a designer who lives and works by her own rules. Her sense of color is powerful, her forms fluid and easy; her work holds together without the aid of fasteners and metal.

After her graduation from NIFT in 1997, she launched her own company, "A Small Shop" and the vibrancy of creations appealed to the young and set her apart from her contemporaries. In 2002, she extended the shop to other cities as shop-in-shops and won *Images*

Anshu Arora

Anshu Arora creation

magazine's Most Admired Young Designer of the Year award at the Lakmé India Fashion Week. Her show brought her to the attention of Selfridges, Ogaan, Cinnamon, Grasshopper, and Kimaya.

In 2006, after a two-year hiatus, her origami-inspired ensembles for Lakmé India Fashion Week were hailed for their innovative design and construction. She then opened a flagship store—"Small Shop"—in Bangalore, and was selected to showcase her work at the Singapore Fashion Festival in March 2007.

Kiran Uttam Ghosh[33]

Kiran Uttam Ghosh uses a variety of handicrafts, with slouchy silhouettes influenced by Dries Van Noten and Marni.

In 1993, Kiran Uttam Ghosh graduated top of her class in fashion design at Sophia College. The following year, she went to London to learn the practical aspects of designing garments with Jasper Conran. In 1995, she approached Ogaan with a collection of garments, but was told that they were too bright for the boutique. She was given permission to leave them there while she went shopping, and when she returned to collect them an hour later, four had been sold. By the next day, the entire collection had sold.

That was the beginning, and before long, Ogaan and Ffolio in Bangalore, Elahe in Hyderabad, and Ensemble in Bombay were selling her clothes. She participated in the first India Fashion Week in 2000, and has been a regular contributor since. She now sells from 18 stores across the country, and in eight countries overseas. In 2001 and 2003, she showed at the Singapore Fashion Week, and in 2007 was invited to the Rome *Couture* Week.

Ghosh has a dedicated clientele across India for her three lines—trousseau, diffusion and ready-to-wear—and works with flowing fabrics such as chiffon and georgette, and amalgamates them with soft linens and cottons. She has plans to launch a premium handbag line in the near future.

Kiran Uttam Ghosh

Kiran Uttam Ghosh creation

Nachiket Barve[34]

Nachiket Barve launched his eponymous label at Lakmé Fashion Week 2007 with a highly acclaimed debut collection, "*Couture* Allure." A postgraduate student at the National Institute of Design, Ahmedabad, he studied at Ecole Nationale Supérieure des Arts Décoratifs (ENSAD) in Paris, and trained with Michael Kors at Celine, a part of the LVMH luxury conglomerate. He has also worked with Abu Jani, Sandeep Khosla, and textile designer Neeru Kumar.

His label aims to express luxury in a contemporary, fresh, and innovative way. He creates his own textiles to bring about an amalgamation of intricate techniques and clean streamlined silhouettes. While his range has an international look, the elements that go into making it are undoubtedly Indian.

Dev R Nil[35]

This collaboration between Kolkata designers Debarghya Bairagi (Dev) and Navonil Das (Nil) came to public attention at the Lakme Fashion Week in 2005, where their clothes were hailed as being off the beaten track. They went on to win the *Elle* magazine Style Awards in 2006 for their debut collection, and were labeled the "Wonder Boys of India."

Dev is a commerce graduate from St. Xavier's in Kolkata. He studied fashion at NIFD Kolkata, and was a "Style File Young Masters" finalist in 2004. Dev is considered to be "the creative one" of the pair whereas Nil is "the entrepreneur" who studied fashion at the Canberra Institute of Technology, Australia, and interned under Akira Isogawa, which helped him understand the importance of art in fashion. At their studio in Kolkata, they have skilfully turned fashion designing to an art form, where it has become a viable business venture.

Nachiket Barve

Nachiket Barve creation

Debarghya Bairagi and Navonil
Das (Dev R Nil)

Dev R Nil creation

Last year, IMG and Lakmé chose them to show at the Rosemount Australian Fashion Week (RAFW) in Australia in April. At the RAFW, they launched their Resort 2007/08 collection, which focused on the relaxed form of fashion with a controlled bright color palette and a breathtaking array of surface texturing, with simple yet effective silhouettes. Their collection at RAFW included tunics and evening gowns, some done with traditional block-printing techniques to create textures, and some depicting the influences of indigenous developed textiles like metallic yarns woven with silk. Their innovation in textiles, surface texturing, and cuts has both national and international buyers.

For their Spring/Summer 2008 collection, designer duo Dev R Nil were inspired by the acclaimed Taiwanese filmmaker Wong Kar Wai and one of his earlier films, *Happy Together*. The collection comprised yellows, pinks, greens, and even dark brown. Flowing fabrics such as cotton voiles, organic cotton, and silk organza with floral prints completed the look. The designers also incorporated satin stripes, metallic, ribbed jerseys, and tie-dyed visuals.

They have now adapted a true corporate model where they are getting foreign investors to help them take the business to the next level. With the acquired funds, they are now in the process of creating separate units catering to separate categories such as traditional, Western, and export markets. Recently, they launched their swimwear collection in Kolkata and at the Lakmé Fashion Week, they launched their menswear line. A foray into the bridalwear market is also on the cards.

Varun Sardana[36]

A definite product of the evolution in Indian fashion, Varun Sardana brings an awakened sensibility and degree of professionalism needed to propel the industry onward and upward. He believes that Indian clothes need to be edgy, experimental in form and style, with a feel

Varun Sardana

Varun Sardana creation

of being created with personal detailing, and a contemporary take on what heritage has to offer.

Sardana's early efforts met with success. Soon after his graduation from NIFT in 2003, and after an apprenticeship with Varun Bahl, he launched his own label in August 2004 just after winning the Bijenkorf Fashion Design Award in Amsterdam. This led him to develop a Spring/Summer 2005 collection for Bijenkorf, the largest chain of stores in the Netherlands.

With acumen not common in creative fields, Varun waited before entering the public eye, "It is comfortable to work for yourself at your own pace, but once you do a fashion week, one is expected to deliver every few months and be better or at least consistent," he explains. Yet when invited by the Fashion Design Council of India (FDCI) to be part of Hi-5 of young first-timers at Fashion Week, he entered the fray on an impulse.

He is inspired by the Belgian designers, who combine craft with caring, and Indian talents such as Sabyasachi and Anamika Khanna, who have "contemporized heritage." He believes he has potential to make the international grade, not only because he is accepted more easily by the Western client who is open to his experimentations with form and detailing, and his way of using embroidery, but also because his creations appeal to a mindset rather than to a demographic. His Indian line is classic, but his Western clothes, mostly diffusion in price point and appeal, are the result of holistic thinking; nothing is incidental, everything is thought out and falls into place.

Samant Chauhan[37]

Coming to NIFT, hailing as he did from a center of raw silk, Bhagalpur, in Bihar, it was only natural that Samant Chauhan responded to his calling in Indian textile tradition as a subject. This was further stoked by the comparative ignorance of many seasoned players in the fashion industry about the fabric that was part of his roots.

Samant Chauhan

Samant Chauhan creation

His research on Bhagalpur silk included ways to contemporize it, to experiment with its feasibility in knitting and in the washes, the structure of the silk, and how it would lend itself to the silhouettes he had in mind. Hand knitting it to prevent the slough and breakage that are inherent in raw silk yarns, he also came to mix and match it with different yarns.

His early success at being selected for Singapore Fashion Week and London Fashion Week gave him enough exposure to understand "what the Western market wants." He also managed second time round at Fashion Week to get a slew of orders, a confirmation for him that he was on the right track. "I do think I will go far," he says. "I do not want to become a huge label and sell everywhere, but to be big enough to be bought and understood by those who understand what I am doing."

His jackets in pure silk sell at between 4,000 and 40,000 rupees, and his clientele includes stores like Tsum in Moscow, Golf & Co. in Israel, Sigassis in Singapore, Leanard & Marvin in New York, Moksha for Earth in Portland in the U.S., Tashi, Boho London, and R.C.K.C. in London. He has his own flagship store, Samant Chauhan, in New Delhi, and is distributed in 20 other multidesigner stores including Ogaan, Elahe, and Fuel.

In the immediate future, he plans to take his eco-friendly experiments a bit further, combining knit silk with Lurex,[38] with metallic feel, and using junk jewelry to embellish silk and leather. Inspired by Abraham and Thakore, John Galliano, and Jean-Paul Gaultier, he hopes that even when he spawns a brood of imitators, his style and his fabric, "which will not be like any other designer's," will stand out and be instantly recognizable.

NOTES

1. In correspondence with the authors, May 7, 2008.
2. Tarun Tahiliani interview, July 2007; <www.taruntahiliani.com>.
3. Rohit Bal interview, July 2007; <www.rohitbal.com>.

4. Time 1996, Special Report on India, March 25.
5. J.J. Valaya interview, June 2007; <www.valaya.com>.
6. Ritu Kumar interview, March 2007 and May 2009; <www.ritukumar.com>.
7. Abu Jani and Sandeep Khosla interview, August 2008; <www.abusandeep.com>.
8. Rajesh Pratap Singh interview, February 2008; <www.pratap.es>.
9. Ashish N. Soni interview, July 2007; <www.ashishsoni.com>.
10. Suzy Menkes 2005, "Furstenberg's 'La Dolce Vita'", *International Herald Tribune*, September 12.
11. Abraham and Thakore interview, July 2007; <www.abrahamandthakore.com>.
12. Narendra Kumar, <www.narendrakumarfashion.com>.
13. Shahab Durazi, <www.shahabdurazi.in>.
14. Wendell Rodricks, <www.wendellrodricks.com>.
15. Savyasachi Mukherjee interview, June 2007; <www.sabyasachi.com>.
16. Anamika Khanna, <http://ana-mika.com/>.
17. Anupama Dayal, <www.anupamaa.com>.
18. Manish Arora interview, May 2007; <www.manisharora.ws>.
19. Gaurav Gupta interview, October 2007; <www.gauravguptastudio.com>.
20. Aki Narula interview, July 2007.
21. Nandita Basu interview, July 2007.
22. Namrata Joshipura, <www.joshipura.com>.
23. Rohit Gandhi and Rahul Khanna of Cue, <www.h2ocue.com>.
24. Varun Bahl interview, December 2006.
25. Sonam Dubal interview, February 2008; <www.sonamdubal.com>.
26. Anand Kabra, <www.anandkabra.com>.
27. Payal Jain, <www.payaljain.com>.
28. Gauri and Nainkia Karan, <www.gauriandnainika.com>.
29. Rina Dhaka interview, July 2007.
30. Monisha Jaising, <www.monicajaisingh.com>.
31. Prashant Verma, <www.prashantverma.co.in>.
32. Anshu Arora interview, February 2008.
33. Kiram Uttam Ghosh interview, June 2007; <www.kiranuttamghosh.com>.
34. Nachiket Barve, <www.nachiketbarvedesign.com>.
35. Dev R. Nil interview, July 2007.
36. Varun Sardana, <www.varunsardana.com>.
37. Samant Chauhan, <http://samantchauhan.net>.
38. This is the brand name for a type of yarn with a metallic appearance, and it may also refer to the cloth created with the yarn.

PART V
CONCLUSION

CHAPTER 13
Where Are Indian Luxury and Fashion Going?

In his 1979 book *The Culture of Narcissism*, the American author Christopher Lasch wrote that the new luxurist "does not accumulate goods and provisions against the future, in the manner of the acquisitive individualist of 19th Century political economy, but demands immediate gratification and lives in a state of restless, perpetually unsatisfied desire." While this may help to throw some light on the triggers driving India's luxury boom, one thing is certain: luxury or the appreciation of the finer things of life isn't new at all (see chapter 2). Throughout its civilization, India has been a showcase for unprecedented levels of refinement, as the 2007 exposition at the Galeries Nationales du Grand-Palais in Paris revealed to us.

This spectacular exhibit of the Gupta era (320–450 A.D.), as described in the gallery's remarkable brochure:

> ... marked the high point of Indian civilization. During this golden age, when religious thinking, sciences, literature and the theatre flourished, art reached an unprecedented level of refinement and perfection; aesthetic canons and iconographic models developed during the Gupta period would endure through the centuries, and their influence would spread into the art of Nepal, of South East Asia and even of Central Asia, while goods manufactured out of India reached even the Roman Empire.

There is a story in the public domain that is ascribed to the elder statesman Pliny. Apparently, Emperor Claudius publicly scolded his daughter for wearing so little clothing on her person, while she was fully clad in India-made muslin clothing (showing the high degree of skill in the textile industry). We state this tongue firmly in cheek, but Roman beauties, apparently decked in even seven folds of muslin, were used to parading themselves on the highways of Rome, and were later considered to be negatively affecting Roman society's morals. The word "muslin" was derived from the name of the city of its origin, Mosul, in Iraq, and through the centuries when India became known as the home of exotic muslins, two Indian cities, namely Masulipatnam in south India and Dhaka in Bengal, became famous for weaving this cloth. It was so popular that the import of Indian textiles had to be banned by Roman Senate. The ban on imports was necessary also because of the balance of payment crisis. It resulted in a favorable trade balance for India, with a stable gold currency for the Kushana Empire.

To satisfy the Roman world's insatiable appetite for luxury goods, Western trade with the East grew immensely in the first two centuries A.D. But because such Roman exports as wool, linen, glass, and metalware to the East did not match in value Rome's imports of silk, spices, perfumes, gems, and other luxuries, the West suffered seriously from an adverse balance of trade. Gold and silver had to be continually exported to Asia. Late in the first century A.D. Pliny estimated that India, China, and Arabia drained away annually at least 100 million sesterces[1] (perhaps US$10 million), declaring: "That is the sum which our luxuries and our women cost us." The discovery of large hoards of Roman coins in India supports Pliny's statement. This serious drain was one of the factors in the general economic decline of the Roman world in the third century A.D.[2]

The point of this little detour is only to reiterate that arguably in the history of textiles, there is perhaps nothing that matches the famous Dhaka muslin. In 1875, when Edward VII, the then Prince of Wales, came to Bengal, Sir Abdul Gani of Dhaka ordered 30 yards of the most superior muslin as a gift to the prince. One yard of this fabric weighed barely a third of an ounce! It is said that a yard of fabric could fit through a ring meant for the little finger because of its fineness. Their weave was so fine that the Egyptian pharaohs used them for wrapping mummies. Even today, fine muslin, known to the locals as *mul-mul*, is the bulwark of many of India's fashion designers' collections, particularly for spring/summer celebrations.

In 2006, Rohit Bal was inspired by the royal courts of Rajasthan during the Mogul rule when he created his Evening Chic collection. Trying to innovate and leave aside the stereotypical image of the Indian bride, he was minimalistic with the embroidery, yet had added bright shades of color and gold and silver leaf printing to reproduce the festive mood that so categorizes weddings. The collection was: "[B]asic elements of *gota* in different forms like stripes, *lehriyas,* and *jharokas.* The fabrics used for constructing garments include muslin, *chanderi,* and Banarsi cutwork, which are quite apt for any wedding."[3]

The irony is that in spite of its luxury heritage, to date there are no globally recognized luxury brands to come out of India. The country is now on the world stage, and the time is ripe for an authentic India-influenced luxury lifestyle brand—an Indian version of Shanghai Tang. On the basis of our research for this book, we would say that a series of converging factors bode well for global fashion and luxury brands in India.

Those brands that have already established a presence in Delhi and Mumbai—the likes of Ermenegildo Zegna, Tag Heuer, Montblanc, Louis Vuitton, Hermès, and Giorgio Armani—have planned for expansion into secondary markets such as Bangalore, Hyderabad, and Kolkata. These are the strongholds for the booming Indian IT industry and a new population of successful and wealthy Indians who will spend on luxury, international or not. However, at present, it is the foreign brands that are being bolstered by the growing number of magazines and newspapers that devote significant space to new fashion looks and trendsetting celebrity styles.

With the increasing number of wealthy Indians, there will be a stronger focus on the arts. While global art purchases continue to reach extraordinary levels, local creations by Indian artists will also continue to appreciate and break records, as happened in 2005 when

Tyeb Metha's *Mahisasura* became the first Indian painting to pass the million-dollar mark when it sold for US$1.7 million. Purchasers are predominately wealthy Indians, but there will be increasing interest from Western and Asian art collectors who recognize the appreciation value to be gained from Indian art.

Natural, home-grown, product extensions will be available in the jewelry, health and beauty, home décor, and Western fashion sectors. Home décor will expand enormously, as home ownership becomes more pervasive. Products such as hand-embroidered silk and cotton bedding, handcrafted furnishings, and art objects reflecting the ancient techniques and traditions of generations past will flourish. As we saw earlier, many of these techniques have been revived in recent years, and this trend will continue and will help sustain highly skilled crafts people in their unique culture.

Rather than simply viewing India as a source of low-cost labor, luxury brands will use Indian craftsmanship. One example is Donna Karan's Urban Zen, a "breakthrough lifestyle brand inspired by the cultures of the world." There is also likely to be an increasing number of collaborations between Indian designers and strong global brands, such as we saw with fashion designer Neeru Kumar's recent invitation to create a line for the cult Japanese brand Muji.

Health and beauty is a key category for India to compete in on a global level. With the world becoming increasingly focused on alternative, holistic, non-Western medicines, India's long heritage of Ayurvedic treatments, yoga, and meditation should come to the fore and be marketed on a global basis.

With its renowned prowess in state-of-the-art high-tech, there is vast untapped potential for international and local brands to use the e-commerce shopping format for fashion and luxury goods. In the meantime, the influx of global companies will result in a weeding out of the weaker local entities. Others, however, will learn quickly how to compete and adapt into brands that may achieve international status.

Major local luxury players will emerge *à la* Bernard Arnault. If Darshan Mehta, for example, maintains the current momentum at Reliance Brands, he will become a force to be reckoned with. Acquisitions will proliferate, particularly in the private-equity sector, with an increasing number of marriages of foreign and domestic companies like that between Louis Vuitton and Hidesign. Jewelry companies may well be the next target of the big players, giving them market entry and a source both of stones and handicraft skills, not to mention access to a client base of families who have been buying their jewelry from the same source for generations. The same process could well apply also in other handicraft areas such as embroidery.

For the Indians themselves, for whom value for money will remain engrained in the psyche, jewelry will remain an investment buy, but the outward representation of status that it confers will feed the business of the foreign brands.

Bollywood will remain a key influence, and adulation of its stars and what they wear will continue to have an impact on the Indian consumer.

Commentaries abound in the media and on a multiplicity of fashion websites offering Bollywood-inspired clothes. Stakeholders are waking up to the business opportunities these are presenting, and many designers are now joining with companies or movie stars to cash in on the retail potential.

The influence of films in India should never be underestimated. Celluloid fashion has long dictated common taste for a large section of fans. The role of the designers became increasingly prominent when they began creating the "look" for particular stars or for an entire film. A great deal of credit for this goes to people such as Manish Malhotra, Karan Johar, Abu Jani, Sandeep Khosla, and Sabyasachi, as film-makers seek to create the "right look" for their work. Being associated with the stars in this way enables the designers to raise the equity in their main business.

BEING INDIAN AND BUYING INDIAN

The arrival of the international brands will undoubtedly inspire and motivate local Indian talent to sign up with these brands until they have acquired the necessary skills and experience to apply their know-how with local firms. This will serve to spur on a new generation of entrepreneurs. The tradition and heritage of being Indian and buying Indian are things the major brands may be overlooking, and locally produced goods will be so much more "reasonably priced" that buying "localikes" may take a bite ant of the big brands' business.

Another drawback to the mass awareness of fashion and luxury brands is the natural extension of counterfeiters producing replicas of the iconic designs for which the luxury brands are known. Counterfeit goods have a way of finding their way into many an emerging market, and not just for tourists. Locals may prefer them to the originals. The heritage brands will work with the government to educate people about the harmful effects of counterfeiting. To reinforce their image and to protect their market and revenues, the international brands will reinforce this with public service announcements using famous Bollywood actors to engage the consumer emotionally with the dangers of counterfeiting.

The tradition of the Great Indian Wedding will have a growing impact on the fashion and luxury sector. Beyond the platform for gift buying and oneupmanship, this ritual has fed the Indian designer market like no other, making stars of a select few. These few will continue to reign but will be joined by others as the good times roll.

INDIAN DESIGNERS

Beyond their obvious talent and place in the future of fashion, the Indian designers of tomorrow will have understood that cutting standards will have to be more in line with those of foreign brands if they are to sell their goods overseas. While some will want to maintain the ethnic "Indianness" of their collections and limit their appeal in other markets, others will aim to compete directly in international fashion markets. Many top Indian designers may well choose to do both. Those who become stars outside India may then have an even greater impact on local buying, both for traditional apparel and for Westernwear. They may also diversify their offerings with accessories and eventually move towards lifestyle branding, including décor.

Designers who have seen what LVMH did for John Galliano or Marc Jacobs will be the next wave of creative types for the major luxury or retail groups. Sooner than many expect, select Indian designers will be hired—either in full-time positions or as free-lancers in head designer roles—by the major international brands, which in turn will acquire shares in the designers' local companies, giving them much-needed capital to grow their business.

MANAGEMENT EDUCATION

The companies involved in today's joint ventures will be the first to understand the importance of applying the rules of branding. They will know that they need either to hire talented designers who already possess this knowledge or to provide the necessary training. The leading companies in the sector will partner with leading businesses schools and fashion institutes to breed a whole new generation of young professionals capable of performing to the required standards.

RETAIL AND DISTRIBUTION ISSUES

The High Street is a concept whose time has come in India, which is something that will evolve as clusters of international brands form. While India's climate may remain an impediment to the shopping experience so well developed in other countries, it is inevitable that standalone stores will develop as "destinations." Beyond the global fashion and luxury brands that will help fuel the growth of luxury malls in India, the next big entrant will be the luxury department stores such as Saks Fifth Avenue and Harvey Nichols, both of which have identified India as a potential market. There will be a stronger growth in local specialty boutiques such as Thanks, Escape, and Kimaya, which carry a broad range of domestic luxury lines. These retailers will ride the wave created by the influx of foreign brands, and expand into many cities to sell the wares of the increasingly competitive Indian designers.

With the proliferation of international brands in the market, there will be increased pressure on infrastructure that is already below par. Major upgrades are required to facilitate the development of retail distribution networks. In 2005, India passed a groundbreaking law permitting governments to form partnerships for infrastructure initiatives with the private sector. It is estimated that over the next five years, public and private organizations will chip in between US$330 billion and US$500 billion for highways, power generation, ports, and airports that will help alleviate these pressures. The US$27 billion National Urban Renewal Mission, for example, will reduce pressure on India's megacities, and create adequate infrastructure in other cities across the country. This government may come to recognize the importance of the luxury and fashion market for India, and there is a risk that it may do what previous governments have done: enter into this world, where there could be conflict of interest, special favors, and movements that could enrich the politically privileged.

On the regulatory side, there is increased pressure from both brands and consumers for the government to further reduce tariffs. Extremely high import duties translate into higher-priced goods. We know that consumers shopping in the luxury boutiques in India are conscious of what the same items cost in Milan, Paris, London, or New York. Luxury players are pricing on par with New York, taking in lower margins to cover the tariff costs. However, some feel that the Indian government may reduce duties for luxury goods, and some expect decreased tariffs in the coming months.

The high costs of real estate will go even higher. Land-use conversion is time consuming and complex, and wrought with legal process for property disputes. Urban planning, combined with rigid building and zoning laws, will not make for an easy future for the foreign brands seeking retail space. The major cities have major retail projects under way, which will continue and extend to the suburban areas. The second-tier cities stand to gain from this, and shrewd foreign brands will be investing in property now. The established Indian companies already have access to prime locations; however, the foreign companies will continue to rely upon rentals. Malls will continue to be the foremost vehicle, and many will face challenging times.

Management the key

Whereas the availability of quality retail space will remain critical for the international brands, even more important will be the need for top-quality managers to ensure the optimization of business development. The increase in the fashion and luxury business overall in India will spawn a whole new level of services specific to the sector. Consulting firms—strategic management, executive search, or other—will create luxury and fashion "practices" to access the burgeoning market. Individual consultants will flourish or fade until their convergence is balanced by local market expertise. Employee training and development will become ever more important, and be key drivers for organic business growth, as well as tools for employee retention. These too will feed an industry to service the specific requirements within organizations.

Talent hunting and the retention of key people will be the determinants of success or failure. Two different mindsets on recruitment will evolve within the ranks of organizational decision-makers: the precautionary, testing-the-waters types who will take the value-for-money approach to an extreme; and the forward-thinking entre-preneurial approach with vision and sagacity. Tomorrow will belong to those who are willing to invest in it, literally. With a paucity of local talent with suitable experience to manage the businesses, senior talent will be brought in from outside. The most logical next best source are Indians living abroad and open to repatriation; then neighboring countries such as Dubai, where a comparable market boom in luxury and fashion has resulted in a talent pool worth attracting. The influx of foreign talent will have an impact on senior executive compensation and benefits, driving the market ever higher.

Investing in the future was not an issue for the four companies that are highlighted in our next and final chapter. We examined sev-eral companies that have already displayed the vision required to thrive. They are not the only foreign brands that have risen to the India market challenge, but certainly represent a strong example of how to optimize their resources and build on their position in the market.

NOTES

1. This was a coin used during the Roman era.
2. Arthur Llewellyn Basham 1975, *A Cultural History of India,* Clarendon Press.
3. *Hindu* 2006, "For the chic bride", November 13, <www.hindu.com/mp/2006/11/13/stories/2006111301020200.htm>.

CHAPTER 14
CASE STUDIES

For our case studies we have selected four brands that have proven successful in entering the Indian market:

- Ermenegildo Zegna
- TAG Heuer
- Montblanc
- Louis Vuitton Malletier

It is clear that each of these global luxury companies has mastered the branding techniques, to which their success in established markets as well as those of other emerging economies bears clear testimony. There are interesting parallels in how and why they have achieved this success, which may serve as a lesson both for other global brands and for Indian companies aspiring to succeed in their own market.

ERMENEGILDO ZEGNA

History in India

If there is one brand that epitomizes successful market entry in India, and serves as a paradigm for every other luxury marque, it is Ermenegildo Zegna. The brand and its principal have paved the way for luxury retail in India as facilitators in government policy changes to infrastructure development. However, this rise to success was not without its share of complexities and failures.

In November 1999, Ermenegildo Zegna was the first of the luxury brands to make a foray into the Indian market (though this accolade is often mistakenly bestowed on Louis Vuitton). This joint venture also entailed elements of technology transfer to the joint venture company for manufacturing processes in textiles and fabrics, capital goods, knowhow, and plant management. India's newly liberalized foreign direct investment (FDI) policies of the late 1990s and the Foreign Investment Promotion Board (FIPB) directives of that era permitted collaborative joint ventures to engage freely in retail operations as free-standing points-of-sale. (This policy was subsequently rescinded in 2001.) At that time, Zegna operated a fully stocked boutique catering to its elite Indian clientele. However, this theoretical format failed to take into account one crucial aspect: guaranteeing an immediate return to the investors capitalizing the venture. Indian venture capitalists were looking for a quick return, which is not possible in manufacturing or retail, especially for luxury goods. Zegna was left with retail ambitions based on its successes in China, but with no partner to fulfill its India dreams. It quickly came to learn the complexities of partnerships in India.

The brand has always had early market entry and new market development as core philosophies. It has achieved several successes as a market leader in previously nonexistent markets such as China, Argentina, Estonia, and Siberia, among others. In India in 2001, its only feasible option was to engage in a local distribution partnership based on a franchisee model. With potential partners lining up to associate themselves with a prestigious luxury brand, suddenly the prospect of opening the first Ermenegildo Zegna boutique was rekindled. The inexperience of these potential partners in retailing—luxury or otherwise—and the lack of adequate infrastructure did not seem to be a deterrent, a fact that would soon prove to be the Achilles heel for the menswear giant. When the Piramals, the promoters of Crossroads in Mumbai, presented floor plans promising adjacencies such as Hermès, Louis Vuitton, Dior, and Armani in India's first mall, the Zegna board in Milan was sold. And in November 2001, Ermenegildo Zegna opened the first luxury boutique at Crossroads, as a franchised operation of MF Fashions. Nobody could have guessed that a year later the tenant mix of the luxury "dream team" would be replaced by McDonald's, Marks & Spencer, and Samsonite. Within three seasons of operation, when the mall failed to live up to expectations, both the Indian franchisee and Zegna felt severely compromised.

The brand was faced with the task of undoing whatever harm had been done to its reputation by regaining control of the brand name and image commensurate with its 100-year-old legacy. The Zegna management had learned from the experience and had the foresight, the wherewithal and the commitment to see the task through. It began by annuling the previous franchise model, and wiping the slate clean by closing its Crossroads store in late 2005. Next was the task of establishing a corporate structure that would enable a majority equity holding and, as a consequence, more control over the brand name and management. However, under pressure from the left, the Indian government was still on the fence with regard to enabling a further easing of FDI restrictions. Its deliberations were protracted, fearing an onslaught of mass-marketers such as Wal-Mart and Carrefour that would wipe out small Indian retailers across the subcontinent. However, Dr. Paolo Zegna, chairman of the Zegna group, championed the cause with great tenacity and his open dialogue with the Minister of Commerce and Industry, Kamal Nath, established a direct line of communication with the policy-makers who could enact the required changes. Making a strong case for the inflow of foreign equity, collaborative partnerships and raising the level of retail standards, he was able to convince the government that single-brand FDI was not the pariah it was made out to be but the harbinger of a new retailing era for the country. Finally, on March 16, 2001, came cause for celebration: *The Economic Times* reported that the government had approved a maximum of 51% foreign equity participation for single-brand retail.

Ermenegildo Zegna had paved the way for others, and, in the process, had set several precedents: it was the first global luxury men's

brand to enter the country, the first to have majority equity participation, the first to have free street access (as opposed to having to go
through the precincts of a hotel) and it was the largest single-brand
emporium.

Current market issues

As with China in the 1990s, Hong Kong and Singapore in the 1980s,
and Japan in the 1970s, India has a luxury retail infrastructure that
is restricted to premium hotel properties. This is generally the norm
in most emerging Asian markets, and is a prelude to Asian-style
malls such as Paragon, IFC, Plaza 66, and so on. Zegna and, indeed,
all other brands are confronted by a lack of adequate retail infrastructure and nonexistent retail space in high-end hotels built in
the 1970s (or earlier) for retailers of local artifacts. However, recent
years have seen an active participation from hotel groups lured by
the high demand from premium brands, and, consequently, the propensity to charge sky-high rentals on a par with Bond Street, Avenue
Montaigne, or Via Montenapoleone. Though every brand aspires
for a free-standing monobrand operation in a colonial or historic
Indian structure, they will have to settle for hotel locations or malls
such as Emporio. Ultimately, as with the Bund in Shanghai, Central
in Hong Kong, Orchard Road in Singapore, or Ginza in Tokyo in
their respective eras of development, Indian cities will see the development of such high streets in Mumbai and New Delhi.

Partnerships

India is a country of failed foreign collaborative efforts over the past
three decades. From Coca-Cola in the 1970s to the now-defunct joint
ventures of Rover, Xerox, Disney/ESPN, and, more recently, Dan-
one, all have ended in bitter lawsuits and compensation payments.
One major factor involved in these and other failed partnerships,

especially in the field of retailing, is the expectations of returns on investment. In a highly bullish market, coupled with the "casino" mentality of the Indian investor, the only benefit of allocating capital in the relatively sluggish luxury retail structure seems to be association with a "fashion" label. To that, add the brand stipulations for capex investments, minimum open-to-buy budgets four times a year, advertising costs, and high real-estate costs, and the only model for success is a joint venture that entails direct capital investment from the parent brand. Only a brand has the propensity to invest in an economic model that is "top line" driven and not the "bottom line" format of a franchisee. Only a brand can bring the necessary expertise involved in retailing luxury. Only a brand can control pricing strategy and markups. And only a brand can destroy leftover inventory that is seasons old.

Tariff levels

India's tariff structure for imports and domestic sales is one of the most complex in the world. The method of calculating countervailing duties based on the maximum retail price (MRP) needs to be reconsidered. This would encourage the growth of luxury brands, both foreign and Indian (which need to import components as well), and counter efforts to evade tax by smuggling goods into the country.

Starting in March 2001, additional custom duties (also called "countervailing duties" or CVD) have been calculated on the basis of the MRP minus abatement. In 2001, the existing method of computation was changed after the method used to calculate excise duties was changed. The authorities have fixed the amount of the abatement at their estimate of the cost structure for locally manufactured goods.

According to WTO regulations, import taxes should be levied on invoice prices and not on an MRP basis, because the importer may have nothing to do with the actual retail (there may be various intermediate distributors). It would make more sense to levy additional customs duties on imported products based on the CIF price. This was the method used before 2001.

The cost structure for imported products is not the same as for locally manufactured products. It follows that to ensure a level playing field, the abatement amount should not be the same. It would be more legitimate to consider increasing the rebate on the MRP to 70%, rather than 30% or 35%, to reflect the actual cost structure for imported products. Today, most foreign luxury products sold in India are priced 20–40% higher than in London, Dubai, or Singapore because of the level of import taxes. If India wants to promote the consumption of luxury goods, as Dubai and Singapore do, to generate revenue from shopping tourism and consumption, the government should reconsider how it levies countervailing duties.

The peak duty has been reduced every year for the past few years. The budget of March 2006 reinstated special additional duties (SAD), 4% of which had been abolished in 2003–04.

These MRP-based components play a substantial role in the calculation of duties. This point relative to CVD is critical. The regulation requiring that imported products be labeled with the MRP is difficult to implement. It should be possible to do this after the import stage.

The Weights and Measures Act stipulates that imported products should be labeled with the MRP. But most importing companies are wholesalers, not retailers. They do not know in which state the imported goods will be retailed, so they cannot label MRP at the customs stage. The act is redundant here. It should be possible to issue the MRP after the import stage. This is done for liquor imports into India or, indeed, for most imports, because the act is applied de facto by Customs officials at port entries.

The Indian government announced in April 2005 that a general VAT rate would be implemented. At state level, VAT is not yet fully harmonized, and companies must register separately in each state.

In some states, VAT has not been fully implemented. Full VAT harmonization in India would facilitate business development.

Investment

Until the infrastructure develops, keeping the intricacy and the quality of Indian production aside, investment in high-end production is like putting the cart before the horse. For luxury goods, the supply chain starts with the procurement and import of high-quality raw materials. Unless the government invests in the development of free-trade zones or special economic zones, the import of raw materials will incur high duties and, subsequently, additional import duties from the countries to which these goods are exported. Even if indigenous raw materials were used, they would have to comply with international standards in the use of such things as nonhazardous dyes and material. Second, warehousing infrastructure at airports would need to be developed, especially considering soaring temperatures upward of 40°C (104°F) or humidity of 100%. Without these, India as a luxury-sourcing destination seems to be decades away.

Counterfeiting

The government needs to take a more stringent approach toward copyright and trademark laws to safeguard intellectual property. It needs to work closely with law enforcement agencies, both domestically and internationally, to implement these measures at an early stage before the proliferation of counterfeit goods becomes a major issue, as in several emerging and developed markets.

Counterfeiting and intellectual property infringements in China and most of Asia have become a full-blown epidemic. In contrast, brand equity that fuels copyright infringement is relatively small in India. Working together, the government and the brands can implement stringent parameters to help minimize future problems.

Buying local or buying abroad?

The concept of people purchasing products outside their home country is not a phenomenon exclusive to emerging markets: Americans buy their Chanel and Fendi in Paris and Milan; Europeans stock up on their True Religion and Juicy Couture in New York; Chinese mainlanders make shopping trips to Louis Vuitton and Zegna in Hong Kong. Similarly, the Indian consumer avails of the competitive price advantage of shopping in Dubai or London. However, this does not preclude them from shopping in India for the same brands that they would have bought abroad. The difference is more in the social cachet attached to where the purchase was made, rather than its price. However, with international travel becoming increasingly available to the masses, trips to Europe are becoming less entrenched in consumer buying patterns and service-oriented purchasing is becoming a larger part of the decision-making psychology. The key to success in the Indian market is more correlated to the service and buying experience that a brand offers than to the mere fact of selling the product. Brands such as Zegna and Louis Vuitton have undertaken extensive staff-training programs and exchange seminars with other markets to propagate best-practice policies at the shopfloor level, an aspect that will eventually determine success.

SWOT analysis

Strengths

- Early market-entry strategy
- Corporate structure with direct equity and management control
- Retail positioning at premium location with large-format flagship
- Advertising and editorial support
- Pricing strategy at par with other markets
- Sales staff with intensive product knowledge and training
- Fast implementation of rollout plan in other cities

Weaknesses
- No women's wear

Opportunities
- Travel retail at airports
- Shop-in-shops in multibrand retailing
- Fragrance and eyewear
- Small and large leather goods

Threats
- Increasingly competitive market within the next 12–18 months
- Brand equity proliferation

Development plans

- Primary metros: Mumbai, New Delhi, and Bangalore
- Secondary markets: Kolkata, Hyderabad, Chennai, and Chandigarh

India-specific product lines

These have not been implemented. Because Indian consumers prefer to purchase products that are available worldwide, the company produces no products specifically for the Indian market.

TAG HEUER[1]

History in India

In late 2001/early 2002, TAG Heuer gained parent company LVMH's support to enter India as one of the key emerging markets for luxury watches. As a comparatively late arrival in the market (other brands had entered the market in the 1990s, and had already created a big enough scale to threaten the entry of a new player) TAG Heuer faced stiff competition.

An additional problem was that the TAG Heuer brand ambassadors were drawn from Western sports—diving, golf, and motor sports, for example—which were relatively unknown in the country.

The launch of TAG Heuer began with the basic premise that Indians would buy in India if the brand could deliver actionable branding promises. In essence, this meant that:

- Product pricing would be comparable with that in Singapore, Dubai, or any other international destination. Given the huge duties and taxes at the time, this was a difficult decision to reach since it meant that TAG Heuer would absorb the duties into its P&L rather than passing it over to consumers.
- A true "international retail experience" would be provided. The company was among the first to create a flagship store in the market (the first for the watch category) while its competitors were in multibrand stores only.
- All new products would be launched in India concurrently with other international launches. The general practice before this had been to "dump" old and nonselling goods in India at a low cost. TAG Heuer has delivered on this promise, ensuring that the assortments in India are the same as in every other major international destination.
- Its aftersales service would be developed before the actual sale. In each new city it entered, the company first opened a center to service consumers and thereafter began the operation of selling.

Current market issues

The availability of the product offer for retail is seen as a critical issue by TAG Heuer, which has demonstrated its willingness to create a network of boutiques to provide luxury goods to local consumers.

Despite the shortage of top retail space, it has opened boutiques at most high-end locations, including Delhi's Connaught Place and South Extension-1. It also has a presence in hotels such as the Sheraton in Chennai and the Grand Hyatt in Bombay. With the advent of luxury malls, it has invested in having a presence in Bangalore's UB City and Delhi's DLF Emporio.

Its margins, which are dependent on duties, remain a key issue for the company.

Partnerships

Distribution is undertaken through both wholesale and retail outlets. Even the company's boutiques are run as franchises invested in and managed by entrepreneurs from within or outside the watch industry. The challenge for TAG Heuer in this business model is that it has to deal with seven different parties who operate boutiques located in various cities. However, this does have the advantage of allowing it to tap into the customer databases of these entrepreneurs, most of whom are players from the watch industry and themselves run various single- or multibranded stores.

Tariff levels

Taxes and duties on watches are as high as 50%, which reduces TAG Heuer's gross margins and its ability to invest in various facilities to increase the business. The policymakers need to understand that reducing duties would make the business more interesting for many players, and would increase exponentially investments into marketing or retail. This, in turn, would increase consumption and broaden the market to the extent that the government would earn much more from indirect taxes than it does from duties.

Once the duties are rationalized and brands lower the prices, consumers will be able to get all the brands they currently get from other countries on Indian soil, greatly benefiting the government and the economy.

Investment

At the outset, TAG Heuer decided on a five-year investment in marketing and human resources with the goal of building TAG Heuer into a position in the top five luxury watch brands in India. To achieve this, it invested more than the turnover for the first year, a very bullish and uncommon practice but one that proved to be very effective: in 2007 TAG Heuer was the fourth luxury watch brand in value in India.

Counterfeiting

Counterfeiting is a big problem for the watch industry. For TAG Heuer, however, it is a manageable problem. Because India does not have a great manufacturing infrastructure, the fakes are generally imported. TAG Heuer keeps eye on the market, and works closely with the government to identify and block these imports.

Buying local or buying abroad?

Traditionally, Indians feel that they do not get the same quality, assortment, price, or choice of brands in India as they do in the Middle East or Singapore, a problem exacerbated by the country's proximity to Singapore and Dubai. TAG Heuer has made every effort to ensure that it offers the same assortment in India as elsewhere and at the same price, reinforcing this message through extensive media and PR campaigns. Each of its stores has a certified Singapore and Dubai price list, which allows consumers to check the prices for themselves. (Many other luxury brands have, as yet, no presence in

TAG Heuer ambassador
Shah Rukh Khan

the Indian market and those that do often attempt to sell obsolete goods or at very high prices.) TAG Heuer has invested a great deal to create retail stores that are of international quality and can provide an international experience.

As the brand has grown in India, the company has seen a significant increase in Indian purchases in Dubai and Singapore or in duty free markets. A lot of these stores use Bollywood star Shah Rukh Khan as a brand ambassador to relate to the Indian clientele.

SWOT analysis

Strengths

- Brand ambassadors: With Shah Rukh Khan as the recognized top star in the Indian film industry, the company has the best possible endorsement for the brand. It helps that Khan is also a passionate fan and collector of TAG Heuer watches, and always wears the products whenever and wherever possible. Priyanka Chopra is another compelling Bollywood celebrity, with deep inner substance and a natural class. Having these two appear together at promotional events emphasizes the brand's feminine and masculine appeal, not to mention the glamor of TAG Heuer.

- Marketing: The company has developed a very high-end image through its association with golf and polo (TAG Heuer is the official timekeeper of the India Polo Association). Its golf and polo events have become benchmarks for the industry and consumers look forward to attending them.

- Distribution: The company has managed to create a 70-door and 10-boutique infrastructure over the past five years. With the economy growing and the market set to witness a boom, it is well placed to ensure its top positioning.

Weaknesses

- While TAG Heuer has managed to carve a place for itself in the men's market, its women's business remains quite insignificant. With new introductions of feminine products such as the Tag Heuer Formula 1 Series (including the Glamour Diamonds watch) and focused marketing efforts, it is working to overcome the weakness and become a reference brand for women.

Opportunities

- With the new wave of luxury malls and so much development happening, strategic retail opportunities abound. The introduction of the Grand Carrera presents a great opportunity to increase market share for products in the CHF50,000+ price point. That all other brands in this price point are only available through agents and do not have subsidiary or a long-term vision should allow TAG Heuer a great opportunity to consolidate its position in this segment.

- With Formula 1 racing coming to India in 2010, TAG Heuer will have a great platform on which to build its brand extensions. TAG Heuer eyewear is already doing great business among celebrities and the broader market. The company expects to launch more extensions and accessories for the stores, all of which offer opportunities to grow the business.

Threats

- The biggest threat to the company is its own rate of expansion. It has grown rapidly and needs to ensure that its positioning does not become diluted to the point where it is perceived as a mass-market brand. When it arrived in the market, it offered watches that were glamorous yet sporty. It needs to ensure that it retains that allure and exclusivity.

Development plans

TAG Heuer's plan now is to become the number one Swiss watch brand in the Indian market by 2010, a goal it is confident of achieving.

India-specific product lines

Despite claims to the contrary, the company has discovered that Indian consumers are amazingly international in their choices and preferences. Its bestsellers in India are the same as its international bestsellers. This has been reassuring, and, consequently, there has never been a need to create products specific to the Indian market.

Nonetheless, it is continuing to work with Shah Rukh Khan on creating another limited-edition watch similar to the 100-piece SRK Monaco 69 that Kahn used in a very successful movie. The entire edition was bought by his fans.

MONTBLANC[2]

History in India

Montblanc is an internationally established luxury brand. With a history stretching back more than 100 years and strong roots in the writing culture, the brand was known in India even before it entered the market.

The history of Montblanc in India is a stunning success, and is a result of early entry, a well-prepared distribution strategy, and—perhaps most importantly—a trustworthy and loyal partner from day one.

In 1993, Montblanc management was introduced to Dilip Doshi, a very successful cricketer and businessman. A business plan was developed and Montblanc applied for an import license as India's first luxury brand.

The new partner, Entrack International Pvt. Ltd., offered two major advantages:

- Dilip Doshi's popularity and fame as a cricketer opened many doors in government, which proved useful because imports of luxury goods were banned at that time.
- Entrack was willing to invest in the brand without the expectation of immediate returns. Only after many years and after the brand was established in India did the business became profitable for Entrack.

The import license was finally approved in 1995. At that time, India was considered to be a sleeping giant, and it was thought that one day it would rise to be one of the key world markets. The next step for Montblanc was to determine the optimal strategy to achieve market share. At the outset, the company's products were distributed through hotel shops within the Taj Hotel group. While this turned out to be a good way to test the acceptance of the products, it was not a long-term option for a luxury brand looking to build the right brand image as the basis for future success.

The first milestone in the company's strategy was the opening of a franchise boutique with Entrack in 1997, when Dilip Doshi used his excellent contacts and influence to persuade a five-star hotel—the Maurya Sheraton Hotel in Delhi—to allow for the first time a standalone boutique for a luxury brand. Over the next few years, many more were to follow, to the point where today the company is the clear market leader with 17 boutiques across the country: in Mumbai (four), Delhi (three), Bangalore (two), Hyderabad (two), Chennai (two), and one each in Ahmedabad, Chandigarh, Pune, and Ludhiana.

Current market issues

With India's real-estate market booming, the investments going into retail structure are changing shopping behavior as customers begin to frequent the new malls, rather than the traditional small street stores. Currently, there are more than 200 malls under construction in India, and both domestic and international companies are actively involved in the process. However, for Montblanc three things are already apparent:

- There is no real strategic approach behind many of these projects. For example, new malls are opening next to an existing mall with the same target customers.

- Because the opportunities are tremendous, there is a market for everything.
- Luxury retail space is still very rare and expensive. The Emporio in Delhi and UB City in Bangalore are the first two malls for the luxury target group.

While the luxury retail market is still active in hotels, it is only a question of time before luxury streets or malls become available. Seeing this, hotels such as the Taj Mumbai are fighting to retain the luxury retailers, and are coming up with more professional approaches and new shopping arcades, which can accommodate more stores.

An increasing number of luxury brands are entering the Indian market, and the fight for AAA space will result in higher rents, but also in more space for the brands in luxury malls and streets.

Partnerships

This remains a key issue for Montblanc, which is quick to acknowledge its great luck in finding the right partner from the outset. Unlike in other territories, it started with one partner, and continues to use the same successful business model. From Montblanc's perspective, it is impossible to build a successful business without a partner that has confidence in the brand; financial power; time to develop the brand; influence in the market (particularly in India); and courage.

Tariff levels

The tariff structure in India continues to limit the growth of luxury businesses with imported goods. Most brands are building up structures for the future, hoping for a more liberal system. High duties and taxes, in combination with skyrocketing rents, are squeezing the margin of the local companies and their international partners.

Montblanc believes that lower taxes and duties, and a harmonized VAT system, would lead to faster growth, more foreign investors in the market, and more employment in many sectors. While international pricing in most markets is set by a net price plus local VAT differences, the situation in India is more complex.

Because local costs outside the high-end locations are often low, the dealers accept a very low margin and compete with lower prices rather than service. Such discounting can damage the image of a luxury brand.

Investment

Montblanc's Indian investment is targeting retail development in prime locations.

Counterfeiting

Generally all successful products across different industries are being copied. Montblanc has developed various confidential tools to protect its interests.

Buying local or buying abroad?

The average Montblanc customer is an educated, cultured person and a frequent traveler. Because Montblanc prices its products at European levels, it is not competing with other markets. However, there is always a component of excitement whenever people travel, and customers often make purchases while abroad. Montblanc feels that customers may have their first experience with luxury brands in foreign markets, and may become loyal customers in India afterward. Because Montblanc has a strong retail network, it is not as dependant on these customers as most other brands, and it has the unique chance to present the brand with the right image in India.

SWOT analysis

Strengths
- Early market entry
- Loyal and strong local partner
- Excellent boutique network in prime locations
- Pricing on European level
- Professional training organization
- Strong links and cooperation with Montblanc headquarters

Weaknesses
- Only limited access to more potential customers because retail business is concentrated in low-traffic hotels

Opportunities
- More than 60 cities with more than a million inhabitants
- Travel retail business just starting
- Jewelry
- Special products targeting local market

Threats
- Complex market structure
- Very limited professional retail space
- Lack of experienced staff

Development plans

Montblanc will continue to expand its retail structure and look for the best locations. The brand's diversification strategy will be developed further.

India-specific product lines

Montblanc rarely develops products for specific markets. However, in the area of small leather goods, it adapts functions to local needs. Next to this they are constantly developing high-end country editions in their writing instrument category (i.e. Churchill limited edition for the U.K.) and they can envision using this concept as well for India in the future.

LOUIS VUITTON MALLETIER

History in India

The Louis Vuitton relationship with India reaches back to the early decades of the previous century when Maharaja Jagjit Singh of Kapurthala, India's most highly decorated maharaja, ordered 54 Louis Vuitton travel trunks, each painted with his name, initials and colors, custom-built to house his royal outfits.[3] These trunks are now on permanent display at the Louis Vuitton store in New Delhi.[4] Other rulers had cases custom made for various non-travel purposes, including a tea-set trunk commissioned by the Maharaja of Baroda in 1926 (now on display at the Louis Vuitton Travel Museum) and a typewriter case built for the Maharaja of Jammu & Kashmir.

Louis Vuitton's orders from Indian princes outnumbered those from elsewhere in the world. When Louis Vuitton visited India on business, he cultivated relationships with many royal families. "This is where the luxury business took off," explains Tikka Singh, great grandson of Maharaja Jagjit Singh and now an advisor to Louis Vuitton in India. "It was a golden era for Vuitton, who bagged big orders."

Louis Vuitton special order for the Maharaja of Jammu and Kashmir
© Archives Louis Vuitton

In the 1990s, Jean-Marc Loubier (at the time the company's deputy general manager) and Yves Carcelle (chairman and CEO of Louis
Vuitton), made several reconnaissance trips to India to explore the
opportunity to launch freestanding stores. They were instrumental
in creating a strategic plan to enter the market. By the time the
import ban on leather was lifted in 2001, Louis Vuitton was well
ahead of any other luxury leather-goods company in its planning.
Yves Carcelle had high hopes and great confidence for business in
India: "The potential is massive in India," he commented, "and of
course there is a great awareness of our heritage...Louis Vuitton
represents, better than any other brand, the world of travel and
beauty. We have always had a relationship with India...It's a way
of acknowledging the brand's origins, and I think the company's
founders would be pleased...I believe Mumbai or Delhi would be
in the league of European cities such as Madrid or Brussels."[5]

Current market issues

After careful planning, Louis Vuitton opted for a similar strategy to that it had employed in China, by entering India through a hotel location because "a hotel is a gathering point for society, and a hub for those who travel."[6] When it opened its first store in India, at the Oberoi Hotel in New Delhi, in March 2003, the company had first-mover advantage. In the following year, it opened another boutique within the Taj Hotel in Mumbai.

According to a study by KSA Technopak, a New-Delhi based management consultancy firm, the size of the luxury market stood at Rs2,400 crore in 2006 and is projected to grow to Rs5,000 crore by 2010. The luxury market, the study shows, is growing at 30–35% year on year.[7]

Partnerships

Because India's FDI regulations at the time didn't permit single-brand retailers to have majority ownership, Louis Vuitton initially established a subsidiary, LV Trading India Pvt. Ltd., with 11% ownership and a local partner. The subsidiary had a nonexclusive distribution agreement to sell the company's branded products in India.

Louis Vuitton approached the FIPB seeking its approval to pick up a majority stake in Indian companies, including LV Trading India. The FIPB loosened its ownership restrictions in 2005 and granted a 51% equity ownership opportunity for single-brand retailers in India.

Tariff levels

Louis Vuitton products cost about 30% more in India than they do in Europe partly because of government levies on luxury goods imports.[8] However, the higher prices do not seem to deter local consumers. When the company shipped 300 of its Suhali bags to India, the entire collection sold out more than two months in advance.[9] More than 90% of its Tambour chronograph priced about US$4,700 sold before they were even launched.[10]

Investment

Louis Vuitton Malletier intends to invest important sums in India. While the publicly stated sum of Rs32.2 crore will be used to acquire 51% equity in Indian entities and for expanding operations,[11] the actual amounts invested may be far more substantial.

Louis Vuitton is still in negotiation to acquire a minority stake in Hidesign, an India-based maker of branded handbags and leather accessories. Hidesign's product range is upmarket, yet much cheaper than Vuitton and its main rivals, Gucci and Prada. In the future, Hidesign will stay managed completely independently from Louis Vuitton, and none of its facilities will be used for Louis Vuitton.

However, Louis Vuitton is also building its own shoe-components factory in Pondicherry. Designed by Jean-Marc Sandrolini, the architect of the company's factory in Condé, France, the Indian plant would specialize in "piquage" (sewing the soles to the uppers) for Louis Vuitton shoes.[12] The shoes would still bear the prestigious "Made in Italy" label because the vast majority of work would continue to be carried out in Italy. The company claims that the reason for its first factory outside Europe or the U.S. is not the low cost of labor in India, and has implied that this factory's presence dovetails with India's emerging wealthy class which consumes luxury goods. It is thought that the factory will serve India and nearby markets initially, but could end up supplying other territories.

Counterfeiting

In 2004, Louis Vuitton fakes accounted for 18% of counterfeit accessories seized in the European Union. Louis Vuitton takes a serious view of all counterfeiting, employing a team of lawyers and special investigation agencies, actively pursuing offenders through law courts worldwide, and allocating about half of its corporate communications budget to counteract piracy of its goods.

Buying local or buying abroad?

To understand domestic potential, Louis Vuitton has closely monitored Indians who would shop for the brand on their visits to London, Paris, Zurich, Hong Kong, or Singapore.[13] Sales growth in India has been outstanding to say the least, with around 50% year-on-year growth in sales. Management expects double-digit growth for the next six-to-eight years.

SWOT analysis

Strengths
- Strong brand awareness
- Historical ties
- Reputation for service (extremely important since the majority of its sales come from personal shopping)
- Control of distribution from the outset
- Excellent PR work with Bollywood and Indian royals
- No-discount policy

Weaknesses
- Limited merchandise assortment—doesn't sell full assortment of bags or items such as women's clothing
- Fewer walk-in customers. Need to drive traffic to stores and make a larger group of Indians comfortable with shopping at the Louis Vuitton boutiques

Opportunities

- Growing wealth in India
- Increasing demand for luxury products
- Broadening the product assortment will provide lower entry-level price points and introduce the brand to a larger percentage of the Indian population
- Improving the overall retail landscape in India through its presence in the shopping malls

Threats

- Regulatory issues
- Infrastructure issues
- Distribution issues (limited to five-star hotel arcades or luxury malls)
- Losing well-trained staff to competitors coming into the market

Development plans

"India is a very strategic market, and the market is close to fulfilling its potential," says Damien Vernet, the company's general manager for West Asia and India.[14]

Louis Vuitton opened its second operation in New Delhi, with 3,000 sq. ft. of space in the new luxury Emporio mall. Along with other global luxury brands—Gucci, Fendi, Montblanc, Van Cleef & Arpels, Ermenegildo Zegna, Rolex, and Omega—it also opened a store in Bangalore's UB City complex,[15] and is open to developing further in Chennai, Kolkata, and Hyderabad if they find the right market and retail space.[16]

India-specific product lines

India and the Middle East are two of the larger markets for its made-to-order trunks, with special models being constructed as part of wedding trousseaux.[17]

While the Suhali handbag collection, inspired by the styling of the handmade trunks first made 150 years ago, is available world-wide, it is named after an Indian desert wind, and is made from goatskin so that Hindu customers will feel comfortable carrying the bag.[18]

Louis Vuitton Malletier exemplifies the luxury industry's global branding techniques put to full force in an emerging country, and with impressive effect. The key issues to ensure ongoing success for the company in India are:

- growing a retail network while maintaining the highest-quality products and excellent service
- building a brand that started at the very top of the social pyramid in India: traditionally the purveyor of goods to the traditionalists (Indian royals), it shrewdly expanded its appeal to the modernists (Bollywood). Broadening the appeal to the next level is a PR challenge
- ensuring sufficient media coverage, particularly editorial. Advertising is less relevant
- bridging the gap with Indian socialites in other countries (the U.K., the U.S., Singapore, Hong Kong) to optimize synergies.

NOTES

1. This case study is based on an interview with Manishi Sanwal in Mumbai in February 2008.
2. This case study is based on interviews with Montblanc's Oliver Goessler in March 2008.
3. *India Now* 2005, "A Bagful of Style", vol. 2(1), June 7, India Brand Equity Foundation (ibef.org).

4. Melanie Rickey 2003, "Louis Vuitton, Meet India", *Fashion Windows*, <www.fashionwindows.com/boutiques/louis_vuitton/new_delhi.asp>, April 7.

5. ibid.

6. ibid.

7. *LiveMint* 2007, "Luxury Brands Shower Gifts on Rich and Famous to Spur Sales", September 13.

8. *India Now*, op. cit.

9. Redif.com 2003, "Have Money, Will Spend", July 12, <www.rediff.com/money/2003/jul/12spec3.htm>.

10. ibid.

11. *Franchise Plus* 2006, "Louis Vuitton, Fendi 'Arriving' in India", vol. 3(3), July–August, <www.franchise-plus.com/n15.asp>.

12. just-style.com 2007, "INDIA: Louis Vuitton to Build Shoe-making Plant", September 21.

13. *India Now*, op. cit.

14. *The Hindu, Business Line* 2007, "French Luxury Brands Bullish on India", March 31.

15. *The Economic Times* 2007, "Mallya Enters Retail; Ropes in Louis Vuitton", November 7 2007.

16. *The Hindu, Business Line* 2008, "Slow and Steady", May 29.

17. *India Now*, op. cit.

18. Rickey, op. cit.

APPENDIX I
How-to Guide for Brands Entering the Market

The following guidelines may serve companies attempting to gauge the right time to enter the Indian market. Many companies are currently adopting a wait-and-see approach that may put their plans on hold for a few years. For example, two highly successful brands—Coach and Prada—are adopting such a strategy.

Entry into India presents some significant operational challenges for any luxury goods player. These include:

- High tariffs: customs duties can make luxury goods anywhere from 15–65% more expensive than in London or Paris
- A pressing need for public and private investment in infrastructure
- Corruption still existing, despite improvements in specific sectors
- A lack of experienced senior managers in retail
- "Multi-brand" stores are not allowed any foreign ownership
- "Single-brand" stores are permitted a maximum 51% foreign ownership (via FDI)
- Market fragmentation making brand development very challenging
- Very poor standards of logistics, transport, and warehousing
- Consumption patterns may be evolving more slowly than expected.

FOREIGN DIRECT INVESTMENT (FDI)

Foreign investment is governed by the government's FDI policy and the Foreign Exchange Management Act (FEMA), 1999. FDI policy is implemented by the Reserve Bank of India, if no prior approval is required, and the Foreign Investment Promotion Board (FIPB), which comprises members of various central government ministries.

Foreign investors may participate in the Indian economy through the creation of publicly held or privately held corporations, partnerships, and sole proprietorships. In most cases, foreign investment is limited to 51% of the total equity. In January 2006, the Indian government allowed foreign companies to own a controlling interest of 51% in joint ventures operating "single-brand" stores. Anyone selling single brands can now enter into a joint venture with a local partner.

Before 1997, FDI was permitted in retailing on a case-by-case basis. There was vigorous opposition from smaller businesses and foreign retailers could only enter India through franchise agreements. Those who did so included Marks & Spencer, McDonald's, and Nike.

Industry watchers predict that restrictions on multibrand stores will also loosen in the near future, which could spark a surge of luxury department stores.

The government has allowed 100% FDI in wholesale trading and sourcing for exports, and in respect of e-commerce activities, subject to the condition that companies listed abroad divest 26% of their equity in favor of the Indian public in five years. Furthermore, these companies are only allowed to engage in business-to-business (B2B) commerce and not in retail trading.

Against this background, set out here are the questions most asked by companies looking to enter India:

- *Is my company's product right for the India market?*
  Knowledge of local buying behavior is key. For example, Indian women would rather spend their money on an expensive embroidered sari than on a Western gown, which indicates that the market is not yet ready for, say, the Donna Karan collection. It is imperative that any company contemplating entry should spend sufficient time getting to understand the "new age"

Indian consumer, who may be more receptive to learning and experimenting with new global brands than the traditionally affluent.

However, understanding the needs, aspirations, and lifestyles of both new and traditional consumers is essential. One starting point for this process would be to run focus groups and interviews of Indian consumers in countries outside India to get a better sense of the "East/West" blend in their buying behavior and preferences. Attending industry conferences and pursuing networking opportunities with government officials and other key industry players, both local and international, at events such as the annual *Hindustan Times* Luxury Conference.

- *Is there already an awareness of my brand in India?*
  Amongst the most recognized international luxury brands in India today are Louis Vuitton, Ermenegildo Zegna, TAG Heuer, Chanel, and Dior. Other major players such as Ralph Lauren are planning on entering. Where does your brand stand in global awareness? Are Indians who travel abroad already buying your products? Has there been any Internet demand for your products for delivery in India?

- *What considerations do I need to keep in mind regarding sourcing?*
  What are the implications for the manufacturing versus handmade aspects of my products?

- *What about location?*
  Prime real estate (in five-star hotels) is increasingly expensive and increasingly scarce. There are currently no true high streets in India and a major upgrade is required in basic infrastructure, to facilitate the development of suitable real estate. Somewhere in the region of US$330 billion–US$500 billion of direct and foreign investment is expected to pour in over the next few years.

- *How high are import duties?*
  India has high tariffs on textiles and leather products because it does not want cheap imports from countries such as China to swamp the market. Depending upon the product category, customs duties on luxury goods still range from 15% to 65%, making the purchase of luxury goods more expensive than anywhere else in the world. This makes things particularly difficult, since Indians want to pay what they would pay anywhere else in the world. This translates either into higher prices for your brand or lower margins for you. Your best bet may be to wait and see what the government's next moves are in the years to come as regards the reduction of imports on luxury goods.

- *Are Indian luxury consumers buying more abroad than at home?*
  The mentality is changing, but it is still limiting the luxury market in the short term.

- *Is there sufficient management talent in India?*
  There is a lack of experienced senior managers in retail, especially at the level of mall management.

- *What is the best ownership structure?*
  Entry can be through traditional licensing agreements, franchising arrangements or, for single-brand retailers, direct 51% ownership. While direct ownership gives greater control, licensing can help mitigate risk. Look at what similar brands are doing.

- *How should I go about selecting the right local partner?*
  Explore potential partnerships with key retailers and local partners and developers. Speak with local companies that have already worked with luxury foreign branded retailers (e.g., Murjani, Planet Retail, Reliance Luxury, Brandhouse Retail, Tata, and Blues Clothing Company).

• *What do I need to keep in mind with regard to real-estate sites and distribution networks?*
There is a dearth of "luxury" retail locations, and an under-developed retail infrastructure. India's economy desperately needs more and better roads and highways, airports, railways, power supplies, and clean water.

According to the Federal Planning Commission, economic losses from congestion and poor roads are as high as US$6 billion annually. For example, 40% of farm produce is lost because it spoils en route to consumers, which contributes to rising prices for staples, such as lentils and onions. In Bangalore, traffic jams mean that workers can spend upward of four hours commuting each day. But the landscape is changing. The government estimates public and private organizations will chip in US$330 billion–US$500 billion over the next five years for highways, power generation, ports and airports.

For example, the US$27 billion National Urban Renewal Mission will reduce pressure on India's mega-cities and create adequate infrastructure in other cities across the country. Under the scheme, 63 cities will benefit from better housing, water, and sanitation—and, ultimately, from the better delivery of other basic services such as health, education, and social security. In 2005, India passed a groundbreaking law permitting officials to enter into partnerships with the private sector for infrastructure initiatives. Governments and companies share costs, risks, and rewards. A good place to begin would be to check where your competitors have selected their distribution sites. These may be in five-star hotels, the traditional safe havens of luxury in India; specialty stores; shopping malls; or department stores (although there are as yet no exclusive luxury department stores, the environment is changing with the recent boom in malls). Some department stores are looking to increase their mix of luxury merchandise, and the Shoppers' Stop's "Verdi" concept and Reliance Retail's luxury store concept may provide some insights in this regard. Another alternative would be to opt for distribution through duty-free outlets, which would provide an opportunity to build international awareness. Explore opportunities in New Delhi, Bangalore, and Mumbai. In any event, check with five-star hotels such as the Taj Mahal Palace Hotel in Mumbai and The Oberoi in New Delhi to see if there are any current vacancies.

Real-estate and mall developers such as DLF Properties, Select Citywalk, K. Raheja Group, and Emaar Properties would be good sources of information on upcoming developments for potential site locations. The current setups in existing malls such as Emporio in New Delhi and UB City in Bangalore may also help clarify your plans. It would be a good idea also to take a look at the operations of specialty stores such as Thanks, Gossip, and Kimaya Fashions.

- *What are the most effective merchandising strategies?*
Varied strategies may be effective, with some limited product customization based on merchandise selection. Evaluate whether it makes sense to develop merchandise specifically tailored to the Indian market (specifically, by region).

Introduce collections with color and embellishments, which have the potential to appeal to Indian consumers' traditional appreciation for precious and semi-precious stones. Indian women are very individualistic in their dress and, where financially viable, it may pay to introduce limited edition or customized products.

WHAT PRICING STRATEGIES SHOULD I ADOPT?

Wealthy Indians have long traveled abroad, primarily to places like London, Dubai, and Hong Kong, to buy their Western clothes. You would do well to price on a par with such places, despite high import duties, because consumers are unlikely to shop at home if it's cheaper abroad.

WHAT ABOUT MARKETING STRATEGY?

Flagship stores bring greater brand awareness. Your marketing efforts should convey a global message but should be communicated using appropriate local vehicles, such as brand ambassadors from the world of Bollywood (such as Shah Rukh Khan for Tag Heuer and Aishwarya Rai for L'Oréal India), which plays a major role in influencing the tastes and preferences of new-age consumers.

Conduct your own research to determine the most appropriate ambassador or ambassadors for your specific brand needs. Attend Indian fashion and trunk shows to meet current Indian designers to consider possible joint ventures or co-promotions. Use the opportunity to evaluate how competitors are targeting the Indian market.

Analyze marketing and communication channels to determine which magazines will be the most effective for advertising your brand to your specific target consumer.

WHAT KIND OF CUSTOMER EXPERIENCE SHOULD I AIM TO CREATE?

Studies have shown that affluent Indian consumers value customized service in stores highly. You must be service oriented and this should be adapted according to both the brand culture and local culture. This, of course, will require specific training for each member of your staff in line with your customers' needs and expectations, which may entail introducing "by appointment only" service at select stores and training sales staff to track loyal customers' tastes and preferences.

GLOSSARY

annas: former money coin worth 16 to a rupee before the decimal system was introduced

asana: a yoga posture

avatar: incarnation of a deity in human or animal form to counteract an evil in the world

ayurveda: ancient system of health care that is native to the Indian subcontinent that includes healthy living along with therapeutic measures that relate to physical, mental, social and spiritual harmony

Banarsi: census town in the Raipur district in northeastern India

Benarasi: refers to cloth from Benaras or Varanasi on the banks of Ganges in Uttar Pradesh

batik: tie-dye design for textiles

chawls: multistorey concrete buildings

chikan or **chikanwari:** traditional embroidery style from Lucknow in India, with the use of one or more pattern blocklets to block print a pattern on the ground fabric

choli: midriff-baring blouse worn in India, and other countries where the sari is worn, which is cut to fit the body tightly and has short sleeves with a low neck

churidaars or **churidaar pyjamas:** tightly fitting trousers worn by both men and women in South Asia and Central Asia

crore: a unit in the Indian numbering system and formerly a unit in the Persian numbering system. An Indian crore is equivalent to 100 lakh or 10 million (10,000,000)

Dalit: word meaning "oppressed" and is a term coined by lower castes to signify that they have been oppressed. Some members of communities involved in weaving could be Dalits

damask: a figured fabric of silk, wool, linen, cotton, or synthetic fibers with a pattern formed by weaving

Dharavi: a mega slum and administrative ward over parts of the Sion, Bandra, Kurla, and Kalina suburbs of Mumbai

Dhokra metalware: one of the earliest known methods of nonferrous metal casting, notable for its strength and shapeliness of design

Duende: mythological term for fairy-like or goblin-like creature, or free spirit

dupatta: long scarf that is most commonly worn with the *salwar kameez*, the trouser suit, and the *kurta*

ghat: refers to a series of steps leading down to a body of water in many parts of South Asia

Ghats: often used in reference to the steep mountain rangers of India—"the Western and Eastern Ghats"

ghunghat: ritual of veiling the face (common in the north of India)

gota: gold tinsel embellishment on fabric

Gujarati: term that refers to anything relating to the Gujarat region in India (e.g. language, people, script, cuisine, or sari draping)

haldi: ritual cleansing of the bride and groom with turmeric

Haryana: state in the north of India

Hindu: a person who follows the philosophies and scriptures of Hinduism

Hinduism: religious, philosophical, and cultural system that originates from India

ikat: style of weaving that uses a resist dyeing process similar to the tie-dye process

jharokas: type of overhanging balcony used in India architecture

kameez: a form-fitted overshirt worn by women

kantha: type of embroidery that forms or outlines decorative motifs with a running stitch

khadi: article of clothing made from coarse cotton cloth

kiranas: word given to describe small "mom and pop" stores

kurta: loose overshirt worn by men

kalamkari: technique of block printing

kathiawari: breed of horse from India, specifically originating in the Kathiawar peninsula in western India

kilims: flat tapestry-woven carpets or rugs

kumkum: name given to the red dot on the forehead that the Hindu population wear

kashida: decorative technique using needle and thread

lakh: a unit in the Indian numbering system, widely used both in official and other contexts. When used to denominate money, one lakh is equal to 100,000 rupees

lehenga: bridal gown or evening gowns

Leheriya: the horizontal coloured stripes used in Rajasthani fabric for *dupattas*

Lurex: brand name for a type of yarn with a metallic appearance and it may also refer to the cloth created with the yarn

Mahim: a neighborhood in Mumbai, one of the seven original islands that make up the city

mehendi: pre-wedding ceremony where henna is applied decoratively on the bride and groom

mul-mul: fine muslin

Mughal: refers to a person from the period of dominant power of the Indian subcontinent between mid-sixteenth and early eighteenth century

paan: a type of Indian digestive, which consists of fillings wrapped in a triangular package using leaves of the betel pepper held together with a toothpick or a clove

papad: also known as poppadom, this food is a dried lentil chip studded with Indian spices that comes alive when grilled or deep fried

phulkari: embroidery technique from the Punjab region in India, which literally means "flower working"; name also given to everyday shawl garments

Punjab: from the medieval Persian for land of the five rivers, this term refers to the geographical region that extends from eastern Pakistan to northwestern India

Punjabi: term to describe the language or the people of the Punjab region

purdah: the custom in some Muslim and Hindu communities of keeping women in seclusion, with clothing that conceals them completely when they go out

saat phere: ritual of walking around the sacred fire while taking vows of togetherness

sagai: engagement ceremony

salwar trousers: trousers that are cut wide at the top and narrow at the ankle

sangeet (or ladies sangeet): event in a Hindu or Sikh wedding that takes place two or three days before the wedding in a banquet hall or at home and only women take part in the event

sesterce: A coin used during the Roman era

Sikh: means disciple or learner; refers to a person who is an adherent of Sikhism

Sikhism: religious philosophy founded on the teachings of Nanak and nine successive gurus in fifteenth century northern India

slub: slightly twisted roll of fiber, as of silk or cotton

streedhan: dowry

Tamil Nadhu: region that lies on the eastern coast of the southern Indian peninsula

tussar: raw silk, where the worm is allowed to fly out as a butterfly before the silk is woven. It is rough and the colour and texture differs from region to region

zardosi: gold thread embroidery

BIBLIOGRAPHY

REPORTS

10 Things You Didn't Know About Luxury (Deutsche Bank, July 2007)

Annual Location Ranking Survey (ECA International, 2007)

Architecting Desire (Condé Net, September 2007)

Brochure from the Galeries Nationales du Grand Palais Exhibition on India (Musées Nationaux de France, 2007)

Building a Strategic Partnership Between EU & India (2008–2013) (The Boston Consulting Group, Eurupee, February 2008)

de T'Serclaes, Jacques and Sanjeev Rao, *Market Report* (Gateway 2 India)

Economic Survey (Government of India's Planning Commission, February 2008)

Executive Summary of A Note on Consumer Spending Patterns in India (ICMR, 2007)

Flash on India Budget 2005–2006 (PriceWaterhouseCoopers, February 2005)

Forbes World's Billionaires (Forbes, 2007)

Global Retail Development Index; 30 Emerging Markets (AT Kearney, 2008)

India and China: New Tigers of Asia – Part II (Morgan Stanley, June 2006)

India Shopping Trends 2008 (The Knowledge Company, Technopak Advisors' Market Intelligence Division, 2008)

Interactive Snap Poll: How Well Do You Know Your Luxury Customer? (Luxury Institute, 2007)

Jewelry: Indian Affluent Consumer Trends (The Knowledge Company, Technopak Advisors' Market Intelligence Division, 2006)

Le Luxe en Inde, du Sur Mesure à la Démesure (Institut Français de la Mode, September 2005)

Le Marché des Produits de Luxe (Ubifrance, 2007)

Luxury Brands in China (KPMG, November 2006)

Luxury Market Report 2004: Who Buys Luxury, What They Buy, Why They Buy (Research and Markets, 2004)

Made in India Made for a Young India! (KSA-Technopak, 2006)

Market Study (Bain & Company, 2006)

Millward Brown Optimor (including data from BRANDZ, Datamonitor and Bloomberg, 2009)

The Bird of Gold: The Rise of the Indian Consumer (McKinsey Global Institute, May 2007)

The Dawn of the India Century (Keystone India, 2005)

The Future for the Luxury Market (Ledbury Research, October 2007)

The Indian Brand and Wallet Share, Consumption Patterns of Indians Premium Consumers (Images in collaboration with AC Nielsen, 2005)

The Rising Elephant, A comparison of the Chinese and Indian Markets (PricewaterhouseCoopers, May 2007)

The Sun Rises on the Indian Executive (Boyden, September 2007)

Vision 2020 (McKinsey and "Bombay first" business group, 2003)

BOOKS

Airault, Régis, *Fous de l'Inde : Délires d'Occidentaux et sentiment océanique*, Payot, 2002

Amartya Sen, *The Argumentative Indian*, Farrar, Straus & Giroux, 2005

Ashutosh Sheshabalaya, *Rising Elephant: The Growing Clash with India Over White Collar Jobs and Its Challenge to America and the World*, Common Courage Press, 2004

Assouly, Olivier, *Le Luxe, Essais sur la Fabrique de l'Ostentation*, éditions de l'Institut français de la Mode, 2005

Badhwar, Inderjit, *Sniffing Papa*, Tara Press, 2002

Basham, Arthur Llewellyn, *A Cultural History of India*, Clarendon Press, 1975

Blanckaert, Christian, *Luxe*, éditions Le Cherche Midi, 2007

Carcano, Luana and Carlo Ceppi, *L'alta Orologeria in Italia*, éditions Egea, 2006

Carrière, Jean-Claude, *Dictionnaire amoureux de l'Inde*, Plon, 2001

Chadda, Radha and Paul Husband, *The Cult of the Luxury Brand: India's Love Affair with Luxury*, Nicholas Brealey International, 2006

Charrin, Eve, *L'Inde à l'assaut du Monde*, éditions Grasset & Fasquelle, 2007

Chevalier, Michel and Gérald Mazzalovo, *Luxury Brand Management: A World of Privilege*, John Wiley & Sons, 2008

Clement, Catherine and Tobie Nathan, *Le Divan et le Grigri*, Odile Jacob, 2002

Clement, Catherine, *Promenade avec les dieux de l'Inde*, Editions du Panama, 2005

Desai, Anita, *Le Jeûne et le festin*, Gallimard, 2002

Dumont, Louis. *Homo Hierarchicus: The Caste System and Its Implications*. Complete English edition, revised. 1970, 1980 Series: Nature of Human Society

Dupuis, Jacques, *L'Inde, une introduction à la connaissance du monde indien*, Editions Kailash, 2007

Eliade, Mircea, *La nuit bengali*, Collection Folio, Gallimard, 1979

Gillion, Kenneth L., *Ahmedabad: A Study in Indian Urban History*, University of California Press, 1968

Hesse, Jean-François and Claudine, *Luxe Mode d'Emploi*, éditions du Rocher, 1988

Jaffer, Amin, *Made for Maharajas: A Design Diary of Princely India*, Roli Books, 2007

Jaffrelot, Christophe, *India's Silent Revolution: The Rise of the Lower Castes*, C. Hurst & Co, Editions Kailash, 1997

Kakar, Sudhir, *Au nom de l'extase*, Editions du Seuil, 2005

Kakar, Sudhir and Katharina, *The Indians*, Penguin Books, 2007

Kakar, Sudhir, *L'Ascèse du désir*, Editions du Seuil, 2001

Kakar, Sudhir, *Mira et le Mahatma*, Editions du Seuil, 2006

Kaldar, Alexandre, *Une promenade en Inde*, Editions Grasset & Fasquelle, 2007

Kamdar, Mira, *Planet India: How the Fastest-growing Democracy is Transforming America and the World*, Scribner, 2007

Kumar, Ritu, *Costumes and Textiles of Royal India*, Antique Collectors' Club, 2000

Lasch, Christopher, *The Culture of Narcissism: American Life in an Age of Diminishing Expectations*, Norton, 1979

Marseille, Jacques, *Le Luxe en France du Siècle des « Lumières » à nos Jours*, éditions ADHE, 1999

Mehta, Suketu, *Bombay Maximum City*, Buchet-Chastel, 2006

Michaud, Roland et Sabrina, *La danse cosmique de l'Inde : des dieux et des hommes*, Editions du Chêne, 2006

Mistry, Robinton, *L'équilibre du monde (a fine balance)*, Editions Albin Michel, 1998

Nath, Kamal, *India's Century: The Age of Entrepreneurship in the World's Biggest Democracy*, McGraw-Hill, 1st edition, 2007

Nehru, Jawaharlal, *The Discovery of India*, Oxford University Press, 1946

Okonkwo, Uché, *Luxury Fashion Branding*, Palgrave Macmillan, 2007

Rivoyre, Christine de, *Archaka*, Editions Grasset, 2007

Seth, Vikram, *Un garçon convenable, première partie*, LGF-Livre de Poche, 1997

Shanghvi, Siddarth Dhanvant, *La Fille qui marchait sur l'eau*, Editions 10x18, Collection Domaine étranger, 2006

Tejpal, Tarun J., *The Alchemy of Desire*, Picador, 2005

Tharoor, Shash, *India: From Midnight to the Millennium*, Harper Perennial, 1998

Umrigar, Thrity, *The Space Between Us*, Harper Perennial, New edition 2007

Index